D1109918

THE GENTLEMAN FROM MARYLAND

THE GENTLEMAN FROM MARYLAND

The Conscience of a Gay Conservative

By

ROBERT E. BAUMAN

A Belvedere Book

ARBOR HOUSE · New York

Copyright ©1986 by Robert E. Bauman
All rights reserved, including the right of reproduction
in whole or in part in any form. Published in the United
States of America by Arbor House Publishing Company and
in Canada by Fitzhenry & Whiteside, Ltd.

Manufactured in the United States of America
10 9 8 7 6 5 4 3 2 1

Designed by Beth Quigley

Library of Congress Cataloging in Publication Data

Bauman, Robert E., 1937–
  The gentleman from Maryland.

  1. Bauman, Robert, 1937–   . 2. Homosexuals,
Male—Washington (D.C.)—Biography. 3. Politicians—
United States—Biography. 4. Legislators—United
States—Biography. I. Title.
HQ75.8.B38A34   1986   306.7′662′0924   86-3345
ISBN: 0-87795-686-3

Grateful acknowledgment is made for permission to reprint:
Excerpt from *Lord Jim* by Joseph Conrad. Copyright 1899, 1900 by Joseph
Conrad.
"S'POSIN' " by Paul Denniker and Andy Razaf. © 1929 by Edwin H. Morris &
Company, a division of MPL Communications, Inc. © Renewed 1957 Morley
Music Co. International Copyright secured. All rights reserved. Used by permis-
sion.
Quotation from Michael Olesker's column published in *The Baltimore Sun.* Used
by permission.
The Church and the Homosexual by John J. McNeill, S.J. Copyright © 1976; 1985
by Next Year Productions.
The Christopher Street Reader, edited by Michael Denneny, Charles Ortleb and
Thomas Steele. Copyright © 1983 by That New Magazine, Inc. Reprinted by per-
mission of the Putnam Publishing Group.
From *The Almanac of American Politics* 1980 by Michael Barone, Grant Ujifusa
and Douglas Matthews. Copyright © 1979 by Michael Barone. Reprinted by per-
mission of the publisher, E. P. Dutton, a division of New American Library.
From *A Challenge to Love: Gay and Lesbian Catholics in the Church,* edited by
Robert Nugent. Copyright © 1983 by New Ways Ministry. Reprinted by permission of the Crossroad Publishing Company.
From *A Portrait of the Artist as a Young Man* by James Joyce. Copyright 1916 by B.
W. Huebsch. Copyright renewed 1944 by Nora Joyce. Definitive text copyright ©
1964 by the Estate of James Joyce. Reprinted by permission of Viking Penguin Inc.

From *How to Save the Catholic Church* by Andrew M. Greeley and Mary Greeley Durkin. Copyright © 1984 by Andrew M. Greeley and Mary Greeley Durkin. Reprinted by permission of Viking Penguin Inc.

Excerpts from *Advise and Consent* by Allen Drury, copyright © 1959 by Allen Drury. Reprinted by permission of Doubleday & Company, Inc.

Tennessee Williams *Memoirs,* copyright © 1972, 1975 by Tennessee Williams. Reprinted by permission of Doubleday & Company, Inc.

From *Reaching Out* by Henri J. M. Nouwen, copyright © 1975 by Henri J. M. Nouwen. Reprinted by permission of Doubleday & Company, Inc.

Quote from *The Washington Times*. Reprinted by permission of *The Washington Times*.

Quote from *The New York Times*, "A New Gadfly Keeps Eye on House," by Richard L. Madden, of April 4, 1976. Copyright © 1976 by The New York Times Company. Reprinted by permission.

Quote from *The Baltimore Evening Sun*. Reprinted by permission of *The Baltimore Evening Sun*.

Quote from *The Washington Post*. Reprinted by permission of *The Washington Post*.

PREFACE

If you persist, what you will read is not the book I would have written. Fortunately for me and you, the reader, wiser editorial counsel prevailed.

The first massive Bauman book (more than 650 pages) was a straightforward chronological history of Bobby Bauman, young Bob Bauman, congressman Bob Bauman, ex-congressman Bauman. It was filled with minutiae any political junkie would love. You could have read about my humble origins, my relatives, my travels to Europe, Africa, China, Central America. You would have heard recounted talks with U.S. and foreign presidents, Ian Smith, Deng Xiaoping, even the dying Shah of Iran. You would have retraced every major theme of my conservative career in the Maryland General Assembly and the House of Representatives. You would have even learned how I got Bella Abzug to shut her mouth, though it took the rules of Congress to achieve that feat.

But I was caught at my own game when a good editor pointed out I really was hiding behind politics to prevent the real Bob Bauman from emerging, a tactic I perfected over many years.

So what you have here is a true story, in my own words, of what some have called a near-perfect Greek tragedy, the somber theme of a "noble person" whose character is flawed by a great weakness, causing him to break a divine precept, leading inevita-

bly to his downfall, perhaps destruction. I wish it were so simple.
I did not want to write this book.

I wrote it because I need the money. A priest friend of mine,
having viewed me on the obligatory "Donahue Show," compli-
mented my appearance but wondered "why you want to expose
yourself publicly to all that?" I didn't. Or at least I don't now. But
I soon discovered in my own difficult way what gay people find
out every day—discrimination. I would rather have spared my
family and myself further public display but the editors of Arbor
House made me an offer I could not reject. Indeed, I would not
have rejected any reasonable offer.

Yet I can conceive that this book will have some beneficial
value to the many thousands of young and older men who have
lived a life of fear and self-hatred, not knowing exactly why they
are the way they are, not wanting to accept the possibility they are
homosexual. For those people, I feel the greatest kinship. I hope
you find comfort in knowing others have gone through similar experiences and even worse. But this is not a "coming-out" story.
This is a "forced-out" story.

For my conservative friends I hope those of you who need it
may find some small degree of understanding and tolerance of a
timeless human issue that will not go away. You liberals could
use the same understanding and tolerance. A year or so ago I was
invited to a Washington all-male party at a posh residence with
the admonition, "We heard you are writing a book and some of
my guests wanted assurances that their presence will not be mentioned." I will go my host one better and not even mention the
party. Yes, some names are renamed here but those people are already out of the closet. Others you may be able to guess, especially if you are close to the "upper echelons" of the Washington
gay scene. What I hope you understand is that roughly 10 percent
of your fellow human beings fall into the category of "gay" and
that could be anyone—your lawyer, your legislator, your child, or
your spouse.

I owe special thanks to Owen Laster of the William Morris

Agency for his diligent dedication, advice, and promotion of this book. He saw me through some dark times and never lost faith. Thanks go to my former Eastern Shore neighbor, famed novelist Jim Michener, who recommended Owen to me, and whose book agent Owen is. For having the judgment and courage to buy and publish the book, I thank John Dodds of Belvedere Books and Arbor House. It is he who labored long and hard to bring logical order to a politician's ramblings, to give theme and heart to a book that was painful at best for me to write. I also thank Alice Fasano for her outstanding editorial assistance and patience.

There are others to whom I owe appreciation for help both in writing the book and help to me during the time it has taken. Roy Childs is one of them. I would like to mention all their names but that might be a disservice to them. But you know who you are and you have my sincere thanks.

Lastly, I owe an inextinguishable debt of gratitude to the many hundreds of gays and alcoholics, and gay alcoholics, who share a special understanding of my journey. They have been there too. Each was encouraging in his or her own way, offering hope, support, and constructive critical comment.

This book is my own and its thoughts and statements belong to no one else. Any blame or credit is therefore mine. As in life.

April 1986
Washington, D.C.

From *The Almanac of American Politics, 1980* (New York: E. P. Dutton)

"Until the completion of the Chesapeake Bay Bridge in 1952, the Eastern Shore of Maryland was virtually cut off from the rest of the State. The "Eastern" refers to the east shore of the Chesapeake, a part of Maryland that remains almost a world unto itself—a region of Southern drowsiness, chicken farms and fishing villages. Its history has been told in James Michener's bestseller, *Chesapeake.* Before the Civil War, the Eastern Shore was very much slaveholding country. Up through the sixties attachment to the mores of the South persisted; until 1964 Maryland had a public accommodations law which explicitly excluded the Eastern Shore counties. Mostly rural, the economy of the area is buoyed by the dollars spent by tourists, summer people and the rich who have built big estates there.

"The Eastern Shore continues to bulk larger than its numbers in Maryland politics. It continues to produce important state legislators and two of its last four governors. . . . But because its population has not grown much—it only slightly more than doubled between 1790 and 1970—the Shore is less and less important politically. The 1st Congressional District is, by reputation, the Eastern Shore district, although only 53% of its residents live east of the Bay. The rest are found in two entirely separate areas. The first is Harford County, a northern extension of the Baltimore metropolitan area; the second is Charles, St. Mary's and Calvert counties south of Annapolis. The latter are where Lord

Baltimore's Catholics first settled Maryland and there is a substantial rural Catholic population there still . . .

"Both the Eastern Shore and the two western parts of the 1st have a Democratic registration which is deceptively high. Although Democrats still hold local and state legislative offices, these are areas which for years have preferred Republican candidates, not only for president but for congressman as well. Fully 19% of the district's population is black—this is the farthest north you will find significant numbers of blacks in rural settings—but their Democratic preferences are outweighed by the whites' Republican majorities. The Eastern Shore has gone Democratic in the House race only twice since World War II.

"The 1st District is currently represented by one of the most staunchly conservative Republicans. Robert Bauman was a founder of Young Americans for Freedom in the early sixties; he served as a Republican aide on the Hill and in the Maryland State Senate. Bauman is as ideologically committed as any Republican in the House; he is also one of the Republican party's masters of parliamentary procedure. He comes to the role naturally; he objects to what he believes government is doing to the country, and he interposes objections when he sees advocates of big government trying to get something through on the floor of the House. Bauman forces the majority to play by the rules and to air fully their reasons for what they want to do; and sometimes by doing so he forces them to reconsider or stop. His procedural talents won him a seat on the House Rules Committee in 1979. He can be counted on to vote against the wishes of the Democratic leadership almost always and against the wishes of the Republican leadership more often than it would like.

"Bauman is not only involved in procedural matters; he has an impact on the substantive issues as well. . . .

"Bauman could continue as an influential figure in the House, or he might run for the Senate in 1980 or 1982 . . . If he ran he would be banking on the conservative leanings of the relatively small number of Marylanders who vote in Republican primaries. This is probably enough to make him a formidable challenger and maybe even a Senator. . . ."

CHAPTER ONE

*T*here are two versions of how, first, the Washington, D.C. Metropolitan Police and then, the U.S. Federal Bureau of Investigation, became highly interested in the private life of the Honorable Robert E. Bauman, member of the United States House of Representatives from the First Congressional District of Maryland.

When the Bauman scandal became public in October 1980, only four weeks before I was to face the voters' verdict at the polls, the most widely published account held that sometime in the winter of 1979–80 I solicited sexual favors from a sixteen-year-old nude male dancer at a Washington gay bar, the Chesapeake House. Fifty dollars sealed the tryst but an unexpected complication was reported to be the young man's seventeen-year-old lover, also a male dancer at another nearby gay bar, the Lone Star. The official government memorandum containing this version and used to justify prosecuting me was authored by Carol Bruce, the young lady who, as one of the assistant United States attorneys for the District of Columbia, was in charge of my case.

The other version reported at the time by the *Washington Post* stated that the Washington field office of the FBI had been conducting an investigation of pornography in the area. They stumbled onto a young man who alleged that he had a sexual encounter with me, hoping that this bit of information about a congressman would help him out of his own difficulties with the law.

Four years later, mostly by chance, I was able to piece together a more accurate account of how I happened to find myself charged with the criminal misdemeanor of solicitation for sexual purposes, a violation of section 22-2701 of the District of Columbia Code, bringing my marriage, my career in politics, and life as I had known it to an abrupt and shattering end.

One source for this more reliable account of what happened to me was a young man I met through our mutual association with groups dealing with our alcoholism. He identified himself as a former male prostitute and drug addict who knew both the young men involved in the events that led to my exposure. Another unexpected source of information was a government official directly involved in the investigation who was willing to talk candidly about it, provided he not be identified.

So now, more than five years later, having lived through the aftermath and having lost nearly everything, it is appropriate to place things in perspective and learn from what happened to me so that I can get on with the rest of my life, whatever lies ahead.

On Wednesday morning, September 3, 1980, I breezed into suite 2443 of the Rayburn House Office Building, tanned and rested after a long Labor Day weekend at the beach with my four children. As I entered my private office, my personal secretary, Nancy Howard, followed me nervously, clutching her steno pad. It required four tough but successful campaigns for Congress before I acquired enough seniority to obtain offices in the Rayburn Building, the most desirable of the three marble mausoleums comprising the congressional edifice complex on the House side of Capitol Hill.

"Bob, there were two FBI agents here earlier this morning wanting to see you. They waited a while and left to get some coffee but said they would be back soon." Nancy had that look of perpetually grave concern she always wore when my personal welfare might be involved.

"Did they say what they wanted?" I tried to ask nonchalantly, an indefinably cold sensation inching up my spine.

"No," Nancy replied, "but you know they are always up here on the Hill checking out security clearances for people appointed to government jobs. Maybe that's it."

As I sat at my desk brooding about what the unexpected FBI visit might mean Nancy buzzed me and at my direction ushered in Special Agent M. Glenn Tuttle and his deferential partner, David R. Loesch. They seated themselves on the massive blue leather couch opposite my mahogany desk. A large gilded mirror over their heads allowed me to watch them and my reactions as well.

I started to ask what this was all about but the tight, grim looks on their faces informed me that this was indeed an official visit. A knot the size of a man's hand began to grow in my chest and breathing became more difficult.

"This is it," I thought to myself, trying to remain calm. A lifetime of acting was about to end.

They knew.

Special Agent Tuttle, who I later learned has made a career of "morals" type investigations, did all the talking. He informed me I had been under investigation "for some period of time" by the FBI. The "facts" gathered included, he said, my repeated nocturnal visits to gay bars where I allegedly solicited sexual acts from various young men, transporting some of them within the District of Columbia for purposes of sexual activity, a federal felony. Additionally, he charged I had used my official influence to obtain a discharge from the U.S. Navy for a young man whose mother supposedly threatened me with exposure unless I helped her son.

I listened as passively as I could until the mention of the navy discharge. I knew this was false and reacted accordingly with a strong denial. But the lawyer in me allowed no comments that might confirm anything Tuttle said. The single denial must have contrasted strongly with my silence on the other charges.

When he finished his dry recitation Tuttle asked if I had any response. I had none. At this point I should have recognized that the agents had come to my office on a fishing expedition, trying to bolster their case. I later learned that they had very little in the way of hard proof that would stand up before a jury under the standard of reasonable doubt. As it turned out, what they did have was the possible testimony of two paid informants, "Steve" and "Eddie," both male prostitutes, both with criminal records, both with drug habits. Their questionable statements would have been balanced against the denial of a respected congressman and national conservative leader whose political demise was devoutly desired all the way from the Georgia Democrat in the White House, through the ranks of many of my opponents in the Senate and House, down the line to the minions in a Justice Department not unknown for its political decisions. Well-meaning advisors told me after the fact that I should have denied and fought the charges.

But the most remarkable aspect of the FBI visit was Agent Tuttle's response to a question I asked after he was finished with his charges.

I tried to retain control as I said: "Gentlemen, obviously I have never been in the position of an accused before. I will have to seek legal counsel. But what do you want me to do? Am I under arrest? What happens next?"

Agent Tuttle repeated something he had said when he first arrived; he had come to see me under the authority of the United States Attorney for the District of Columbia, Charles Ruff, who had jurisdiction over the investigation. There would be no arrest.

"My understanding of what Mr. Ruff proposes, Congressman Bauman, is that you plead not guilty to a misdemeanor charge of solicitation for prostitution under the terms of the first offenders statute which allows such a plea for those with no previous criminal offense. The government will accept that plea and agree to a six-month probation, which the law allows for those with no previous criminal record. No jail sentence will result." Tuttle rattled this off as if he had memorized it.

"And what if I do not agree to this course of action?" I wanted to know.

"In that case," Tuttle replied, "it is my understanding that the U.S. Attorney will seek your immediate indictment before a grand jury on any and all possible charges, including felonies, even though it might not be possible to prove all the charges." He added in his businesslike tone: "We feel we have enough evidence to prove our main case."

Although the FBI is an investigative arm of the Justice Department, and its agents do not represent the U.S. Attorney, in my case it was obvious that complete discussions between the investigative agents and the official prosecutors had produced a decision as to what my legal fate would be. "They" had made up their minds.

As I ushered the two men out of the back door of my private office my brain swirled with the horrible possibilities this twenty-minute meeting had suddenly imposed on my life and the lives of those around me. Though I hardly realized it then, nothing would ever be the same again. Just as suddenly, what had been the most important objective in my life, my reelection to Congress now only eight weeks away, dwindled into relative insignificance.

My first call for help was to Thomas M. O'Malley, a friend since college days and a former assistant U.S. Attorney himself, who within two hours met me outside the House of Representatives Chamber. With the FBI involvement I did not want to talk over the phone. We crossed the hall to the ornate private office of the Republican Whip. As we sat in these plush surroundings signifying congressional power, I related my sad tale to Tom. After questioning me closely, he agreed to represent me, with or without a fee, since I insisted that he know my precarious financial position along with all the other bad news. And I did tell him everything, knowing that to be successful in representing a client, the attorney must have no surprises. I had already talked briefly with U.S. Attorney Charles Ruff, who asked that I have my attorney contact him immediately. Tom would do that quickly so that we could both get an estimate of just how bad this was.

Next I had to confront my wife, Carol, but I knew it had to be immediate, that very night. Minutes after the FBI visit I also called Reverend Father John F. Harvey, a Catholic priest of the order of the Oblates of Saint Francis de Sales, a saintly man who had been Carol's friend before our marriage and both of ours since. I told myself his presence would help Carol but I wanted him there as much for my own support. As we drove from Washington toward my home in Easton, Maryland, I gave him the details of the FBI visit. Many months before Father Harvey had heard the entire story of my life, sex included, in the form of my confession. After absolution we had both talked about the possibility of public exposure, which then seemed remote. Now it had come.

The quiet dark of the auto ride, broken only by the soft light of the dashboard and our conversation, now gave way to the cheerfully warm light of the library at Glebe House, our home on Maryland's Eastern Shore. But there was no cheer as we sat down. Carol knew something awful had happened to bring Father Harvey into our home unannounced on a week night. He had concelebrated our wedding mass, presided at our children's baptisms, many times been our guest but never as a witness to such sadness. Haltingly I told Carol what had happened and what likely lay ahead in the coming days and weeks. As I spoke softly, trying to contain my own emotions, she began to sob, tears rolling down her cheeks, "Oh, God! Oh, God!" I tried to comfort her and finally Father Harvey motioned for me to leave the room so that he could talk with her alone.

I stepped out into the late summer night, already with an autumn chill in the damp air, and walked slowly down the long lane of trees leading from our house to the nearby country road. I tried to calm my feelings in this setting in which I had often sought solace before, many times when I was drunk. But now painful sobriety was stark and total. The actual sight of my weeping wife seemed to confirm the terrible future.

When I returned to the house, Carol had regained her composure and began to ask the practical questions an experienced political wife thinks of in such a crisis. After the countless hours and days of suffering I had inflicted upon her, miraculously she was still able to summon untapped reserves of stamina to deal with yet another personal disaster.

Would I be able to do the same?

There was a terrible poignancy in my past coming back to haunt us now.

Almost nine months before Carol and I had a major personal confrontation about my "problem." Not for the first time, she had discovered a copy of a gay publication under the front seat of my auto. But it was the last. Highly agitated she insisted that I see Father Harvey immediately to discuss fully whatever it was that was wrong with me. "I just cannot go on like this any longer," she told me angrily. And I knew she meant it.

Out of her proper desperation came months of counseling with Father Harvey and a Washington psychologist he recommended, whom I shall call Dr. Kay. Kay specialized in problems of alcoholism and homosexuality, often treating members of the Catholic clergy with whom Father Harvey worked in his own counseling. With Kay's advice and guidance I had taken my last drink on May 1, 1980, and had been regularly attending meetings of self-help groups dealing with alcoholism. I had also stopped frequenting the Washington gay scene. Central to my thinking was the salvation of our marriage.

In those months prior to September 1980, the spiritual and psychological guidance I received from Father Harvey and Dr. Kay brought me to a new plateau of personal equilibrium unequaled in my lifetime. Carol, our children, even our colleagues in the House of Representatives commented on the newly relaxed ease which marked my conduct. One political writer commented that "the rough edges" had come off of Bob Bauman. I had high hopes that personal peace might finally be at hand.

All that ended with the visit of Agents Tuttle and Loesch. Now it was useless to speculate what might have happened had the issue of my personal life not been forced out into the open. Carol and I had talked about getting through "just one more campaign" and even whether I really wanted to stay in politics at all, something I never thought I would doubt. Once the 1980 victory was achieved we could consider our future calmly and maybe we would be able to do finally all those things we talked about but my demanding schedule rarely seemed to permit.

But that was all gone now.

And yet there was a certain sense of personal relief that descended upon me. It was much like the feeling I had experienced at the meeting one evening when I had summoned up the personal courage to utter the words at last: "Yes, I am an alcoholic." Now at least I would not have to hide the major problem of my life anymore. Although I was many months from accepting it, circumstances were forcing me at last to deal with my sexuality.

Whatever the exact origin of their interest in my private conduct, other than the nature of my actions, it seems that I was caught up in a wider problem that came to occupy Washington police attention in the late 1970s. The government informant willing to talk with me said the police were becoming increasingly alarmed at the growing number of male juveniles, most of them runaways, flooding into Washington from all over the U.S. Many of them joined the ranks of the male prostitutes who line New York Avenue N.W., and the more fashionable P Street area in Georgetown. At first the police took these young men into custody and released them to their parents or put them on a bus back home.

But soon rumors began to surface of organized rings of imported male prostitutes and, more disturbing, the names of prominent government officials appeared in the stories the young men were telling police. A D.C. police squad known as the "juvenile sex exploitation unit" began to be concerned that what they were hearing "was too hot to handle."

Mine was among those names.

And so were the names of nine other members of the U.S. House of Representatives and U.S. Senate. We were not alone. The young men under police questioning named high officials of the federal government, the District of Columbia government, aides to the White House staff of Jimmy Carter, as well as men well known in Washington military, business, and professional circles. One Carter aide was seen getting out of his chauffeured government limousine late at night in front of a male brothel on 13th Street N.W. The "mister" of the house had the good sense to demand that the large black car be parked around the corner. A few weeks later the police raided the house and its records but the case never came to trial. In another instance, the police discovered that a high D.C. government official owned and rented a downtown house used as a brothel by male street prostitutes and their customers.

Little wonder such interesting discoveries caused Washington police a case of the nerves.

There has always been extreme sensitivity on the part of the Washington Metropolitan Police Department about dealing with "very important persons" who may commit a less serious crime. This is particularly so if the act involved is drunken conduct or consensual sexual activity. "This is a town," my informant told me, "where the police officer never knows who he is dealing with when the person is apprehended. If a D.C. officer or an FBI agent wants to keep his job, he'd better be very careful not to step on any important toes." He recalled the case of a rookie D.C. traffic patrolman who stopped a car late at night going eighty miles an hour on a downtown street, only to discover rudely that the driver, high on drugs, was the child of the President of the United States. "This kid was traveling so fast that the assigned Secret

Service detail lost the car. By the time they caught up the D.C. officer was placing the young driver under arrest. Secret Service intervention put a quick end to that and the youngster was chauffeured home to Mom and Dad at 1600 Pennsylvania Avenue."

Most D.C. police call this "go easy" policy toward government officials and their families a form of "job insurance." This is especially true when members of the Senate or House are involved. Unless an offending congressman commits some public criminal offense they are usually not arrested for misdemeanors or traffic offenses. Often no charges are brought even when the problem becomes public. Some years ago the then Speaker of the House, Carl Albert of Oklahoma, sideswiped a parked car while driving drunk on Connecticut Avenue. No charge resulted even after the story made the press. When a leading conservative Democratic congressman, Joe Waggoner of Louisiana, was arrested and booked for soliciting a female prostitute (who turned out to be an undercover policewoman), his identity, once discovered, resulted in dropping the charges and alteration of records to cover the fact. When the story came out a few years later Mr. Waggoner's long House career came to an end.

As the famous names began to multiply in investigative files in 1979 and 1980, Washington police became collectively nervous in the extreme. The juvenile sex unit decided to buck the matter up the traditional next step to the "intelligence unit," a group that considers issues of a "sensitive" or "political" nature. Often the charges die there. But this time the police officials mulled over the problem, the famous people involved, the aspect of youthful sex, the possibility of press interest and exposure, and they too acquired a case of nerves.

The upshot was the formation of a "special task force" after consultation among the several federal, local, and special law enforcement units that operate in the nation's capital. Sometime in 1978 the task force began operation with twelve members from the FBI, U.S. Secret Service, the U.S. Attorney's staff, and from the Washington police, representatives from the vice, sex, juvenile, and prostitution squads. As part of the FBI contingent, Special Agent M. Glenn Tuttle was involved.

The same Agent Tuttle who had been paying a number of informants, including one named "Steve" and another named Eddie Regina, both male hustlers. Tuttle was particularly interested in the private lives of public officials, especially homosexual activity. Once gathered, Tuttle presented the preliminary information about me to the United States Attorney for the District of Columbia, Charles Ruff, a Carter appointee, who assigned the matter to the "Major Crimes Unit" of his office, the same unit that handles all "big" cases involving federal officials whether Hamilton Jordan's alleged drug use or Watergate. Here an assistant U.S. attorney, Carol Bruce, became involved, charged with eventual prosecution of my case. The Washington police were only too pleased to have this hot potato removed from their sensitive fingers. Indeed, when my case came to public view, the D.C. police were at a loss to explain what had gone on. An unidentified D.C. police official told a reporter: "They [the FBI and Justice Department] did not want anyone else to research this one. They only do this themselves on special occasions."

But all such delicate matters require a certain amount of political clearance before mere law enforcement officials charged with statutory duties feel confident in upholding the law. U.S. Attorney Ruff refused to discuss my case with reporters, even after its court disposition, but he did feel a need to defend his decision to act. Asked why federal prosecutors would be interested in the private conduct of any citizen, much less a congressman, Ruff protested that "the matter was pursued in a wholly professional manner and it was brought to fruition in the normal time in the normal fashion." He acknowledged to the *Baltimore Sun* that before he decided to proceed with my investigation "he had consulted with his superiors in the Justice Department about it." At the head of that department in 1980 as attorney general was a prominent lawyer-politician from Maryland, one Benjamin Civiletti.

On Capitol Hill political clearance probably was sought and obtained before Ruff proceeded with my case. With nine other members of the Senate and House known to Washington police to have been engaged in homosexual conduct, singling out one Republican from the Eastern Shore of Maryland might raise questions. The former official who was involved in my case told me: "The big guy with the white hair who runs the House knew about and approved of what was going to happen to you." I assume, but have no proof, that he meant House Speaker Thomas B. "Tip" O'Neill, my chief antagonist in the House political wars.

Whoever gave their official and political approval, what followed was worthy of a major Federal case of espionage, treason, murder or corruption. The private sexual life of one congressman became the focus of a major FBI investigation eventually condensed into a report exceeding thirty pages. Agents fanned out over Washington and surrounding areas interviewing every male hustler they could find, asking if they knew me (showing them my photo) and if so, had they ever had sex with me. Arrangements were made with a Chesapeake House employee to notify the FBI if I came into the bar. I was followed leaving the House office building some evenings and night photography was used. One young Washington hustler was pursued by Agent Tuttle to his home in rural Virginia where the surprise FBI visit was the first the young man's mother knew that her son was in any trouble or gay.

The nature of the FBI case against me was starkly revealed by the type of witnesses they sought to employ. In his search to find almost anyone who would provide proof against me, Tuttle did not have to look far.

One of his regular paid informants was a twenty-six-year-old male prostitute and self-admitted heroin addict, Eddie Regina, who coincidentally happened to come from rural Dorchester

County on Maryland's Eastern Shore, only a few miles from my own home in Talbot County. Unfortunately for me, Eddie was the same young man who had introduced me to the Chesapeake House one evening in 1979.

Eddie was a coarse-featured, muscular young man with shoulder-length blond hair. His father, a convicted murderer, was dead. His mother, Janet, remarried Ralph Stanley Hall, a waterman from Fishing Creek, a remote village out in the marshes of the Chesapeake Bay. Eddie was known locally as a misfit who did not hide the fact that he was "queer," not exactly an acceptable attribute in his area. His teen-age years were marked by numerous runaways from home and by the time he was thirteen or fourteen he was already into the Washington hustling scene, living on Capitol Hill with a gay congressional aide, by his own account. By 1979 he had worked as a nude dancer at the Chesapeake House and a bar man at the Naples on New York Avenue. At the old age of twenty-six, Eddie had been around the Washington gay bar scene for a long time. And those who remember him then used such terms as "weird" and "strange" to describe the young man who was chosen to be the star witness in the case against me.

Not only did Eddie confirm to Agent Tuttle that he knew me, he boasted that he had been my "lover" for years, frequently dating me since he was a teen-ager. He even claimed I had given him gifts. But various news reporters who talked with Eddie concluded that his stories of how long he had known me varied widely and were inconsistent with the facts they could prove. And Eddie willingly agreed to do whatever Agent Tuttle wanted, in return, of course, for continued payments from the FBI.

Eddie's mother and stepfather were to tell the *Baltimore Sun* that "their son often tells wild stories and 'you should only believe part of it.' " They also said that in the summer of 1980 Agent Tuttle twice visited their modest frame home at Fishing Creek asking numerous questions about Congressman Bob Bauman and whether they knew that I was engaged in homosexual conduct with Eddie and other young men. According to Eddie's stepfather, Ralph Hall, "Mr. Tuttle said Eddie was working for him on other cases and was helping him now on this Bauman thing." During a second visit to the Hall home Eddie accompanied Tuttle and was later to tell the press that Tuttle and another FBI agent had asked him to arrange "to get Bauman in a hotel room with me." Eddie added: "They wanted him to resign (from Congress) but they didn't have enough evidence yet."

Regina later told the *Baltimore Evening Sun* that he cooperated with Agent Tuttle ". . . because the agent promised him money for his information. He said the agent paid him several times, mostly small payments of twenty-five or thirty dollars." But Eddie added: "They promised me big money when this (the Bauman case) was over."

Unfortunately the FBI money Eddie was getting was not big enough.

On July 24, 1980, he was called to testify before a Washington federal grand jury. The declared purpose of the grand jury meeting was possible violations of child pornography laws. But when he got there Eddie was told by assistant U.S. Attorney Carol Bruce and Agent Tuttle that his testimony would not be needed that day. And the big money was not forthcoming. So Eddie, drawing on his native wit, looked around for a new source of finance. His fertile imagination did not fail him.

He called me. The phone call came to my Easton congressional office on September 23, 1980, three weeks after I had been confronted by Agent Tuttle in my Washington office. After wringing what they could out of poor Eddie, Agent Tuttle had not informed him that federal prosecutors were proceeding without his expert help. Had he known my desperate situation Eddie might have realized that I was now the last person in the world who could be subjected to blackmail.

At first refusing to identify himself, Eddie talked with my Easton office assistant, Don Anthony, who carefully took notes. The nervous voice on the phone said he must talk with the congressman about "a grand jury meeting in Washington" which involved me. A second call a little while later contained the open admission that Don Anthony was talking with "James Edward Regina of Fishing Creek," who gave two telephone numbers at which Mr. Bauman could call him. Eddie ominously announced to Don Anthony that he was "in hiding from the FBI" and must talk immediately only with me about the grand jury. He told Don that we had met at the Chesapeake House in Washington.

Don, faithfully efficient as always, immediately phoned me in Washington and I in turn called my attorney, Tom O'Malley, who had been negotiating with the U.S. Attorney's staff for my own welfare. I suggested to Tom that since we had heard nothing of any grand jury meeting perhaps this caller might have some information that could help my defense. O'Malley, ever the prudent professional, told me that the only course was to inform the U.S. Attorney of what had happened.

Within an hour two FBI agents were in my Capitol Hill office, this time setting up wiretap equipment which I gave them permission to place on my phone. A call to the numbers which Regina had left produced the news that he was not there, but one was his parents' home. The FBI agents told me that if Regina made another contact I should try to set it up so that they could record when I called him back. The next call came on Friday, September 26, but I was campaigning in my district. At a time he named I called Regina from a Salisbury pay phone at his parents' home in Fishing Creek.

Regina identified himself by name and said ". . . you have been with me a couple of times, if you know what I mean." I let him talk and didn't confirm that I knew him or the truth of anything he said. He told me that he had been called to testify before a July 24 grand jury meeting about his relationship with me. (I was later informed he never did testify.) He said that he had been working with FBI Agent Glenn Tuttle and Carol Bruce of the U. S. Attorney's office. Then he said: "They are out to get you at all costs. They have watched and followed and photographed you. They even asked me to get you into a compromising situation so that the FBI could arrest you when we were together in a hotel room."

Then I was startled by what he said next: "If you don't believe me, I can prove what I am saying. I know just what deal they have offered you. They told me they want to get you out of Congress and you will be able to plead not guilty to soliciting prostitution, you won't have to go to jail, and you will get probation." Now I really was concerned. How would a male prostitute be privy to the legal strategy of government prosecutors? Then came the hook. Eddie said: "The FBI is hounding me to testify against you but I don't want to do it." He said he was "hiding out" at his mother's home but that he wanted to get away. "I really need to get out of the country," he said. "Could you give me two thousand dollars to go to Hawaii? Then I won't bother you anymore and I won't have to testify against you. Please think about what I have said. I want to help but I need the money right away or they'll force me to testify against you." In spite of the serious implications of what he had said the tone of the conversation had been surprisingly friendly, almost solicitous.

My only reply was that I would carefully consider what he had said and get in touch with him as quickly as I could.

I reported all this to my attorney who informed the FBI. I agreed to allow FBI agents to pose as my congressional staff members who would make contact with Regina in order to trap him. But before he called to set up a date for the payoff, friendly Eddie turned decidedly hostile. In a letter postmarked September 30 that arrived in my Easton office on October 2, the day before I was to appear in court, Regina openly threatened to tell my wife, my family, and the press ". . . who I am and what we did." He gave graphic descriptions of what he intended to say unless I purchased his silence. He demanded two thousand dollars "in $100 bills" and closed with the cheery note: "After all, you have a lot to lose; I don't. It's your neck, not mine. So hang yourself if you dare."

Ever since the first Regina phone call O'Malley had been trying to get the FBI and the U.S. Attorney to seriously pursue the arrest of Regina for the obvious crimes in which he was engaged. But looking back now, I suspect that Agent Tuttle and Carol Bruce were in no hurry to have their paid informant–star witness against me arrested before they got me into court. I had been forced into the anomalous position of having my attorney attempt negotiations on my behalf with the U.S. Attorney at the same time that the U.S. Attorney's possible witness was being investigated for attempting to blackmail me. The same U.S. Attorney and FBI agent had been using Eddie for months to obtain evidence against me. Until the matter of Congressman Bob Bauman was disposed of in court the last thing they wanted was Eddie Regina blabbing all about his role in the government's investigation.

On October 9, almost at the same hour I was holding my first press conference since my court appearance on October 3, Eddie Regina was arrested by FBI agents in Annapolis, the Maryland state capital, on the State House lawn. He thought he was about to receive two thousand dollars from my congressional staff members to buy his silence. Ever a man of his word, Eddie had arranged to meet a reporter from the *Baltimore Sun* a few minutes later and instead of the promised interview, the press witnessed him being taken into custody.

Ultimately I had to appear before a federal grand jury the day after the election to testify about Regina's blackmail attempt. He was indicted for numerous federal crimes, including blackmail, and later served a three-month sentence after a plea bargain arrangement with the U.S. Attorney on the charge of using the U.S. mails to threaten.

From that morning on September 3, 1980, when the FBI paid me a visit until 9:30 A.M., October 3, 1980, when I appeared in the Criminal Division of the Superior Court for the District of Columbia, the official prosecutorial establishment of the United States Attorney for the District of Columbia, personified by Carol

Bruce, never budged from the deal first described to me by Agent Tuttle and later by Eddie Regina. No amount of argument or discussion could convince Ms. Bruce or her associates to deviate from the outcome they wished to dictate in the case of *United States of America vs. Robert E. Bauman.* The two alternatives were, plead as I was directed or, have "the book" thrown at me in multiple indictments by a federal grand jury. My attorney, Tom O'Malley, did his best to bolster my legal situation but drawing on his own experience in the U.S. Attorney's office he deemed the chances of lessened pressure to be almost nil. "They've made up their minds and I doubt that they will change," he said.

But he tried. Responding to Carol Bruce's expressed concern that my past conduct constituted an opening to blackmail, O'Malley patiently explained the details of my personal battle to recover from alcoholism and to solve my sexual problems with professional help. He underscored that this self-help had begun long before any investigation was known. My drinking had stopped on May 1, 1980, and I was no longer cruising the gay bar scene. Father Harvey met with O'Malley and the U.S. Attorney's staff to confirm these facts and Dr. Kay submitted an affidavit that I was his patient after a personal visit by him was rejected by the staff. O'Malley's argument was straightforward. The First Offenders Act was supposed to promote rehabilitation, the kind I had already done. "This man has faced his problems," Tom said. "A court appearance can only destroy his reputation and possibly his political career."

The brutally frank answer to that central question came inadvertently from a member of the U.S. Attorney's staff in an unguarded moment. In the presence of O'Malley and Father Harvey the staff member denied a request for a delay in the court date until after the election with this curt reply: "The people of Bauman's congressional district have a right to know what kind of man he is before they cast their votes."

In an explosive response Tom O'Malley was just as blunt: "If this criminal proceeding is based on politics then you can haul us

18

into court on whatever charges you wish. I will not be a party to using the judicial system for a political lynching. I'm sure the public will want to know this is your motivation."

Realizing this fundamental mistake the staff member retracted the statement by saying that any delay would constitute "special treatment" for me. Besides, he said, the case had been under investigation for many months and was ready for court action. Political motivation was strongly denied.

O'Malley then pointed out that the First Offenders law allowed for court proceedings to be conducted *in camera,* that is, in closed session. That request was also denied. Not only would the appearance not be in secret but I would be required to make a "public statement" which Carol Bruce described in an October 2, 1980, letter to O'Malley as ". . . a full disclosure of the facts of the charges, the circumstances leading up to his involvement in this crime, and the agreement reached with this office concerning the disposition of the charges." This "full disclosure" requirement was sprung on me only hours before I appeared in court and only after I had been led to believe that no such statement would be asked of me. I had been told that the U.S. Attorney would simply file a confidential statement with the court which would remain a part of the closed record of the case that only the judge would see. Since the prosecutors were simply filing an "information" which requires no factual statement I had believed assurances given to Tom O'Malley by Ms. Bruce that the U.S. Attorney would make no statement. I would appear in court, plead not guilty as a "first offender" to the single charge of solicitation, and the judge would place me on six months' probation during which I would receive counseling for my "problems."

Before the court date O'Malley had asked for any supporting documents or other information the government might possess in my case and was told there were none to which I had a right under the law. At my insistence I obtained a written statement from Ms. Bruce that once I met the terms of the agreement no other charges would be filed.

But on the evening of October 2, the day before I was to be in court, the thirty-page FBI investigative memorandum which I had been denied was in the hands of reporters for the *Washington Post.* Neither O'Malley nor I had ever seen it and it was filled with wild charges against me. The October 5 *Baltimore Sun* reported: "Mr. Bauman's lawyer, Mr. O'Malley, reacted angrily to the reports disclosing details of the FBI's investigation, material which he said was never presented to him in his discussions with the U.S. Attorney's office . . . during those negotiations prosecutors presented him with no documents and no witnesses to substantiate the allegations (in the FBI report), only generalizations. They were extremely vague."

The *Sun* said further: "The lawyer said he was 'sick at my stomach' that 'raw data' which he characterized as 'unevaluated crap' contained in the FBI report was leaked to the press. 'Everybody knows that the FBI puts everything but the kitchen sink in their reports,' he said. Mr. O'Malley said he felt it was a violation on the U.S. Attorney's agreement—which provides that no materials pertaining to the case will be disclosed and the charge will be dismissed upon the successful completion of the probation—if 'the U.S. government can't take better care of their documents in this case.' " In response, U.S. Attorney Charles Ruff told reporters that 'no one in his office leaked details of the investigation or the FBI report to the press.' "

Two weeks later, right in the midst of my difficult reelection campaign, the *Washington Star* featured an article entitled: "Susceptibility to Extortion Brought U.S. Charge Against Rep. Bauman." The story was based solely on the "confidential" memorandum Carol Bruce had written as an internal staff argument of justification for prosecuting me. The *Star* wrote: "The report, which was obtained by the *Washington Star,* provides a detailed explanation of the rationale used by the prosecutors for charging Bauman earlier this month . . ." The article then went on to quote all the juicy, lurid details, including such phrases as "closet homosexual" and "pederast," "blackmail" and "extortion," "violation of public trust" and "abuse of public office." When O'Malley called Ms. Bruce to protest the next day her airy reply was that in an age of copying machines it was difficult to control such leaks. She assured him that she knew nothing about it.

The blatant leaks of the FBI investigative report and the Bruce memorandum brought about just the situation I had sought to avoid by agreeing to plead and not stand trial. I had stupidly believed that avoiding the prolonged agony of a public trial with daily press reports and media coverage would spare Carol, the children, and myself the humiliation and embarrassment that a court fight would have insured. Now all the sensational charges had been placed before the public even though most could never have been proven in court. And it was done intentionally in the worst possible manner, leaving me without any means of answering except under the merciless grilling of the news media that cared nothing about legal concepts such as "due process of law" or "proven beyond a reasonable doubt." To add to the irony, Carol Bruce again refused to give Tom O'Malley copies of the two documents that had already appeared in substance and direct quotes in the press, saying that the law exempted them from a defendant's request since they were internal documents in the case used by the prosecution and law enforcement officials. To this day I have not seen them.

In retrospect, I seriously doubt that those bent on prosecuting me ever intended that the matter be handled quietly, in spite of their specific assurances to the contrary. Their purpose was not strict and impartial application of the law, but rather to make sure that my personal conduct was exposed before the 1980 elections. Under the pressure of my situation I had wanted to believe their promises. My mind was so dazed by the deepening horror of my circumstances that I actually had thought that the news coverage and the resultant public uproar could be minimized. That I ever believed such a thing was a measure of my desperation. While it in no way diminishes my personal culpability, it is a fair question whether I was singled out while others in Congress were ignored, and whether the timing of my case was delayed to affect the election.

On both counts my belief is that the answer is "yes."

The source who was directly involved in the investigation at the time told me that the police task force interest in me had produced an investigative report that "in most respects was finished by March 1980." The same person told me that several times he had made informal inquiries of the U.S. Attorney's staff as to what was being done with my case as the summer passed and was told that it was taking more time than expected to bring to trial. In response to inquiries as to whether anything was being done about investigations into the nine other senators and congressmen he was told "that decisions in each case have not been made yet." And they never were.

That the FBI investigation of me had concluded by March 1980 would certainly fit with the attempts made later by Agent Tuttle to get Eddie Regina to entrap me. Lack of hard evidence would also explain why the July grand jury never heard any evidence against me, or if they did, why they failed to act. "If they wanted to haul you into court they should have been able to do so any time after March 1980," my informant said.

Instead, exactly sixty days before the 1980 elections, months after its conclusion, I learned of a criminal investigation of me that had been under way for more than a year.

The same source assured me: "They did not act in your case, either at the FBI or the U.S. Attorney's office, without political clearance from the top. Self-protection means they at least got an okay from the Justice Department and maybe even higher. Prudence dictates that much, so that when the pressure hits those lower down the line don't become scapegoats if something goes wrong." Then he added, as if an afterthought: "It may be no consolation to you, but the truth is that the same kind of conduct by congressmen, senators, and other government officials is still going on in Washington and the police know it. Some of the same people known in 1980 are still involved. Things never really change in this town, only some of the names and faces."

One possible proof of that assertion is a stunning bit of evidence provided to me by the late Congressman Larry MacDonald of Georgia. The very conservative Democrat died thirty-three thousand feet over the Sea of Japan in Korean Airlines flight 007 on August 28, 1984, when the Russians shot down the plane. MacDonald, who at his death was national chairman of the John Birch Society, was a dedicated anti-Communist whose office files contained interesting information about many famous people. I worked for MacDonald as a consultant in 1981–82. One day he called me into his office to ask a question: "For some time I've wanted to know why you didn't tell me about your personal problems in 1980. I think I could have helped you." I had never been personally close to MacDonald although we were friends. I explained that, caught up in the predicament, I really had little time to talk with anyone except those immediately involved. "But what," I was eager to know, "could you have done to help?"

In his soft, southern, matter-of-fact accent MacDonald replied: "A very prominent Democratic congressman was involved with the same young man you were. I only learned later that it was the same young man but I have known about our colleague's private conduct for some time. Had I known of your situation I would have gone directly to him and told him that if Bob Bauman was going to be singled out then he would receive the same treatment."

Frankly I was stunned at the name Congressman MacDonald had uttered. I protested that he surely must be mistaken. He didn't back down a bit: "My sources are reliable and there were more than one. I am as sure of this as anything in my life." I left his office not knowing what to believe. But then few people ever expected to discover Bob Bauman in such a situation. The Democratic congressman Larry MacDonald named continues to this day in a position of major prominence in the House of Representatives.

And as further evidence of what MacDonald, my informant in the government, and others have told me—and what I have seen myself in the last few years—there are many men in leading positions of power who are homosexuals and yet appear regularly in the media as the leaders of our nation. Gay and closeted, many of them are married and have families. They serve in Congress, the Reagan administration and White House, the judiciary, military, and Washington power circles. Many of them are not so closeted and are known to a wide circle of people, even those in the press, who protect their secret. And often it is not so secret. One of them took the political precaution of acquiring an attractive young wife after the rumor started that he was gay. He can still be found some evenings in Washington gay bars smirking with his companions at the nude male dancers. Another is more cautious: he sends out one of his staff aides to recruit male hustlers for a price, thus avoiding being seen in public places that might raise questions. In Georgetown, on Capitol Hill, in Foggy Bottom and Alexandria, all-male parties are often graced by some of the big names of our times. The participants include Democrats, Republicans, liberals and conservatives, labor union officials, and business leaders. Sometimes they bring their younger male friends with them (derisively known as "twinkies") and sometimes they are accompanied by lovers of many years. Some are close friends of the President, some serve on the staff of the national political committees of both parties, and some aspire to higher office. Some regularly appear in public as leaders of the conservative movement and some few even resort to the hypocritical tactic of attacking homosexuality and gay people in their public role. Later the same day they retire to bed with another male after spending an hour or two at a gay bar.

As my informant says, in Washington things don't really change that much.

* * *

It is pointless to deny the truth. I was guilty of criminal conduct in engaging in sexual acts, soliciting sexual acts, and far worse, I must accept responsibility for betraying my wife, our marriage vows, and dishonoring my family. I compromised my religious beliefs and my personal honor.

But those personal failings were not the reasons on which those who held legal power and authority based their decision to bring me to public account.

Was it simply, as Attorney General Civiletti later said, a matter of routine law enforcement? Or was it a calculated act of politics in both content and timing?

As the one who suffered the punishment I think I have the right to offer my own opinions after five years of living the consequences of not just my own acts, but others' decisions as well.

Obviously, some one person or persons within the Carter administration made a calculated decision to finger me for action.

Was this decision made because I was indeed, as some said, susceptible to blackmail?

In that charge resides a supreme irony. The only blackmail attempted against me was on the part of the government's own paid informant and possible witness against me, the grasping Eddie Regina, who wound up in a federal prison for his efforts. Several years before all this I had been contacted by an official of the Soviet Embassy in Washington who asked for a meeting with me after hearing me speak at a conservative conference. I granted him the meeting after checking with the FBI who informed me that the man was a KGB or Soviet secret police agent. As the FBI instructed I gave them a full description of what was discussed; the Russian wanted to know about Ronald Reagan's chances of becoming President and whether all conservatives really were so violently anti-Communist. The only other allegation of possible blackmail in my case, that made by Agent Tuttle that I had obtained preferential treatment on a U.S. Navy discharge case because of a threat to expose me, was later admitted by both government spokesmen and the press (much later) to be false. In fact, the discharge was handled in a routine manner by my staff without my knowledge at the time.

So there was no blackmail and had there been any attempt it would have failed, as Eddie Regina's attempt did.

Far more likely, whatever your sympathy with my political views, is that Carter administration officials were not nearly so interested in protecting the virtue of male prostitutes, preventing blackmail, or even the fact that others in the Congress were doing it too. The pleasing prospect in getting Bauman was that my private conduct could be justifiably employed to end my admittedly irritating public career.

Here was a chance to remove one of the most vociferous critics of the President, of his hapless brother, of his unpopular gasoline tax, of his confused energy policy, and of his floundering administration in general. The so-called "New Right" was already deeply involved in the threatening Reagan presidential campaign. I was one of that group's congressional leaders and a longtime Reagan supporter. By his own repeated admission, I was near the top of his list of those who inflicted massive political irritation on the Honorable "Tip" O'Neill, the highly partisan Speaker of the House of Representatives. Under all these unique circumstances what political animal, given such a chance, would fail to come down with force on a vulnerable adversary? Men, particularly politicians, do not resist such temptations.

Add to the general political considerations a personal factor at the Justice Department when it came to Congressman Bob Bauman of Maryland.

The U.S. attorney general was then one Benjamin Civiletti, a leading liberal Democrat from Baltimore, Maryland, formerly, and now once again, partner in one of the major establishment law firms of that city. Civiletti had a long record as an active participant in the state's Democratic politics and is a close personal friend and supporter of the incumbent junior senator from Maryland, Paul Sarbanes. The attorney general owed his cabinet position not just to his considerable legal talents and standing within the profession, but to Paul Sarbanes and his service as the senator's fund-raiser and political confidant. In 1980 Sarbanes had served four lackluster years in the Senate and was tagged by the experts to be the most vulnerable Democrat up for reelection in 1982. Polls showed him to be virtually unknown and among those who could identify him his image was of ineffectiveness. Already the National Conservative Political Action Committee (NCPAC) had targeted him for extinction. The sympathetic editorialists for the *Baltimore Sun* were warning the senator of his precarious future. A well-financed, articulate conservative candidate could be a real threat to Paul Sarbanes' return to the Senate even in a "moderate" state such as Maryland, especially if Ronald Reagan made a strong run for the White House and carried the state.

And throughout the Maryland press and media for almost two years the name most prominently mentioned as the likely Sarbanes 1982 opponent was the gentleman from Maryland, Bob Bauman.

CHAPTER
TWO

*T*he homosexual scene in the nation's capital is not that different from gay life in any large metropolitan area with the exception of the openly hospitable attitude displayed by the mayor and city government toward the gay community. Perhaps exceeded only by San Francisco, the policy of Washington's mayor, Marion Barry, is to support gays, who form a large, cohesive block of Democratic party voters, many of whom he has appointed to municipal office.

Barry, a liberal black activist and civil rights veteran, pledged in his first campaign to end police harassment of gays which had included regular raids on gay bars and entrapment of individuals by undercover policemen. Barry kept his word. After he won, police vice squad activity against gays was curtailed. Solicitation for prostitution, that venerable misdemeanor in most countries of the Christian West, ceased to clutter the Washington police blotter. Where once there had been hundreds of cases each year, only three or four had occurred since Barry took office prior to my own case.

In 1953, when I came to Washington as a fifteen-year-old page boy in the U.S. House of Representatives, confident that I was not queer (only confused), I heard rumors that there were places that such people gathered such as a nondescript restaurant on L Street N.W., called the Redskin Lounge. It was not until the early 1960s that openly gay bars appeared, one appropriately near the U.S. Marine Barracks at Eight and Eye Streets S.E., called Plus One. By 1980 there were gay social establishments of every description, including baths, movies, burlesque houses, bars, and more bars. The local gay publication, the weekly *Blade,* lists perhaps a hundred such places.

Although free-market economics always dictate change, the gay bar scene in Washington has not changed that much since 1980 when my difficulties occurred. Periodically some venture-some businessman opens a new bar or club and some prosper and some die. Popularity runs in cycles with the collective gay desire to always be "in" at the supposedly most fashionable establish-ment of the moment. Which one is the "in place" occupies much discussion over drinks.

For the leather types there is the Exile. But for the large Wash-ington group of "preppies," the button-down crowd that seeks to imitate the latest from *Gentleman's Quarterly* in their manner and dress, there are many places. On the way home from your govern-ment job the young collegiate can stop off at Rascals on Connect-icut Avenue above Dupont Circle, the "in" gay neighborhood. Here Oxford cloth shirts, three-piece suits, and wing-tip shoes are the uniform for a homeward-bound drink, until later in the eve-ning.

The preps and beautiful young men also favor the Lost and Found down among the warehouses and railroad tracks in south-east Washington near the Navy Yard. Covering half a city block, the club is a gay oasis in a slum section of the capital. Nearby is a more recent arrival, Tracks, a "New York–style" club imitating Studio 54, with thundering sound systems, dazzling light shows, bubbles and smoke, video screens, all to the incessant beat of New Wave or other recent dance crazes. High door fees tend to weed out the sleaze factor and at Tracks gays and straights mix with little friction. Two blocks to the south is a major lesbian club and the Follies, a male strip joint for gays. Next door is La Cage Aux Follies, a gay pickup bar. Few straight Washingtonians know about these gay establishments in the slums and gays prefer it that way.

At the Lost and Found, Tracks, and other clubs you can view the parade of beautiful people, including gay congressional aides, Reagan administration officials and workers, Republican National Committee and Democratic National Committee staffers, and lower echelon politicians of all ideological shades. The gay staffer of one of the furthest right senators can be seen chatting over drinks with a junior lobbyist for one of the most leftward causes. The unifying factor of being gay submerges all else for the evening. And you might meet a congressman.

All this is light years from the ancient days when discreet whispers were heard about Franklin D. Roosevelt's notoriously gay Under Secretary of State, Sumner Welles, or the later time when not so quiet rumors were spread about Senator Joe McCarthy of Wisconsin and his staff members. Today, Congressman Garry Studds of Massachusetts has been censured by the House for having a homosexual affair with a teen-age page boy. He has also been reelected by his constituency. His Massachusetts colleague, the witty liberal Barney Frank, appears at Washington's annual Gay Pride Day in a tank top with his usual young companion and their picture appears in the *Blade* without comment. Most gay members of Congress choose to be more closeted but their names are known to many in and out of gay circles, including the media, which has its own gay contingent.

There are others of note who appear in public at gay establishments; the top federal consultant on one of the major international issues now current, often seen with a young hustler on his arm; the son of one of the top U.S. intelligence agencies officials whose father always knows where his son has been the night before because he has him watched; the leading union official; the corporate lobbyists; the journalists.

There are also several bars that cater especially to the middle-aged and older men who are known as "chicken hawks," a crude designation for their taste for younger men, of which there are many eager and available in Washington. The well-known demand for such hustlers has greatly increased the supply. They gather each evening about nine at places such as La Cage, the Lone Star or, the scene of my own denouement, the Chesapeake House, 927 Ninth Street N.W.

I surely did not know that the Chesapeake House would be the scene of the crime.

This establishment's existence, location, and general social function were made known to me by Eddie Regina. After a fateful brief encounter with Eddie, probably in the winter of 1979, he urged me to go with him to the Chesapeake House, where he said he was a nude dancer. He seemed amazed that I did not know of this infamous place where young men danced nude atop the bar to the fervent disco beat so popular with the gay crowd. But his invitation came as the booze wore off and my returning better judgment made me decline. I let him out of my car at the curb.

After all, even in my alcoholic haze I remembered that I had a wife, four children, and a seat in the Congress to think about. Whatever I had done earlier in the evening I was not about to be seen in some notorious gay bar, or so I thought. I chose to drive off into the night toward the Chesapeake Bay Bridge, the Eastern Shore of Maryland, and the only real home I have known in life.

Weeks later, after preying on my mind, the Chesapeake House and its possible action drew me back like a magnet once I had fortified my courage with a large quantity of alcohol, my standard operating procedure before such forays. The mind-altering chemical was essential to what I had to do.

And so it began, sporadic nocturnal visits to the House that would lead to my political demise. And my liberation as a human being, some would argue.

It was on one of these adventures to the Chesapeake House that I noticed the angels. They must have been a whimsical purchase from some second-rate antique shop.

Painted on a large oval canvas, four feet tall and two and a half feet wide, there they were, Raphael-like, a pair of cherubs, dancing and floating in a midair columnar formation, faint pink clouds misting around them. The childlike faces were smiling, seemingly bent on nothing more sinister than the roles an omnipotent creator has assigned all seraphim and cherubim; as it was said of Shelley, "a beautiful and ineffectual angel, beating in the void his luminous wings in vain."

Coated with sepia-toned grime, I doubt that many people noticed the painting hanging close by a neon Budweiser sign over the busy cash register. It was a while before I saw them. Usually my mind was too clouded to realize that my unofficial conduct was being observed by a couple of itinerant angels.

But just as it is a hallmark of the lives of closeted homosexuals, incongruity abounds at the Chesapeake House.

The squat, two-story brick building sits in an uneven expanse of asphalt parking lot only a few hundred yards from the impressive Doric columns that form the Greek Revival facade of the National Portrait Gallery, once the Patent Office. One of the first public buildings to be erected in this federal city built on a swamp, in Abraham Lincoln's time the Patent Office housed the Interior Department and later was filled with inventors' models and other curiosities. By 1980 the old Patent Office housed a national collection of portraits of America's heroes, scholars, politicians, and military leaders. A block away at the Chesapeake House their latter-day descendants often gather.

My usual reason for visiting the Chesapeake House was not to evaluate the decor. Like other men of my age, the crisis years of the early forties, I was there to drink and seek quick and hopefully anonymous sexual encounters with young men, the hustlers who came there for the same purpose. The "Peake," as it is called, is one of the thousands of "over and under" cruise bars that have sprung up in cities throughout the nation. (To "cruise" is to look for a sexual partner. "Over and under" means roughly over forty and under twenty-five years of age. Whatever the age, the customers know why they are there.)

The name Chesapeake House had an ironic meaning for me, representing as I did the Chesapeake Bay area of Maryland in Congress, now famous because of James Michener's epic novel of the same name. There is another Chesapeake House, a well-known fishing resort and hotel on Tilghman Island in the Bay, owned by an old line family of Democrats, the Harrisons, always my strong supporters.

You enter Washington's Chesapeake House through vaguely Spanish-looking double doors to be greeted by a sign informing you that admission will cost you two dollars. It cost me a lot more.

It is not a very large place, guaranteeing that it will be crowded most evenings. The entire bar on the first floor of the Communications Workers of America Building (their local office is upstairs) measures no more than 30 feet across and perhaps 250 feet deep. As you enter, on the right is a dark wood bar with stools over which hang four imitation Tiffany lamps.

On the bar top each evening from 9:00 P.M. to 2:00 or 3:00 A.M. (the later hour on weekends) three or four young men, guaranteed by the management to be eighteen years old or older, dance, strip, and display their nude masculinity. The Tiffany lamp chains serve as convenient display racks for the dollar bills handed up as a mark of appreciation by the ogling viewers. "Street-smart" dancers greet each donation with a perfunctory kiss on the lips, encouraging further investment and perhaps a more lucrative meeting after hours.

Mirrors line shelves behind the bar with the limited stock of alcoholic beverages a preoccupied clientele requires. People drink here but that is obviously not the main reason for their presence. The careful eye catches another incongruity; imitation bronze plaster statues of a man and woman locked in heterosexual embrace, the closest many customers will ever come to such an act. A glass Tower of London guard watches over the couple and touts the virtues of Beefeater Gin.

On the wall over the bar some forgotten spirit of Christmas

past has festooned barren tree branches with tiny electric lights. The twinkling garlands also decorate the antlers of several quizzical deer heads—glassy eyes staring dully into murky space. Deer hooves (cloven?) hang mounted on plaques, each daintily turned upward either in supplication or as a sign of luck for "all ye who enter here."

Beyond the bar at the rear of the large room there is a much wider space with a runway-stage on which dancing boys take turns performing. A smaller platform in the corner serves a similar purpose. Both areas have large wall mirrors which replicate and multiply the gyrating male bodies, allowing the dancers to simulate obscene rituals with their reflected selves, the ultimate public narcissism. Smiling down from the wall on all this are the angels.

And on one wall hangs a huge gilt-framed pastoral scene in oil reminiscent of Albert Bierstadt and the Hudson River School. What is that doing here?

And what exactly are they doing here? These older and younger men?

The older ones lounge near the men's and women's restrooms, used interchangeably by all the male clientele. Sometimes a woman is present but never a lady. The young men, many appearing barely old enough to gain entrance to a place that serves alcohol, circulate in the crowd, greeting other hustlers and past and present customers (known in the trade as "Johns"). The eye contact usually important in a gay bar is unnecessary here. Everyone knows what is going on and only the newcomers are hesitant.

The older men's costumes range from the conservative businessman's three-piece suit of the visiting conventioneer or the late-working husband to the sadly macho jeans and sleeveless muscle shirt that glorifies the youthful body but betrays the sagging physique of the middle-aged. The younger men favor jeans and T-shirts but some choose the neater preppy look. The emphasis is always on displaying the body, a form of advertising.

34

Young and old mix easily here except for the first timers whose nervous glances betray them. Most people here know what they want, what they have to sell, and what they can get in return.

Two factors pervade and dominate the scene: the loud, pulsating, deafening blast of disco or rock which makes serious conversation all but impossible. ("Can I buy you a drink?" "Sure, why not.") The other factor, an overwhelming impression of smoke, darkness, even decay. If the night is black the bar itself seems even darker. Through the haze of cigarettes and an occasional joint of grass there is the faint odor of urine, stale beer, and musty industrial carpet. A very strange place, you might well think, to find men prominent in government, journalism, the military, business, even the clergy. But unless their faces are well known they can travel incognito here. That is the code.

With a few drinks, a drag on a joint of pot, a snort of cocaine, the mind transforms this tawdry scene. Slightly built young physiques gradually become competition for the Junior Mr. America contest. Post-adolescent faces acquire the quality of Michelangelo's *David* as the evening wears on.

And the inhibitions and moral restraints of a lifetime vanish in seconds.

I have not the slightest idea when it happened, what night of the week or the date. And neither did the U.S. Attorney's staff when they came to draw the accusation against me. "... on or about ..." was the best they could do.

It was probably the fall or winter of 1979.

My visits to the Chesapeake House seemed to be increasing by no special design on my part. I was drinking a lot more and that seemed to influence the frequency.

On the evening in question a muscular young blond was dancing on the bar top, tossing his curly hair and snapping his fingers as he swayed to the rock beat. Without the slightest hesitation he shed his T-shirt, blue jeans, and bikini briefs, giving the crowd the show they came for, an eyeful plus. Not strikingly handsome, he was definitely "good looking." In a profession requiring brazenness he retained a certain air of innocence, which appealed to me.

Noticing that he was actively hustling the customers during the breaks between his dance sets I introduced myself and bought him a drink. We sat in the back of the bar with another hustler friend of his with whom he lived.

Speaking of incongruity.

Here was a conservative member of the U.S. Congress attired for that role in a suit with vest, sipping bourbon with two scantily clad young hustlers in a noisy, smoke-filled barroom only blocks from the U.S. Capitol. One A.M. in the morning and a million miles from home and reality.

The young blond's name was "Michael." (If you know the gay scene you might well ask, "Aren't they all named Michael?")

He said he lived in the Capitol Hill area with his friend and another older guy. He would be off work at 2:00 A.M., if I wanted to wait.

I did and he was.

My drinking was, as usual, heavy that night and I'm not sure exactly what happened or whether events from other nights are jumbled in my mind. The official government memorandum written by Carol Bruce says that Michael's seventeen-year-old lover "Steve" (an alias) ". . . through his own brand of moral indignation, jealousy, and a dose of machismo" informed me that he intended to tell the police what I had done, that he knew I was a congressman. At that point I allegedly invited him outside in the parking lot where I offered to buy his silence for one hundred dollars, a crude offer he refused because "he could not be bought," man of honor that he was. My own sources later informed me that "Steve" was not seventeen but twenty-four and a veteran hustler and drug user. (He has twice been arrested on drug charges since 1980. He was also a paid informer for the FBI, who saw me as a lucrative bit of salable information.)

Straightaway Steve communicated his interesting knowledge to his police friends and was told to keep a lookout for me should I again come into the bar, since he did not know my name. He had seen my congressional license plate and in due time the police found out who "Maryland Member of Congress 1" was.

I never saw Michael again after that evening. Not in person. I did see his shy face in a snapshot provided to my attorney by Carol Bruce. We had demanded it so that I would at least know who my accuser was. Taken by Agent Tuttle, Michael's photo made him look even younger and more innocent than I recall him that night at the Chesapeake House.

Unfortunately that night was not my only visit to the Chesapeake House. One evening in 1979 a young federal employee, Craig Howell, was conversing over drinks with friends at a table in the bar. As Howell lifted his glass he stared uncertainly through the haze at a well-dressed, perhaps even dapper man leaning against the dingy bar wall. As the naked dancers strutted to the music's beat Howell blinked in amazed disbelief.

The man he thought he saw was a most unlikely patron of an establishment such as this—yours truly, the Honorable Robert E. Bauman of Maryland.

Not just the Honorable Bauman, member of Congress, but convert to Roman Catholicism, married and the father of four, a leader and spokesman for the American conservative movement. Friend of Ronald Reagan, William F. Buckley, Jr., parliamentary scourge of House Speaker Tip O'Neill and the liberals on Capitol Hill.

Howell was later to tell a reporter for the *Baltimore News American* that the man he saw that night was "one of the loneliest people I have ever seen."

I did not know Craig Howell that evening though I have met him since. In the bar setting I rarely saw anyone as an individual, only as a first name to be forgotten when the brief encounter was over. Booze dulled both memory and awareness, making alcohol essential to my goal.

But Howell was correct in his instant assessment.

The lonelines and isolation he sensed had long been a dominant feature of my introspective life. Often I was so removed from reality that I could boldly visit a place such as this without any real appreciation of the disaster I was courting for myself, my wife, and my family.

Maybe "Steve" had known me only as an auto license plate, but any day Craig Howell and his friends wanted to see the "real" Bob Bauman in his own arena I was not far away. A short five-minute auto drive down Ninth Street, left on Pennsylvania Avenue, and then up Capitol Hill. There in a much larger chamber with a dark wood motif they could have viewed me working diligently at my chosen profession of parliamentary politics.

The Hall of the House of Representatives in the United States Capitol was my home for much of my life; three years as a teenage page boy, ten years as a floor staff member, nearly eight years as member of Congress representing Maryland's First Congressional District. I knew every pockmark gouged by the Puerto Rican Nationalists who fired on the House on March 1, 1954; I was there. I knew the cattle ranch brands still to be seen on the Texas cowhides that cover the chairs in which I would eventually sit as a congressman myself. I memorized the stories of the "famous lawgivers" whose faces grace medallions on the Chamber wall. I could even identify each of the state and territorial seals that surround the enormous glass skylight in the shape of an American eagle.

Once I became a member of Congress after a special election in 1973 I also made it my business to expand my knowledge of the procedures and precedents compiled in great volumes by the past parliamentarians of the House, Hinds, Cannon, and Deschler. As a page and staff member I had used this arcane body of knowledge to aid others. Now I would employ it myself. I also made it my business to know the individual and collective weaknesses and strengths of the congressional cast of characters. I kept up on all the daily legislative rumors and tips in order to exploit the odds and achieve conservative victories. I believed deeply in those conservative principles and here was the ultimate place in which to put them to use. And even in frequent defeat, those around me came to know that Bob Bauman was there.

Always there.

Day after day, and many nights, between September 5, 1973, and January 3, 1981, you could find me in my favorite arena, the floor of the U.S. House of Representatives. For nearly eight years my attendance record on all roll calls was better than 98 percent. Many years it was 100 percent, much to the chagrin of my colleagues who would have enjoyed a little relief from my unrelenting presence.

And what an impressive stage it is. Long before cable television made the House of Representatives as familiar as daytime soap operas, many Americans had seen the chamber in photos of joint congressional sessions about to declare war or hear some famous world leader speak. Each year there is the President's State of the Union address and on special occasions visits by Winston Churchill, Charles de Gaulle, General Douglas MacArthur, Anwar Sadat; they all came to speak to America from the rostrum of the House.

Only a few yards away, four rows from the front, was my self-assigned seat at the corner of the Republican leadership table. There I waged my own personal war of conservative objections and legislative attrition against political liberals in both parties. Often alone, I was sometimes able to command a majority of my colleagues, especially when I forced a current hot issue to a roll call which provided a record for the folks back home to inspect.

A typical day might have been one in the hot 1980 summer when "the gentleman from Maryland" and other conservatives mounted a major assault on President Jimmy Carter's Nicaraguan policy. The President had, in my view, irrationally chosen to give hundreds of millions of dollars of taxpayers' money to the Communist Sandinista regime which only months before had shot its way to power with Cuban and Russian help. Six months after the Sandinistas staged a successful revolt against the long-time right-wing dictator Anasatasio Somoza, I paid an official visit to the impoverished capital city of Managua. I returned to Washington and the debate convinced of my suspicions; these were not "agrarian reformers" but hard-core Communist revolutionaries working hand in hand with Fidel Castro and his Moscow sponsors. Their wider goal was Red revolution and terrorism throughout Central and South America.

When President Carter's Sandinista aid legislation came before the House, I and others offered a series of restrictive amendments seeking to force the Sandinistas to grant human and political rights or lose the money the bill granted. Carter wanted no restrictions. As State Department lobbyists huddled outside in the halls and Speaker O'Neill stalked the House floor trying to stem the loss of Democratic members' votes, the acerbic House Majority Leader, Jim Wright of Texas, took the floor.

As our conservative amendments had triumphed one after another Wright had had enough of losing for one afternoon. Furrowing his bushy eyebrows in my direction he employed his biting eloquence to personally castigate me as the leader of this right-wing band, finally inquiring with heavy sarcasm whether "the gentleman from Maryland has now become the Republican secretary of state or perhaps the Republican Leader of the House?"

As if to answer the Majority Leader's rhetorical question my Republican colleagues spontaneously rose from their seats and turned toward me, raucously seconding Wright's unintended nomination with cheering and applause.

Surprise, immense pleasure, and mild shock made my cheeks burn. Not given to blushing modesty I suddenly felt like the school boy who does well in his class recitation and knows it. My pride of accomplishment must have been obvious. My good friend, the late Congressman from Ohio, John Ashbrook, leaned over and whispered in my ear, "You love it!"

And indeed I did.

This was not the first time my congressional colleagues had granted me their approval and acceptance, something I had never been able to give myself. I had forced the world around me to deal with Bob Bauman even as I could not deal with myself.

CHAPTER THREE

The criminal division of the Superior Court of the District of Columbia had no difficulty in dealing with Bob Bauman. It was all prearranged.

Three weeks of "negotiations" between Tom O'Malley and Carol Bruce produced not a wit of give on the part of government prosecutors. And so on the appointed morning of October 3, Congress having adjourned the evening before for the six-week election recess, I appeared with my attorney at Ms. Bruce's office in the United States Court House at Constitution Avenue and John Marshall Place N.W. The "Major Crimes Section" of the United States Attorney's office turned out to be just another dingy bureaucratic warren, heavy on spent coffee cups, cigarette butts, and impersonality. My wife, Carol, was with me, both of us trying to put the best face on the worst situation. As I glanced out the window of Ms. Bruce's bare office I noticed a small bookshelf below. There were a number of books on homosexuality but one caught my eye; something to the effect of "Male Juvenile Prostitution and Pederasts." The prosecution was obviously ready for any eventuality.

Carol and Tom were sent off to the courtroom but I had to take a humiliating detour. Accompanied by two plainclothes detectives I was whisked down the elevator and across the street in a police car where I was escorted into the police lockup in the basement of the D.C. courts building. I went into a dingy room where tight-lipped uniformed police motioned me to take a seat in front of a stationary camera. Just as with any cheap hoodlum they went about their business, cellblock doors clanging in the background. They placed a rack of numbers on my chest and the light flashed. Front face. Side face. Then I was fingerprinted and courteously given a Kleenex to wipe away a stain all the perfumes of Arabia could not eradicate.

From there I was escorted back to the police car, driven over to the courthouse, up a back elevator and down a long silent corridor to a private entrance of the assigned courtroom. There I met a probation officer who did his best to make me feel at ease, even as I heard the ominous buzz of a packed courtroom beyond the door. He told me he was a former Catholic seminarian and that he knew Father Harvey, my close advisor through all this. He asked what my probation terms were and I told him I knew of no restrictions beyond the fact that I would be under Father Harvey's care. "That's more than I knew," he said. "Your paperwork doesn't indicate what the U.S. Attorney's office proposed." (In fact there was no probationary supervision and after six months the charge was dropped without another court appearance. Had I been reelected they might have decided to watch me much more closely.)

After what seemed hours the black judge, David Norman, who is blind, arrived at the rear door from his nearby office and ascended to the bench. I was the first item on the court calendar. As my case was called I walked out into a jammed courtroom and stood before the judge's bench. The crowd was so packed that Tom O'Malley had trouble getting through to the front of the room. Carol never did make it after all our pains to arrange that my wife be there with me. The judge asked if I understood the misdemeanor charge, my rights as a first offender and what my plea was. "Not guilty," I said quietly. He then announced the six months' probation as agreed and it was all over. It took less than five minutes. Throughout I experienced a detached reality as though I was a disembodied soul viewing my own funeral.

As I was driven from the private parking garage a lone press photographer waiting at the top of the exit ramp caught the full side view of my glum face staring straight ahead in the traditional "criminal leaves court" picture. It graced the nation's Saturday breakfast newspapers the next day.

The courtroom ritual had been a decided anticlimax to the month-long personal horror through which I had just passed. After the shock of the FBI visit, telling Carol, revealing what lay ahead to a few close associates, I had been forced to lead a truly double life.

Outwardly I continued to function as husband and father, vigorous candidate for reelection traveling my district, and during the days the House was in session, the "watchdog of Congress." Internally I was struggling to stay afloat. With flashes of hope, I talked often with Tom O'Malley about the legal situation, the Eddie Regina blackmail attempt, the possibility of postponement of my case until after the election. I made contingency campaign plans for the changes that would occur as soon as the news got out. And I lived in dread of the time when the press would get hold of the story.

Yet I knew it was inevitable. My world was crumbling under me and I was obliged to act as though everything was all right.

A few days before the end I gathered my congressional staff members in my Washington office and told them about my alcoholism, that it had led me to do things I greatly regretted, that I would have to appear in court. A similar meeting was held in my congressional district with about twenty of my long-time key political supporters. I could not bring myself to tell any of these good friends and close associates the whole truth. I simply did not have the courage though I owed it to them. And so, forewarned of trouble, they had to read the sickening details in the newspapers.

Worst of all, I had to face my children. Carol and I agreed they must be told something since they too would soon be engulfed in the flood. Our oldest son, Ted, was away at Loyola College in Baltimore, and his mother talked with him by phone. Our youngest son, Jimmy, eight, and our two daughters, Genie, fifteen, and Vicky, thirteen, gathered in Glebe House's library for a "family conference." In gentle, general terms I told them that their father was in trouble, that it would be public and embarrassing, that although I would still run for Congress that might end in defeat. As children are able, they sensed the gravity of the situation and were naturally upset. The girls wanted to know whether we would have to move away from Glebe House and whether they would lose their ponies. Little Jimmy was silent. Their innocent reaction and continuing trust in me made me realize how great a hurt I had visited on my family. Both Carol and I emphasized what would eventually become a falsehood; that "no matter what happens, our family will stay together." I tried as best I could to reassure them but I am afraid I was not very convincing. As they embraced me they repeated what I had heard so many times before, "Daddy, we love you. Don't worry."

Thursday, October 2, was the last day of the congressional session before the election recess. Though I could not talk about what lay ahead for me I felt the compelling need to say something "for the record." This would be the last day of my life that my reputation would remain intact. Choosing Russell Kirk's phrase I entitled my remarks before the House "A Note of Optimism; The Permanent Things." I doubt that few of my colleagues noticed the difficulty I had controlling my voice, emotions, my hands gripping the lectern tightly to prevent trembling. And as he had so many thousands of other times, the Chair recognized the gentleman from Maryland:

> **Mr. Bauman.** Mr. Speaker, I have listened this morning with great interest to all the gloom, doom, politics, and other disasters on both sides of the aisle and it prompted me, since

this is probably the last day of our session before the recess, to make some observations about other and different things. I learned long ago in politics to always close on a note of hope.

Mr. Speaker, the harvesters are in the field on the Eastern Shore of Maryland and the corn is coming in. It has been a bad summer and the drought has reduced the bushel yield, but there is corn and the beans look good. Along with the coming election ads I have already seen ads for Thanksgiving turkeys. The pumpkins have appeared at the roadside stands and the cider is on sale.

Mr. Speaker, the other morning I heard for the first time this fall the voice of the Canadian geese which to us in Maryland is a promise of hope and a good future. They have come home again.

No matter what we do here in the closing days or have done for the last two years, perhaps this Congress ought to think about these things too. They are, perhaps, more enduring and permanent.

I had to give some, even cryptic explanation to the House of what was about to happen to me. I owed it to this respected institution which had been my home since I was fifteen years old.

Fate had decided at an early age that politics and the Congress were to be my life.

On my tenth birthday, April 4, 1947, my Aunt Louise from Baltimore sent me a children's book entitled *Abraham Lincoln's World,* by Genevieve Foster. Lincoln's story fascinated me from the first reading. He conquered personal tragedy, poverty, his mother's death, his father's weakness and alcoholism, his wife's erratic emotions, the death of his children. He led America through its most terrible war and died a martyr for the cause. In Lincoln's coarse features I saw strength and beauty. I shared his personal sadness as though it were my own. Here was my own exemplar; an exceptional man who showed the world what could be achieved against the odds.

Aunt Louise had given me more than just a birthday gift. In the Lincoln story I was presented with my life's plan. I determined that I would become a lawyer, join the Republican party, and enter politics.

And I managed to do it all.

In 1948 I misguidedly handed out Dewey-Warren buttons before I realized the meaning of party domination by the Wall Street liberal Republicans. In 1952, as an Easton, Maryland, teen-ager, I organized a group of young people who campaigned furiously for Eisenhower and Nixon. My real love was the conservative leader, Senator Bob Taft of Ohio, but after he lost the nomination battle I had to be loyal to the party. Shortly after Ike's victory I read a small story in the *New York Times* about the impact of the Republican takeover of Congress. All the Democratic patronage jobs, including the high school–age pages, would go to deserving Republicans. Unable to imagine any one more deserving than I, I went to my fellow townsman, Edward T. Miller. Ted also happened to be, in 1952, our third-term Republican congressman. I asked him for a page job and, noting my campaign work, he said he would do what he could.

And so at the tender age of fifteen I became a page for the U.S. House of Representatives. Two days before the first presidential inauguration of Dwight D. Eisenhower in 1953, I raised my right hand to be sworn in as a page boy in the House. For the next sixteen years the House was my home as a string of staff jobs financed my way through high school, college, and then law school, all at night. When at last I was forced to tear myself away from Capitol Hill in 1969 I soon found a comfortable seat in the Maryland State Senate and then, quite suddenly in a 1973 special election, I awoke one morning to find that the people of the First Congressional District of Maryland had chosen me to be their member of Congress.

Always the ideologue, I did not neglect my conservative beliefs along the way. I was a founder and national chairman of Young Americans for Freedom (YAF), at one time the nation's largest conservative youth group. I founded and later became national chairman of the American Conservative Union (ACU), serving on its board for twenty years.

I am not sure just when it began, but once in Congress I found myself the subject of an increasing number of press stories about my parliamentary activities on the floor of the House. I was dubbed "the watchdog of the House." Gavel to gavel during every session, I was there in the House Chamber making sure my colleagues could not escape my unrelenting presence, questioning, prodding, demanding explanations, often stopping proposals cold with my single objection. In a body of 435 members where even seniority does not guarantee recognition, I rapidly became a force with which to be reckoned, if I could believe my press notices.

The respected *Congressional Quarterly* surveyed the scene and informed their readers that in terms of who made things happen in Congress I was one of "five most influential congressmen." In one year more Bauman amendments were adopted by the House than all but those offered by two other congressmen, both senior committee chairmen and majority party Democrats. I became, *C.Q.* said at one point, the "de facto Republican leader of the House." The actual Republican Leader of the House at the time, John Rhodes of Arizona, offered the opinion that ". . . Bob Bauman is indispensable. If we did not have him we would have to invent him."

Even my constant target, the Speaker of the House, Thomas B. "Tip" O'Neill, admitted in a fit of rare objectivity that "every Congress needs a Bauman." That got reprinted in one of my campaign brochures. But in a more typical moment during House debate O'Neill referred to me as "cheap, sneaky, and sly." For this breach of parliamentary etiquette, I had his offending words ruled out on a point of order and stricken from the *Record*.

What made me different from most other members of Congress was my interest in and knowledge of the complex arcane rules and precedents which govern congressional deliberations. I learned the rules simply by doing my job. As page and legislative staff member working on the House floor for years I always had to know what was going on. My duty was to advise congressmen what the exact legislative situation was at any given moment.

From this working knowledge of the rules came a grasp of intricate parliamentary maneuvers that could be used to good political advantage, especially in blocking legislative actions I deemed to be inimical to the best interest of the American taxpayers and the Republic. It seemed elemental to me that I should apply this rules knowledge with a tenacious will to advance the conservative principles in which I believe so strongly. After all, I reasoned, why even be in Congress if you fail to use every possible weapon to battle for the cause?

The press and media always love a good fight and the acerbic wit and biting tongue considered my stock in trade soon made me one of their favorites, though few Capitol Hill reporters agreed with my conservative views. Anticipating the needs of the media, I always was ready with a succinct thirty-second quote on the events of the day which often found its way on to the evening network news. Whenever a major battle developed on the House floor I could be found in the thick of it, often starting the fight. Among my accomplishments which gained national notice was a successful single-handed torpedoing of President Jimmy Carter's proposal for a national gasoline tax boost, the initiation of a rare "resolution of inquiry" leading to the revelations concerning brother Billy Carter's Libyan oil deal activities, the defeat and then resurrection of the Panama Canal treaty implementation legislation, and the imposition of tight restrictions on the millions of dollars in aid President Carter insisted on giving the Communist Sandinista government in Nicaragua.

National recognition began with an article by Richard L. Madden in the *New York Times* on my birthday, April 4, 1976.

What he wrote set the tone of the many media stories that followed:

> Each day, just before the House of Representatives convenes at noon, a dark-haired man takes up position near the Republican leadership table on the House floor within grabbing distance of a microphone and begins his afternoon's vigil.
>
> On any given day he can be seen jumping up, demanding an explanation of some bill that is being rushed through without debate; raising parliamentary obstacles to other legislation he deems a boondoggle; or forcing roll call votes on measures that many representatives would just as soon not be recorded as voting for.
>
> It is Representive Robert E. Bauman, a conservative Republican from Maryland's Eastern Shore, engaging in what he calls "a sort of guerrilla warfare." In less than three years in Congress, the thirty-eight-year old Mr. Bauman has become the new gadfly of the House, its most active nitpicker, its hair shirt, its leading baiter of its most powerful members.

The article went on to recount my verbal battles with Tip O'Neill, my successful effort to force a roll call on a 5 percent congressional pay raise. It even noted the suggestion of Ohio Congressman Wayne Hays that I was "an idiot." My reply: "The gentleman from Ohio is well qualified to judge idiots."

The Madden article closed with a quotation that still applies:

> "I love the House. I spent most of my life here. I really feel uncomfortable not being on the floor every day."

Soon scores of other articles, radio and television interviews followed once House sessions began to be broadcast on cable television. Phone calls, mail, and even campaign contributions began to trickle in from around the country. Before long I had compiled a political mailing list of more than ten thousand names, only half of them in Maryland.

And of course I made more than an average congressman's share of enemies. President Carter, campaigning against me in 1974 when he was governor of Georgia, said I was "a good example of all that is wrong with the Republican party." When I recalled this charitable remark to the President at a 1978 White House dinner he displayed his ample teeth in a sweet smile and added, "My goodness, wasn't I prescient?" For my conduct as a very partisan Maryland state senator the press secretary to then Governor Marvin Mandel, a Democrat, variously referred to me as a "pesky Eastern Shore mosquito" and "a bastard."

But most conservatives loved me. In 1980 the readers of the *Conservative Digest,* the monthly bible of Richard Viguerie's "New Right" movement, voted me as one of "the ten most-admired conservatives in Congress."

While the House was my home, I had many interests in the years from page to congressman. In 1955 I graduated from high school at the Capitol Page School in the Library of Congress, in 1959 from the School of Foreign Service of Georgetown University with a bachelor of science degree in international affairs, and in 1964 from the Georgetown Law Center with a juris doctor degree.

Obsessed with things political, I did manage a private life. In 1959 I met and in 1960 married a beautiful young blonde who shared my Catholic faith, my political conservatism, and my zeal for the cause. Carol Dawson was from Indianapolis, daughter of a noted journalist, and a fellow Republican political activist. Over twenty-one years of marriage we had two sons and two daughters.

A phone call on the morning of May 24, 1973, informed me that Congressman William O. Mills, who would ultimately turn out to be my immediate predecessor in the House, had committed suicide. On September 8, I was sworn in to replace him, but only after a special primary and hard-fought general election in the midst of the Watergate hearings.

If the inspiration of Lincoln made me a Republican I worked hard over the years to keep my party credentials in order. Starting in the ranks of the college Young Republicans I served in many party posts before being elected a Barry Goldwater delegate to the 1964 Republican National Convention in San Francisco. For the next sixteen years I served as a delegate or alternate to each national convention and in 1980 at Detroit was co-chairman of the Maryland delegation. A Reagan supporter in 1968, 1976, and 1980, it was at Detroit that Ronald Reagan called me in to consult about who he should choose as his vice-presidential running mate. As fate would have it, Reagan, his staff and I worked together to deflect North Carolina Senator Jesse Helm's bid for the vice-presidency, preserving party unity and allowing the senator a dignified withdrawal speech to the convention after I nominated him.

I became friends and worked with not only Reagan (who spoke and campaigned for me in my congressional district in 1975) and Helms, but most of the known and unknown leaders of the conservative movement of the sixties and seventies; Barry Goldwater, William F. Buckley, Jr., Richard Viguerie, and the late congressman John Ashbrook of Ohio, and Larry MacDonald of Georgia.

During eight years in the House I gradually learned the virtue of some limited discretion and toned down my one-man guerrilla warfare to the point that I was selected by the Republican leadership to serve on the powerful House Committee on Rules, one of only four members of my party granted this honor. Shortly before the 1980 Republican convention in Detroit I let it be known informally that I would stand for election as Republican Whip of the House when Congress reconvened in January 1981.

After decades of labor in the political vineyards, my wife Carol and I flew back from the Detroit convention with the distinct feeling that the day of victory was at last at hand. My own re-election to a fifth term in the House seemed assured. Our polls showed a possible 70 percent majority. With President Ronald Reagan in the White House in just a few short months, my triumph, personal and political, awaited.

At the tender age of forty-three I had reached a pinnacle of success few would have ever predicted for me, and certainly I would have never predicted for myself.

Shortly after my court appearance on October 3, Carol and I were on a chartered plane headed from Washington's National Airport back to Easton. Discussions with close advisors dictated that for the first few days I remain in seclusion at Glebe House until the political damage control estimate could be assessed. As the small plane droned down the Washington runway, climbing out over the Potomac River to the east, rain squalls and turbulence hit us and we bounced toward the Chesapeake Bay. All around us hung low black clouds.

Raindrops beat against the windows with the intensity of small bullets. Soon I could see the Bay below and then the irregular beauty of the Eastern Shore coastline. Carol and I said little, avoiding eye contact. Alone in my thoughts I remembered all the thousands of miles and thousands of people in eight years of travel by car, boat, train, and parade; the good and bad times; all the hopes now fading.

As we circled to land in Easton I could see a Baltimore television station truck pulling away from the hangar below, ignorant that their intended prey was so close. On the ground the airport manager, Bill Newnam, told me he lied to the reporters that I was not coming in. Showing his Shoreman's independence, he said, "To hell with them. All they want to do is kick a guy when he's down."

In retrospect it is difficult to understand how I could have miscalculated so badly what the press and news media would do with the Bauman scandal. I convinced myself, because I wanted to believe it, that the story could be minimized with the assurance of the U.S. Attorney's staff that the case would be handled quietly. Not only was that never their intention, as proven by the leaks to the press from that office, but any reasonably detached person would have instinctively known the intense interest in a story like this one; a leading conservative member of Congress caught up in a homosexual scandal. It was a story destined to make headlines nationally and abroad and it did, for days and weeks afterward.

In the late afternoon of October 2, the press calls about the next day's court appearance started coming into my office fast and heavy. The Bauman story raced across Capitol Hill like wildfire. The late Congressman Phil Burton of California, a very liberal Democrat and a close personal friend, called, weeping over the phone: "Oh my dear friend, my dear friend, God help you through this." Another call came from Congressman Phil Crane of Illinois, a long-time friend and fellow leader of the conservative movement. (His own congressman-brother, Dan Crane, was defeated in 1984 after revelation that he had sexual relations with a female House page.) Soon Phil was in my office giving advice and suggestions on how to deal with the press.

He tried to encourage me, insisting that I keep fighting. He asked about Carol's attitude and when I told him she was reluctant to accompany me to court the next day he insisted on calling her in Easton immediately.

Phil had known Carol for years and he and his wife Arlene had visited our home. Twice Phil spoke for me in my district. I heard him saying into the phone in his accented midwestern nasal voice: "You two have been in this fight together for twenty years and you can't stop now. You can win it if you stick together." Within minutes he had Carol's agreement that she would be with me the next day.

When I told Phil that a *Post* reporter had given my aides a summary story they intended to run including totally false statements, he advised me to call the editor, the patrician Ben Bradlee. Phil, always the joker, quipped: "Bradlee ought to understand sin. He lived out of wedlock with Sally Quinn long enough." Eventually I got through to Bradlee and to his credit the story was altered to reflect a much more factual account. I experienced only a hint of the pain that was to come as I talked with Bradlee, responding to questions about my personal life that would be appropriate under no other but these bizarre circumstances.

Crane also suggested that I call at least one friendly reporter in Maryland and give him the statement I intended to release the next morning. "That way at least they will have to give both sides in tomorrow's newspaper," he correctly predicted. I chose a liberal Democrat who served both as an editor of the *Baltimore Sun* and the editor-publisher of a weekly newspaper in my district. Peter Jay is an excellent writer whose intuitive grasp of a subject rarely fails.

I reached him at his home and he patiently took down the entire text of the statement. The next day it was the lead story in the morning *Sun,* almost without addition or comment. As our phone conversation was about to end, Peter said to me: "Bob, whatever happens, you've been an excellent congressman even though we have not always agreed. I wish you the best." (A few days later Peter Jay's weekly newspaper was the first to endorse my re-election. Four years later, in 1984, Jay wrote a column commenting that he thought revealed homosexual congressman Garry Studds of Massachusetts should be defeated. Recalling my own 1980 problems Jay stated that in retrospect he had been wrong in giving me his editorial support.)

The statement I gave Peter Jay and released to the press at the time of my court appearance was originally drafted by me but revised with suggestions from Art Fincklestein, my pollster and campaign advisor, and Dick Ribbentrop, my administrative assistant. Carol also gave me her thoughts.

Rereading my statement five years later it appears as a masterpiece of self-deception, the product of a muddled mind in intellectual shock. At the time my political advisors' collective wisdom was to tell as much of the truth as possible without mentioning homosexuality. Laying the blame for my conduct on my alcoholism only looked like a phony excuse. I told the public I indeed had an increased problem with my drinking in late 1979 and early

1980, reaching what I called "the acute stage of alcoholism." I truthfully said a family crisis forced me to seek professional help from my priest and a counselor, that my last drink had been on May 1, 1980. I then noted the U.S. Attorney for the District of Columbia "several weeks ago informed me that allegations had been made concerning my conduct during the period of my heaviest drinking . . ." Then came the one and only mention of the heart of the matter: "The charge involved is solicitation." No mention of whom or what I had been soliciting.

I gave a brief resumé of what I considered a laudable career in Congress assuring the people that whatever might have happened it had "nothing to do with my office or duties as a member of Congress." Noting the help I got from Carol and Father Harvey, I added words that particularly rankled some: "I have confessed my sins as my religion requires and I am in a state of grace and will remain so with the help of God. For the first time I have come to terms with my personal problem, admitted my faults, and am trying to make amends."

In retrospect, as some have advised, it probably would have been much better political strategy to call a press conference in early September as soon as I learned of the investigation, lay out the charges against me, explain my attempts to address my alcoholism and sexuality, and let the chips fall. At least that would have defined the terms of the debate and given the people of my district several more weeks to consider the issues, both personal and political, involved in their vote.

As it was there was no debate.

My self-serving statement was lost in the lurid details leaked in the FBI and Bruce reports. My own guarded words were contrasted with the rumors of "unnamed sources" that instantly turned the spectacle into a major press circus. Typical of many newspapers, the *Washington Post* ran the initial story on the front page and then began a daily series on the Bauman scandal, Washington's gay bar scene, male prostitution, and related matters.

Photos of teen-age boys lounging outside the Chesapeake House and other bars were published alongside photos of Reagan, Bush, and Bauman shaking hands. On all the local television and radio stations I was the lead story for days and the national networks gave similar though briefer treatment. Hundreds of calls demanding interviews came from news sources ranging from the BBC to Barbara Walters of ABC's "20/20." Patrick McGrath, a reporter for a Baltimore TV station, had the gall to knock on our door at 1:00 A.M., after guards at my lane left for the night.

Within an hour of my court appearance my hometown of Easton was overrun by a plague of newspaper, radio and television reporters that swooped down like locusts. My Easton office, my home, my children at their school, the homes and business places of my friends and supporters were besieged. Easton townspeople almost had to take turns being interviewed by TV reporters as the price for walking down Washington Street. State and local police had to be called to keep the press from trespassing on my home grounds. A police roadblock was set up at the end of my country lane where a traffic jam of reporters' vehicles quickly developed. Press helicopters and chartered planes crowded into Easton airport and even buzzed my house.

I had appeared in court on Friday, gone straight home to Glebe House, and stayed there until 11:30 A.M. Mass at my Easton church, Saints Peter and Paul, the following Sunday morning. Ever vigilant reporters figured I might attend Mass and camped out at the church door. I entered through the rectory with my youngest son, Jimmy, and left early by the same route. But reporters in the rear of the church spotted me and mobbed us in the parking lot. They blocked my car and upset both Jim and me as they shouted questions and popped flashbulbs in our faces. I was so defiantly furious that instead of returning home as planned, Jim and I went to a local garden shop, Hilley's, to buy our traditional Indian corn and pumpkin for the coming Halloween and Thanksgiving season. It was there I first experienced a new and demoralizing sensation. Some dear lady was staring at me as though I was a two-headed freak. It would not be the last time I was to see this look of curiosity and contempt.

For five excruciating days those of us at Glebe House in the relatively calm eye rode out the news media storm. Jimmy, Genie, and Vicky stayed home from school to avoid press harassment and for a couple of days they went with Carol and Father Harvey to a friend's beach-front apartment in Ocean City. The quiet at Glebe had an air of unreality as I purposely ignored newspapers and avoided TV and radio. I did not want to know what the world outside was being told about me. My only contacts were the comings and goings of members of my congressional staff tending to business and politics that absolutely demanded my attention. Their truncated, rosy accounts of the news would have been unbelievable to me had I been listening carefully. But I wasn't.

At first I engaged in what I was later to learn is a not uncommon psychological reaction by one caught up in a major personal crisis. Unable to deal with the enormity of what was happening to me and my family, I simply formed a defensive mental block against reality, circling my intellectual wagons in a sort of *krall*, as the Afrikaners call it. Although unconsciously on my part, I blotted out events that rapidly and irrevocably were changing me, my wife, our children, and our future. The election was less than four weeks away and instead of campaigning I was brooding in my country home on the waters of Glebe Creek gazing out at thousands of Canadian geese bobbing in the October mists. My focus was on the flame red of the huge maple tree in the ring of our driveway, the browns, golds, and oranges of the damp, fast-changing trees and fields. Amid all this familiar beauty real events were pushed far away, part of some horrible nightmare that must vanish upon waking. All this just could not be real. I even managed to sleep soundly, perhaps because of exhaustion.

Truthfully, as much as I had tried to steel myself throughout September for what was coming, nothing prepared me for the extreme press reaction to what to me was an intensely personal crisis. No amount of political experience or tough election campaigning ever provided me with a basis for a calm and rational response to these events. And so I withdrew. At least for a time. The political plan was this: I was expected to act as a worthy candidate who months before had met his problems, sought help, and was well on the way to recovery. His loyal wife by his side, he was expected to ask his constituents to understand the dimensions of human frailty, consider his record of faithful accomplishment, and continue their support. At least give him a chance. But this public image, discussed and rehearsed by the experts who loyally advised me, was not really me. I had no real faith in myself. Months of counseling and therapy had filled my mind with unanswered questions about my sexuality, my religious faith, and some things I never doubted before. Many of these internal issues would go unresolved for months, years, perhaps forever. Instead of time to deal calmly with these fundamental questions, I was expected to take to the road, acting as if I was just another good old member of Congress, shaking hands and patting backs, confident that my old friend, the new President Ronald Reagan and I would be working together once again come January 1981.

The crush of the news media began at the courthouse door in Washington but I slipped away. Tom O'Malley was left to answer. "The experience for Mr. Bauman and his family has been traumatic in the extreme. He is going to go on living," Tom told the eager crowd. But how does one do that under such circumstances? With a less public person the storm would have blown over in a day or two. But on me the spotlight never wavered and the longer I remained in seclusion the brighter it became.

In the relative privacy of Glebe House, Carol and I talked about what was happening. A flood of encouraging messages from supporters assured us that a chance for electoral victory remained. Many people considered the press reports so at variance with the Bob Bauman they knew that they refused to believe it. With few notable exceptions Republican political leaders in my district stood by me, many suggesting the obvious; the timing had been political and defeating Bauman for Congress was a high priority for the opposition Democrats.

Three days into my self-imposed exile I began to get itchy. I could not just sit there and permit a seat in Congress to go by default. And I began to think in terms of vindication. By God, I was a good congressman and I was trying to get my personal life in good order before all this hit. It was too late under Maryland law to withdraw from the race and to do so would have left my name on the ballot and the party without a candidate.

At such times the mind tends to extremes and I had indeed considered suicide. Driving home the night before my court appearance with my staff member, Kevin Sard, I gazed down at the dark waters of the Chesapeake as we crossed the Bay Bridge near Annapolis. It would have been so easy to just end it all. But then I thought, "Why give the bastards the satisfaction?" Kevin told me that one night, a year before, driving over the same bridge I had fallen asleep after drinking much too much. As we approached the center span I awoke suddenly and tried to jump from the moving car. It was all he could do to restrain me with one hand and stop the car with the other. I remembered nothing of the incident.

Now, after several days of brooding at Glebe House, the thought of self-destruction flickered in my mind again. But my Catholic teaching quickly asserted itself, reminding me that suicide is the only sin which God cannot forgive, allowing no chance for contrition or absolution.

I seriously considered resigning from the race and from Congress. Carol and I talked at length about this possibility. I told her frankly that if she wanted me to quit I would. That would be one sure way of avoiding the grueling campaign that lay ahead. She later told a reporter: "I thought about that for a day and told Bob that a lot of people depended on him as their congressman. I didn't think he should let those people down. He had responsibilities to them as well as to his family."

After a call from Tom Winter, the editor of the Washington conservative weekly *Human Events,* I agreed to have an old friend, Jeffrey Bell, from New Jersey, come to Glebe House to advise us. Jeff, one of the bright young stars on the political right, had defeated the veteran liberal Republican Senator Clifford Case in the 1978 primary only to lose the general election to Bill Bradley. A brilliant political strategist with an encyclopedic knowledge of politics, Jeff would help us write any statements we needed.

Meanwhile phone calls to my office from friends were returned by me on a selective basis. The consensus was that things were beginning to calm down and, most importantly, I had to get out in public immediately and let people see me and know that I was all right. A meeting on October 6 of key campaign leaders was held in my living room and in the presence of Carol, Father Harvey, and Tom O'Malley, I frankly discussed my situation, both personal and political, and we all answered tough questions. After several hours without dissent the group recommended that I get going toward election victory with their unanimous support. All agreed that I must immediately meet the press and get that hurdle behind me.

One thing Carol made clear. Her summary was succinct: "You cannot pull a Teddy Kennedy. You must tell the whole truth, or it is pointless to go on with the campaign." Her reference to the Chappaquiddick tragedy where Mary Jo Kopechne's death was followed by the senator's evasive answers was not lost on me. Carol and I both knew I must publicly admit not just alcoholism but the homosexual problem as well. Jeffrey Bell, Father Harvey, and Carol all went over my original draft and it was Father who opposed the use of the word "homosexual." After some debate he suggested, and we agreed upon "homosexual tendencies," reflecting my then admitted belief I was not a homosexual but my conduct had been.

In my statement I reiterated my progressive alcoholism but made it clear "I do not claim alcoholism as my defense." I said: "I have also suffered from homosexual tendencies although I do not consider myself to be a homosexual." Then a phrase the press latched on to: "Together, the alcohol and these tendencies, these twin compulsions, led me into a pattern of conduct which I know to be wrong . . ."

I made it very clear I was in the congressional campaign to stay and hoped to win.

The press conference was scheduled for 4:00 P.M., October 8, at Easton's Tidewater Inn Crystal Room, the location of so many of my election-night victory parties.

When we arrived through a kitchen entrance the scene out front resembled swarming sharks awaiting an injured swimmer. At least two hundred reporters, cameramen, assistants, technicians, and just plain folks had gathered. Most of the reporters were out for blood and local people several times responded to brutal questions with jeers. Some physical altercations were narrowly avoided.

As I read my statement, Carol and Father Harvey sat at my side, grim-faced, with eyes downcast, as much to avoid the blinding TV lights as an expression of their inner feelings.

"Congressman Bauman, when was the last time you had sex with a boy? Are you a homosexual? How long have you been cruising downtown Washington? Can you identify other gays in Congress? Are you going to divorce him, Mrs. Bauman? Are you really an alcoholic or is that just an excuse? What do your children think of this?" And so it went.

After nearly forty-five minutes, during which I tried to answer all questions lest I be accused of dodging, I saw an old friend, Bill Esham, from Berlin, Maryland, motioning me to cut it off and I did. As we fled the press through the hotel's kitchen entrance police had to clear a path and Carol broke down and began weeping. Pursuing cameramen nearly knocked us to the ground as we got into the car with Father Harvey. When we were in the car and drove off I wept myself.

We went to our nearby Catholic church where Father said

Mass for Carol, Jeff Bell, and myself, and when he offered me wine with communion, I smiled sadly and declined.

The three weeks that remained in the 1980 campaign mercifully have become a blur in my memory.

The strategy was that I should see and greet as many people as I could so that the electorate would be reassured I was still the same man they voted for many times before. I was to avoid formal press conferences and contacts except on a selective basis. Jeff Bell and I composed a letter which was mailed to every registered voter explaining in some detail my situation and apologizing for my personal problems. Campaign workers worked overtime and previously used techniques such as our phone banks were intensified.

The Washington-Baltimore press, and one newspaper in my district, the *Salisbury Times,* kept up their sensationalism, but traveling around my district I found genuine empathy and understanding. Hundreds of times I heard the Biblical quote "Let he who is without sin cast the first stone." Younger people were particularly eager to volunteer the information that "I would not want my personal actions exposed to the public." Of the thousands of people I encountered only two refused to shake my hand or exhibited any unpleasantness. And when Carol joined me on a daily basis the press made much of this, portraying it as an act of campaign desperation. She told one newspaper: "Among Bob's most ardent supporters women are the most upset and I cannot blame them. If there is anything I can do to alleviate their doubts about the kind of person he is today then that's what I want to do." She also said in the same interview, sitting by my side: "In my opinion he had already resolved this thing personally. Between the two of us and between God and himself it had been resolved. I saw no need for the whole world to know about it. It's between himself, his God, and me."

But that defense of privacy was lost on the press. After one public appearance Carol made on my behalf the campaign reached a low point. As I stood by her side, Warren Strickland of

Washington's Channel 9, WDMV-TV, thrust a microphone in Carol's face and demanded: "What do you really think of this man?" Carol returned his stare and replied: "Bob and I share many beliefs and we have worked hard together for twenty years to support them. He's been an excellent congressman and he should be reelected."

Frankly I did not know what to expect from one quarter crucial to any chance for my reelection, the conservative and Republican party leadership. Party leaders and key people in Maryland and my congressional district had, with few exceptions, stuck by me. Dr. Allen Levey, the Maryland Republican party chairman, was out front in my defense and an Annapolis press conference was organized where he, Louise Gore, the Republican National committeewoman, and other elected and party officials rallied to my side.

But what about national leaders of the movement in which I had labored so long and hard? Would they understand or bail out?

The answer was not long in coming. Congressman Guy van der Jaght of Michigan, chairman of the Republican National Congressional Committee, the key House campaign group, pledged his full support and additional funds eventually amounting to over thirty thousand dollars. Republican National Chairman, Bill Brock of Tennessee, an old friend from YR days, said on October 6: "I'd like to support Bob's race in any way I can. He's a very able person." Brock indicated that up to seventeen thousand dollars might be available. The Maryland Right to Life Committee's twelve-member board again endorsed my reelection without dissent. The Maryland Conservative Union chairman issued a statement of support and national leaders of Young Americans for Freedom joined with their backing. "We conservatives would be in a very hard way if we lost Congressman Bauman," said the chairman of the group, Conservatives Against Liberal Legislation. A spokesman for the National Rifle Association said: "We're very definitely supporting Congressman Bauman, no question about it." And they proved it by giving an additional five thousand dollars to my campaign. Terry Dolan, chairman of the National Conservative Political Action Committee (NCPAC), pledged his support and an additional five thousand dollars. The chairman of the Young Republican National Federation, Rick Abell, gave me his backing and Dr. Mildred Jefferson, the black Boston obstetrician who headed the National Right to Life Committee, said: "We are not fair-weather friends ... the love and concern I would extend to an unborn child I would extend to a born congressman who has worked so valiantly for our cause." Congressman John Ashbrook, head of the Conservative Victory Fund, sent his group's additional donation with his personal endorsement. Other members of Congress volunteered their support, including Henry Hyde, John Rousselot, Henson Moore, and a liberal Republican, Pete McCloskey of California.

The editors of *Human Events* gave a very even-handed account of the Bauman matter indicating their hope for my reelection. Observing that my future rested with the verdict of the voters of my district, *Human Events* said: "If the answer is yes, as most conservatives hoped it would be, Bob Bauman might yet return to the House, still able to do battle for the many causes he has championed over the years."

And from the Congressional Club of North Carolina, headed by Tom Ellis, Senator Jesse Helms' close friend and advisor, came several thousand dollars in donations with his best wishes. Indeed before the month of October was over our campaign committee raised over one hundred thousand dollars, an amount never before given to any of my campaigns in a similar period.

Two responses from public figures to my predicament surprised me and others.

On October 6 came a handwritten note from one who, better than most, understood the depth of my anguish. It read:

> Dear Bob,
> I know nothing about the incident which has been reported in the press. I *do* know that you have been a loyal

friend and one of the most courageous and effective spokesmen for the cause of responsible government ever to serve in
the Congress. For that, along with your other friends, I shall
always be grateful.

The letter was signed "Sincerely, RN." It was indeed a generous gesture from the former President of the United States.

And on ABC's "Issues and Answers" one of the press-indicated
leaders of the "New Right," the Reverend Jerry Falwell, was
asked about his attitude toward Congressman Bauman. Falwell
correctly said he did not know me personally (we had only met
once briefly) but that he did know my voting record in the House.
He praised me for my pro-life and conservative stands and declined to call for my resignation, offering instead his "prayer and
forgiveness." He added, "I think it would be inconsistent for me
to do so [ask that I resign] . . . I didn't call for Mr. Kennedy's resignation after Chappaquiddick." Indeed, perhaps as evidence of
loving the sinner and hating the sin, in recent years Mr. Falwell
has invited Senator Kennedy to his Thomas Road Baptist Church
in Lynchburg, Virginia, where they appeared on the same platform together.

Paul Weyrich, it is not too much to say, is one of the genuine
architects of what has become known as the "New Right."

I never knew Weyrich very well. His rise coincided with my
own preoccupation with my service in the House. I would see him
at conservative meetings but we were not in any sense close.

When the story broke Weyrich wrote me a long and thoughtful
letter suggesting I consider resigning from Congress and aban-
doning my race. "Please don't look on this as some sort of moral
pronouncement by me, as in judgment of you. Actually I am suggesting this because I do believe that you care as deeply about the
cause as I do. . . ." Weyrich, in his October 3 letter, assured me he
"would have no public comment" on my problems and "I am not
going to send copies of this letter to anyone, nor am I going to
comment on its content."

On October 5, I received a telephone call from Richard Viguerie in Washington. Viguerie, who publicly supported me, told me Weyrich had talked with him and planned a press conference to call for me to quit the race and Congress. I asked and Richard agreed to try to get Weyrich to stop his actions, which Richard felt were wrong. "But you know Paul," he told me. "When he gets something in his mind it is almost impossible to change him." Richard called back later to say that Weyrich would not change his plans and did not want to talk with me, an offer I made, hoping to explain some of the outlandish charges appearing in the press.

On October 6, the same day I received Weyrich's "confidential" letter, he met reporters at the National Press Club in Washington. He was joined by Bill Marshner of the Religious Roundtable and Jack Clayton of the American Association of Christian Schools, both unknown to me. Weyrich told the press I should resign because I had "done considerable damage to the movement" and I was "no longer a creditable spokesman for conservative causes." He referred to his letter to me saying that he had not intended to go public but that charges that I "may have already submitted to blackmail" caused him to act.

As if to justify his stand, Weyrich told the press: "I got tremendous pressure not to hold this press conference. There's a good old boy network among conservatives and they believe that they should close ranks behind one of their own. There's also another strain of thought which says that, as Christians, we have to be forgiving. Well, it's not that I don't forgive him. It's that he has brought dishonor to the movement in which he has been involved." Weyrich added the hope that I would ". . . repent and redeem himself. However, the cause which he has helped to represent is greater than any one individual."

A gay leader, Adam deBaugh, commenting on Weyrich's statement, wrote: "The thing that is most striking about this statement from Paul Weyrich is the notion that the cause is more important than the individual. It seems to me the essence of conservatism that the individual is of primary importance ... Yet Weyrich is espousing very eloquently one of the major tenets of any totalitarian system: 'The cause is greater than any one individual.' This has been the basis for totalitarian oppression from Caesar's Rome to Nazi Germany to Stalin's Russia. ... Weyrich says the cause is all important. Bob Bauman has become an embarrassment and therefore a hindrance to the cause and he must be removed ... Weyrich's dictatorial mentality is frightening in its implications."

But Weyrich was not alone in his attitude. In spite of Republican National Chairman Bill Brock's statement of support, an underling at the same committee, Alex Ray, told the press: "As a matter of principle there will be no financial support for the first congressional race in Maryland." Ray, an assistant to the party's deputy chairman, added: "This involved a sixteen-year-old boy and that's the cutting edge as far as we're concerned. If Bauman has problems with alcohol, Congress is not the place to go for treatment." I later discovered that Ray had lived in my district for some time unknown to me.

And way out in Arizona, where he was involved in what would be the closest election race of his career, Senator Barry Goldwater was heard from: "If I were Bauman I would bow out. I'm not passing judgment on whether or not being gay is evil but I am sure the people of his area are very anti that. He should resign from the House and the chairmanship of the ACU."

Quietly joining him was the Veterans of Foreign Wars (VFW) with whom I had voted 100 percent of the time during my congressional service. They said they were withdrawing their endorsement and were "sorry."

But perhaps the blow from the right that hurt the most came from my old friend Bill Buckley.

Marvin Leibman, a personal friend of us both, called from New York to tell me that Buckley had asked his opinion of a newspaper column asking for my resignation. Marvin argued strongly against it saying nothing justified it. But upon reflecting

Bill decided he must do it and Marvin assured me he would. I immediately tried to reach Bill by phone in New York but his faithful "gal Friday," Frances Bronson, told me he was "on his way to Seattle for a speech and I cannot contact him." I asked if he would be calling in and she said he might. I insisted that he call me and told her that it was of the greatest importance to my campaign and my personal future. I made it clear that I knew about the pending column and felt that I could explain to Bill enough of the true facts to get him to withdraw it.

But Bill never called. I was later told that he did not want to speak to me because a few years before, under similar circumstances, Vice-President Ted Agnew had talked Buckley out of such a column only to have my fellow Marylander appear in court a few days later and plead *nolo contendere*. Instead, Bill sent me a copy of the column and a note dated October 6, 1980: "My thoughts and prayers are with you and Carol."

The Buckley column was personally devastating to me. It contained a glowing account of my accomplishments in the conservative movement and public office and his personal friendship with Carol and myself. He commented sympathetically on my dealing with alcoholism, which he accepted. Then the kicker:

> Robert Bauman should resign from Congress, and resign, also, from his various positions in conservative organizations. . . . In part he should do this as an act of contrition. In part as an act of loyalty. These are institutions he sought to serve and did serve. But in doing so, he ordained standards of conduct which he himself transgressed. . . . But the cause of Robert Bauman, which he served with such passion, such buoyancy and charm, exacts of its spokesman a certain spiritual candor, a spirit of meekness toward abiding truths. Bob Bauman is as welcome in my home today as yesterday. But to his friends and supporters he owes an obligation . . . to accept retirement from public life, with the assurance that only so will he effect that complete recovery that his friends confidently pray, he will find in private pastures.

Indeed Carol and I had been welcome in Bill's home in the past. We once spent the night at the Buckley residence in Stamford, Connecticut, where we enjoyed not only a late supper but an invigorating swim at midnight. In 1969, we had traveled with him, quite by chance, from Washington to New York along with James Burnham, another *National Review* editor, discussing for several hours the state of the world. I had talked with him, dined with him, introduced him more times than I could recall at countless rallies, meetings, conventions, and events. He was and remains one of my life's heroes. And that is why his judgment hurt most of all.

Human Events editors found Buckley's attitude "puzzling," since he had not only failed to call for Senator Ted Kennedy's resignation after Chappaquiddick but instead had concluded that the ordeal might make him better qualified to be President. In a famous 1979 column Buckley wrote about Kennedy's personal conduct designed to protect himself after the accident, saying: "In a grotesque kind of way, this is testimony to Kennedy's political skill and these qualities are desirable in a President."

In spite of *Human Events* comments on the Buckley column, *National Review* magazine itself reiterated its editor's view in its October 31 issue. In an editorial entitled "The Bauman Case," it stated: "Robert Bauman of Maryland has been one of the House's—and the nation's—most able and effective conservative leaders." It went on to say: "All his political allies are victims of an act some might choose to call victimless . . . at this point it behooves the conservative movement to distance itself professionally from him." *NR* then suggested that I run for reelection, win the election, and resign so that a new election could be called, thus saving the seat for the Republicans.

Ignoring the majority support from conservatives and their organizations the press focused on the negatives. Headlines in the daily papers blared that "Conservatives Abandon Bauman" and "Right Dumps Leader." I expected rabid attacks from the left and yet some of those who knew me best (or thought they had) felt most betrayed and reacted most strongly. And from the liberal end of the spectrum came a defense. The *Baltimore Sun* lead editorial of October 9 said in part, commenting on Buckley's statement that I should resign: "That is nonsense. May only healthy people advance conservative causes: In this instance it would be disloyal for Mr. Bauman to resign from his congressional seat now. He would be selling his party out ... The public must assume that Mr. Bauman is a man of professional integrity and honesty, unless new information shows that not to be the case." The *Sun* also noted that there had not been "... any evidence that Mr. Bauman compromised his office." Noting that it would be for the voters to decide, they offered the opinion: "It is inevitable. And it is not necessarily wrong. We believe it is beneficial for voters, who are human beings first, to contemplate the human condition, even as they contemplate inflation, unemployment, war and peace and constituent assistance." On the same day, a columnist for the *Sun*, Michael Olesker, offered his opinion: "Robert Bauman is entitled to our compassion. We should not deny it to him on political grounds or any other grounds. He is no less entitled to weakness than any of us. And we should show him precisely the kind of compassion that Bauman failed, again and again in his political career and his life, to extend to people in the same kind of trouble he now finds himself in."

Local Maryland editorial reaction was mixed, with many newspapers urging a wait-and-see attitude. Typical was the *Cambridge Daily Banner,* which reviewed the facts and concluded: "While we are sympathetic with Mr. Bauman's plight, we are also baffled, hurt, and angry that our trust has been betrayed." One newspaper, the *Daily Times,* of Salisbury, the largest city in my district, immediately called for my resignation and began a daily journalistic crusade to destroy me. Any story on the wires or in the Washington and Baltimore press was reprinted, usually on the front page, often with an eight-column headline above the masthead. The editor injected comments and asides in the body of the news stories explaining the meaning of such novel words as "pederast" and "sodomy."

Some of the most interesting reactions to my situation came from my own Maryland congressional colleagues. The only other Republican, Marjorie Holt, declined to comment right after the revelation, but she said she was "shocked." She sent me a letter of support but publicly said I should resign. One of the bright young liberals in the delegation, Democrat Michael Barnes, said: "It's a very bad situation for Bob and his family, a very tragic personal situation." A conservative Democrat, Rep. Beverly Byron, told the press: "I think Bob Bauman is a very able legislator. There is probably no other member of Congress better prepared on a day-to-day basis for his work in the House. I'm glad he decided to stay in the race." Several others, including Senator Charles Mathias and Paul Sarbanes, declined comment. But perhaps one of the most humane reactions was that of Congresswoman Gladys Spellman, a very liberal Democrat from Maryland's Washington suburbs. I can almost hear her now speaking in that slow, methodical, and gentle voice: "I was truly, truly, truly sorry. I am sure it has been a torture for him probably all along, not just now that the problem is identified. There are people in the House whom we recognize as having problems and with some it impairs their work; with others it doesn't. With Bob, we had no such indication. There are those—how should I say this? There are those who will be very happy about this because Bob Bauman has been a very definite personality in the Congress. There are people who have run up against that personality, his philosophy, and the manner he went about implementing his philosophy. I personally like Bob," Mrs. Spellman added. "I think he is brilliant. But there are others who do not feel that way. I have never felt the sting of his tongue, but there are others who have felt that lash, and they didn't forget."

A few days after those comments, Gladys Spellman, while

campaigning in a suburban shopping mall for what would be certain reelection, suffered a massive stroke and never regained consciousness. She remains in a coma at this writing five years later.

And then began the Bauman jokes. Local scatological radio disk jockeys, such as Howard Stern, had a wonderful time ridiculing me as undoubtedly my children and their friends listened. Others had jokes too:

- Mrs. Spellman was in a coma; she was reelected and Bauman had been defeated. Why? Because Maryland voters prefer a vegetable to a fruit.
- How do you separate Bauman from the boys? With a crowbar.
- Bauman was born in Maryland but reared in Washington.
- Do you know what position Bauman will have in the Reagan administration? Solicitor general.

And my familiar red, white and blue billboards all over my district bearing my name and the slogan, "For All the People," suddenly began to be altered. In spray paint the word "blows" was substituted instead of "for."

The most direct beneficiary of the Bauman scandal was a then twenty-nine-year-old bachelor member of Maryland's lower house of the legislature, the House of Delegates. Royden P. Dyson, elected to the House of Delegates in 1974 at the tender age of twenty-three, had dropped out of the University of Maryland and worked for the Democratic National Committee and the Committee on Labor and Education for the U.S. House of Representatives in minor jobs. It was at the Democratic committee that he met the man who was to become his political manager, friend, and eventually his top congressional aide, Tony Pappas. Dyson once told a reporter for the *Baltimore News American* that he had entered politics because, without a college degree and no training in a trade, it seemed an easy avenue to pursue and he liked it.

In 1976, the eager Dyson, after less than eighteen months in the legislature, announced as a candidate for Congress against me. In a campaign marked by acrimony and charges that I was "a tool of big oil," anti-worker, anti–old people, anti-everything, he gained a respectable 46 percent of the vote. Labor unions bankrolled his race, perhaps as appreciation for his compiling the most pro-labor voting record of anyone representing the area of my congressional district in Annapolis. His 1980 COPE (Committee on Political Education, AFL–CIO) rating for his House of Delegates voting was 100 percent correct as unions saw it.

Suddenly, on the evening of October 3, 1980, while attending a Democratic dinner in Somerset County, Maryland, Roy Dyson got word that Bob Bauman was in big political trouble. He said it was the first he had heard of it. The next morning he told reporters he was just as "shocked" as everyone else and he "had tremendous empathy for Congressman Bauman and his family." He added: "But we are going to run a positive campaign based on the issues and I am not promising not to bring that issue up." Thereafter he continued to promise that he would not bring up "that issue" every chance he got. Within a few days his tone changed somewhat. He told the *Baltimore News American*'s John Farrell: "A man's character is something his constituents have to judge. I feel his constituents are bringing it (the issue) up themselves."

The next day, October 10, he told a reporter for the *Washington Star* that he had "serious questions" about allegations that I had abused my public office to get a navy discharge for someone under threat of blackmail. Dyson said: "His private life is separate. But that part wasn't his private life, that affected his congressional duties. I was hoping that he would answer that at his press conference today." I had answered it, of course, denying I had been blackmailed or used my office, a conclusion several newspapers, including the *Baltimore Sun,* had reached on their own already.

During the interview, the *Star* reporter, Michael Isikoff, observed the following scene: "Look at that," said Dyson campaign manager Tony Pappas, holding up a copy of the *Baltimore Sun* with a picture of Bauman and his wife on the front page. "I don't think there's any way that can help him. Look at the pain he's caused his wife."

Dyson himself told the *Star* reporter: "It's really unfortunate because there are other issues in this campaign ... it's a shame that a sex scandal has to cloud them." Dyson continued, saying that he did not think that I had helped myself by "appearing to blame homosexual tendencies" on alcoholism. Dyson added: "It was very hard for people to understand because most of his colleagues never saw him drink. You know, in the legislature, it doesn't take very long to know who's drinking." As if to prove the Dyson family's rejection of my alcoholism, a few days later Dyson's twin brother (who often campaigned in his place) came up to me and Carol at a Catholic church dinner in his home area of St. Mary's county. In front of many people Leroy Dyson loudly asked, as he grinned and thrust out his hand with a can of Budweiser in it: "Here, Congressman, would you like a beer?"

Indeed, Royden P. Dyson seemed like a man acutely concerned about his own personal status during our 1980 race. As if trying to set the scene, he told the *Baltimore News American* on October 9: "Bauman is in a very desperate situation. I hope the race doesn't get dirty. They'll have to do something. I wonder what it will be?" With an almost maternal protection Dyson's campaign manager, Tony Pappas, told a reporter: "The people of the first district are a very moral and conservative people and so is Roy Dyson."

Throughout the three weeks of the 1980 campaign one of the most difficult things I had to deal with was not the attacks on me but the issue of Roy Dyson's private life.

I will never know just how far I really fell in terms of support from the good people who voted in Maryland's First Congressional District, one of the most conservative areas in the East.

In August 1980, a professional poll by my long-time political advisor Arthur Fincklestein (pollster for hundreds of conservative candidates including Ronald Reagan) predicted I would win the 1980 election by a margin approaching 70 percent. After October 3 and the scandal, a poll taken by two television stations claimed that it was Dyson 51 percent, Bauman 29 percent and the remaining 20 percent undecided. A *Baltimore Sun* poll a few days later claimed my support dropped to 19 percent. My own poll, taken on October 11 and 12, showed Bauman 34 percent, Dyson 42 percent, and the rest undecided. Art Fincklestein told me: "It doesn't look good but it can still be pulled out. Keep fighting."

As election day, November 4, neared, I and those around me in the campaign got the distinct feeling that I had rebounded significantly. Our telephone canvassing showed this as did our many contacts. As if to prove my surge, Dyson's attacks on me suddenly became openly personal. He told the press that even if I did win reelection I could never again be an effective congressman, that he knew the House Committee on Ethics would investigate me if I returned to Congress. He hinted that I might be expelled from the House. He also repeatedly refused to debate me.

As was my custom I spent a quiet election day at home after Carol and I voted early in the morning at the Easton firehouse. I tried as best I could to keep the butterflies in my stomach quiet but they persisted. As much as anything I was resigned to the presumed inevitability of defeat. At least it was a relief that the campaign was over and, hopefully, with it, the stress and pressure that had become almost unbearable for both Carol and me. I knew that the election turnout would be large; it was a presidential year and the Reagan-Carter race had generated considerable interest although in my own area there was no doubt as to which was the major contest.

The polls closed at 8:00 P.M., and the returns started to trickle in. I got them at home over the local radio and in a series of phone calls from my staff at the Tidewater Inn "Bauman Victory Headquarters." The first results from selected precincts in my home county, Talbot, and the neighboring county, Caroline, had me winning but by greatly reduced margins. For hours the returns seesawed back and forth and finally, well after midnight, it came down to what the largest county might do. Harford County, on the Western Shore, had been a strong point for me in the past and if I did well there I could still win. In Harford, a computer malfunction stalled the vote count and nearly an hour after midnight a call from my county chairman, Chester Price, confirmed that I had narrowly lost the county.

The final tabulation gave me more than 10,000 votes over any previous total I received in winning, 91,143. But Dyson amassed 6,600 more votes, 97,743, to win by 51.8 percent. My share was 48.2 percent. I was one of only three Republicans in the nation to lose their House seats in 1980. It was exactly four weeks from the day I appeared in court.

Even though it was nearly 2:00 A.M., my aide, Dick Ribbentrop, urged me to come to the Tidewater Inn and meet the many reporters who remained, demanding I say something. Carol had suffered enough and she went to bed, but only after an emotional scene in which she cried: "My God, what a tragedy! A beautiful family, a great career in Congress, a lovely home on the water. It's all gone. All gone." There was little I could do but try to comfort her as she finally fell asleep, exhausted from the ordeal.

My oldest daughter, Eugenie Marie, then fifteen, insisted she would accompany me to the hotel. "I've been with you at the Tidewater when you won and I'll be with you now," she said emphatically, a grim determination on her young face. Truthfully, I was glad for her company.

The news photos the next day showed me standing on a chair in order to be seen and heard in the early morning crush of press, friends, staff, and campaign volunteers. Some were weeping, others had obviously drowned their sorrow in spirits I had to avoid. My arm is around young Genie, whose lower lip protrudes slightly in a characteristic Bauman pose. My eyes are tired and sad but there is still a look of faint defiance on my face as I said: "You might not have Bob Bauman to kick around anymore, but then again, you might."

CHAPTER
FOUR

On January 3, 1981, at the stroke of noon, I was no longer a member of the Congress of the United States. As the moment passed, I was gazing out the window at the winter wind making icy ripples on Glebe Creek. The world continued just as if nothing had changed.

What does one do at the young age of forty-three once you have been to life's mountaintop only to awake one morning to find power, honor, reputation, all gone?

Unless you are a total coward you go on living.

For the casual observers preoccupied with their own problems my situation may have produced a mild sense of the deep personal desolation I experienced in those days after the election. What an exquisite mess; powerful congressman, national conservative leader, husband and father, officially repudiated by the voters, privately by friends, out of a job, exposed for the world to see as an alcoholic, hypocrite, even worse, a homosexual, a queer. The end of the road.

For breaching the very imperatives of my existence justice was now exacting a price. I had made certain of that by my own conduct.

What to do?

Life taught me the practical habit of sizing up a situation, analyzing all the factors, and acting. Now forced to survey the wreckage of my own life, there was a swift realization that most things of greatest importance to me had vanished suddenly without hope of retrieval. The few people and things remaining were those I habitually took for granted, my wife, my family, our home.

For years my world included public adulation, news media attention, parties at the White House, chats with the President and foreign leaders, winging on jets to Europe, Africa, China. Now that world shrank down to a century-old farm house on Maryland's Eastern Shore and soon-to-be vacated Washington office strewn with packing crates and memories. In thirty days I had gone from a respected national figure to a scandal-smeared, defeated politician.

Months before when Carol and I had our confrontation over my "problem" I agreed to undergo psychological counseling and Father Harvey's spiritual regime with one goal in mind: saving my marriage. I dearly did not want to lose Carol and our children. Now in exposure and defeat that goal intensified. I went to frequent Mass and Communion and Lord, how I prayed for the grace and strength to get through this. There were some small signs of hope. At least I had endured what was likely to be the worst crisis of my life without resorting to my old crutch, alcohol.

I consulted with Dr. Kay, telling him that in order to preserve my marriage I wanted to pursue a "cure" for my homosexual "tendencies." His response was a frank restatement of what he had already told me some months before; with my long history of homosexual conduct, at my age, any supposed "cure" was highly unlikely. I was most probably gay. To try and change a lifelong orientation would take lengthy, in-depth psychiatric analysis and he was not able to give me that. He suggested the names of several psychiatrists who might be able to help. I tried first one, and then when that did not work, a second. I did not want to believe Kay. What I wanted was a cure, the quicker the better.

I eagerly told Carol of my plans as if to prove my good intentions about our future. She did not discourage me but her mild approval might have warned me of things to come had I been more perceptive. I needed hope and some goal I could cling to in the wake of tragedy. A lost life, a lost campaign, was to be replaced with my new campaign for "the cure."

My public life was winding down and the next few weeks were spent packing the accumulation of a decade in public office. The scandal put an abrupt end to invitations and previously scheduled events began to be canceled one by one. Their organizers had invited a different Congressman Bauman months before.

As fate would have it another possible humiliation lay in my path. The Democratic House leadership, hoping Jimmy Carter would be reelected, had scheduled a special or "lame duck" session of Congress for late November after the elections. Within a few weeks of my ignominious defeat I returned to the floor of the House to face I knew not what. I expected the worst, possible personal snubs, ridicule. Instead, a steady stream of congressmen from both parties came over to my traditional seat on the House floor, quietly expressing their sympathy, many of them praising my past service. "I don't know what we'll do without you" was a phrase I heard repeatedly. More than a hundred members spoke to me, a statistic I know, because, ever the good politician, I sent each a thank-you note.

I tried to continue as if nothing had happened but from the day I returned for the special session the press hounded me for my reaction, election post-mortems, more questions about the scandal. I finally just avoided them telling one *Washington Post* reporter as he pursued me down a hall that one of the virtues of defeat was not having to talk to the press anymore.

And one evening, as the House adjourned, Speaker Tip O'Neill came down from the rostrum, walked over to me, put his huge hand on my shoulder, and told me: "I really am sorry about what happened to you." I still wonder whether he meant it, but the gesture was appreciated.

Before, during, and after the House special session I searched for some appointment in the new Reagan administration. I contacted everyone I could on the new "transition team," reminding them that I was one of the few conservatives who backed Reagan over Nixon in 1968, over Ford in 1976, and again in 1980. Surely, I argued, there must be some post for me with my distinguished record in Congress, my national conservative leadership. What I got was polite demurrers from people like Bill Timmons, head of Reagan's "transition team." "Gee, I just don't know, Bob, but I'll get back to you." My colleagues in Congress rallied around, made calls, signed letters to the President-elect, but nothing happened. Led by my friend, Congressman John Rousselot, all his California congressional delegation signed a joint letter to Reagan urging my appointment to some position, but still no response.

In late November the board of directors of the national group I founded in 1964, the American Conservative Union, met, and I was allowed to preside as chairman for approximately five minutes, turning the gavel over to Tom Winter, the vice-chairman. The board declared my two-year term at a premature end. It took considerable persuasion from Phil Crane and especially John Ashbrook to prevent some board members from moving to impeach me. In my place they elected Congressman Mickey Edwards of Oklahoma.

Things were going better for Carol. She was named to the interim group overseeing the Office of Personnel Management for the incoming Reagan administration, a nonpaying job which required her to be in Washington every day. She began a search for employment herself, and I reasoned this would be at least some economic help since I was having such a difficult time.

In late December it was announced that Governor Jim Edwards of South Carolina, my old friend from our joint service on the Federal Hospital Council, was to be appointed to the Reagan cabinet as secretary of the Department of Energy. After much politicking and my personal intervention with Jim, Carol was finally named as deputy press secretary of the Energy Department—at a substantial salary. This brought press and editorial howls that assumed Carol was nothing more than a housewife of an about to be ex-congressman, that this was a political payoff for me. It angered me so much that I answered several complaints with nasty letters that brought some apologies. I wanted the world to know that Carol in her own right was very well qualified for the job.

Christmas, usually a time of ritual and fun in the Bauman household, came and went. We went through all the motions and although I tried to put my heart in it, Carol seemed unusually reserved. I did everything as I always did with the children, the Advent wreath, cutting the tree ourselves out in the woods, decorating it, hanging all the garlands and wreaths, wrapping the presents. Jimmy even left milk, cookies, and carrots for Santa and the reindeer.

But while mother had a job, father was unemployed.

With the likelihood of a Reagan administration job receding into infinity I turned toward the profession I always before had little time for, the law. With the exception of my three years in the Maryland State Senate, 1970–73, I had abandoned my practice, especially after I went to Congress. So there was nothing to which to return in Easton, no profession, no savings, no investments. How we would survive extended unemployment without Carol's income was unknown. Thank God she had gotten a job.

My difficulty in those transitional months after my 1980 defeat was that I could not grasp the full reality of what had happened to me. I reasoned, wrongly, it would turn out, that my past accomplishments, my obvious political talents, my friends were enough to outbalance the impact of scandal. As time accumulated without a drink, as I listened to professional and spiritual counseling, I began to feel better than ever in my life. I was out from under the terrible burden of secrecy and fear. I knew that I still labored under "the twin compulsions" of alcoholism and "homosexual tendencies" but I somehow forgot how horrible this had been to me for so many years. As I at last began to deal with myself, my problems now horrified others who would not, or could not, attempt to deal with them at all. They saw me as many things, God knows, but not as a possible government official, attorney or employee. Better to avert their eyes.

For the first few weeks of her new employment at the Department of Energy Carol commuted to Washington from Easton, retracing the long daily trek I followed for nearly eight years. I stayed at home, at last acting as father for our three youngest children who were in school, Genie, fifteen, Vicky, twelve, and Jimmy, eight. I moved into a small two-room "law office" in the same building that had housed my spacious congressional home office, unable to afford even a secretary where once I had had a staff of eighteen people. I began hunting for clients, surveying the local legal fraternity grown from about twenty to more than forty in my eight-year absence. Discreet inquiries quickly gave me a clear picture that my association was not wanted by any existing firms in Easton.

And then one cold Saturday in February 1981, Carol said, "We have to talk." I had heard that ominous phrase before, usually prior to some personal crisis over my drinking, late nights, "the problem" or finances.

This time it was far more serious. The eventual outcome produced perhaps the greatest consequences of all that happened to me. We sat on the small settee in front of the fireplace in the living room of Glebe House. As Carol spoke I felt again as a child at the beach, the waves washing the sand from under my feet as I slowly sank.

In careful, measured phrases, almost rehearsed, she told me she had discussed our "situation" with a local lady attorney. Carol wanted us to begin what she called "a trial separation" as soon as possible. Perhaps trying to avoid the worst, she told me "this does not necessarily mean that I want a divorce." As part of the "trial" she requested that I move out of Glebe House. I was incredulous.

"How do you expect me to move with no money and no job? You know the state of our finances and even with you working we probably won't be able to continue paying our mortgages unless I get a job very soon." Even if I had the money, where was I supposed to live? She did not know. She just felt that being apart for a time would give us both a chance to reassess our lives and decide what we wanted to do in the future.

"But I want to keep our marriage and family together," I protested, a note of desperation creeping into my voice. "That's why I've been seeing a psychiatrist and doing what Father Harvey has suggested." She said she had talked with Father about her plans. Soon I would be approaching a full year without a drink. She had wanted me to have that time of sobriety before she informed me of her plans. Evidently she began formulation of these plans long months before, perhaps at the time of our early 1980 confrontation. Meanwhile, I went on blissfully thinking things were improving even though an attempt to resume sexual relations was rebuffed tearfully by her in the late summer. Soon afterward the scandal, campaign, and defeat engulfed us all. Only later had I considered the state of our marriage. But Carol had been thinking about what must be done for a long time. In retrospect it seems that much before the FBI and my defeat, she determined that our marriage must end. At some point "when?" became her only question while I was in my dream world thinking about "cures" for my "problems." As usual my supreme ego assumed that Carol would go along with what I wanted. She always had before, hadn't she?

I slowly began to realize this was a new Carol who confronted me. This was not the compliant wife and mother who for long years suffered in relative silence, promoting my career while enduring my heartless, cruel self-indulgence. This was a new and forceful person who finally summoned within herself the courage and good judgment she possessed but often failed to exercise. The classic enabler had come to her dramatic end but I had yet to grasp the fact.

I once encountered a definition of "love" as a passionate, emotional, spiritual, and sexual bond between a man and a woman, both of whom highly value the person of the other. That is not the love I felt for Carol when we first met. Nor was mine the story-book "love at first sight." In the past five years I have often thought about the meaning of "love." I have concluded that throughout most of my life I was incapable of loving anyone, least of all myself, certainly in that definition's deep sense.

I first met Carol Gene Dawson after my 1959 graduation from the Georgetown University School of Foreign Service in Washington. I remember only one thing about that ceremony on a hot, humid afternoon on the lawn of the Healy Building.

Bishop James Wright of Pittsburgh, Pennsylvania, later to become a Prince of the Church and leader of the Roman Curia, was the speaker. He may have secretly harbored thoughts of his future cardinalate but the good bishop did not let it deter his sense of humor. A popular song of his youth in the Roaring Twenties, he recalled, recommended the daily virtue of "a little love each morning, a little love each night."

"There are those of us in life," intoned his excellency with a twinkle in his eye, "who have managed to sustain ourselves without this recommended daily ritual."

The audience, glad for a momentary diversion from the heat, laughed appreciatively.

But the line stuck in my mind. I could identify.

That September I began three more years of night school studies, this time at Georgetown Law School. For the first time I had time to engage in extracurricular activities; I ran for and was elected president of the G.U. Young Republican Club. The brief campaign was a precursor of my political career. I charged that my opponent, a bright young student, Bob Hall, was really a liberal. He responded by characterizing me as a Fascist. But we conservatives signed up more new YR members and I was elected handily.

I savored my first election victory. My total constituency consisted of a few more than one hundred college students. Armed with the title "Mr. President" (it had a certain appeal), I found myself meeting other area YR student leaders as part of a growing effort to head off New York Governor Nelson Rockefeller's 1960 presidential nomination bid. We were all for Vice-President Richard Nixon. Our goal was Nixon's endorsement by the annual District of Columbia College YR Convention over the despised liberal Rocky.

On a late Friday afternoon in November 1959, conservative students from area colleges gathered in a basement room of the Coleman-Nevils Building, part of Georgetown University, for the mass manufacture of Nixon signs.

I remember clearly the moment when I first saw Carol Gene Dawson.

And I was impressed.

She entered the room, stage right, wearing a businesslike navy blue suit, short jacket, and white blouse. Her dark blond hair was nearly shoulder length, framing a pert, genuinely pretty face with prominent cheekbones, wide-set brown eyes, and a bow-like mouth, the upper lip slightly protruding. It gave her a quizzical smile, yet the impression was of serenity and confidence. "Damned if she doesn't look like Grace Kelly!" a thought which I soon found others shared.

Carol tossed her head like a young filly, flashing her eyes around the room, drawing in her breath before she spoke as though needing an extra supply of oxygen to fuel her burst of words. She seemed self-assured, certain of her purpose and her place in this room full of her political peers, most of whom greeted her.

My fellow student, Doug Caddy, introduced Carol to me, using her title as president of the Young Republican Club of Dunbarton College of the Holy Cross where she was a student. I remember her smile as we shook hands. She said something about "having heard about you."

Indeed she had heard of me, I later learned.

Several months before, Doug Caddy, its editor, had published a feature article about me in the *Foreign Service Courier,* extolling my conservatism and featuring my job in the House Republican

Cloakroom on Capitol Hill. It was all there: Catholic, anti-Communist, pro gold standard, balanced budget; you name it. Carol's younger sister, Nancy, read the article and called it to her attention with the statement:

"You've got to meet this guy. He sounds just like you."

We found we did have much in common.

Our religious faith, our mutual passion for politics and conservatism. Our zeal for advancing the cause, our strong distaste for liberalism. We both came from modest, middle-class homes, both our fathers were alcoholics, both of us had to work to put ourselves through college.

Looking back now I could make no objective claim to maturity at the age of twenty-two when we met. I was lonely, unsure of myself despite the outward bravado, and, though not fully aware of it then, suffering from my own acute case of low self-esteem. I pushed all this aside and what the world saw was an active, aggressive, powerful personality; a facade as intricate and insubstantial as those built by Prince Grigori Potemkin when ordered up by Catherine the Great.

I really had no confidence that anyone, much less this beautiful young lady, could love me because I could not love myself. The concept of loving me for myself was a stark contradiction in terms.

I felt an inner powerlessness I tried to abate by control, manipulation, domination, and coercion of those around me. That certainly included the major figure in my life, my wife. I could not rely on any reserve of inner strength because at my core there was a void I had no idea how to fill. Long years before I recently achieved some degree of serenity by living one day at a time, I lived from minute to minute, always on guard against the internal dread I did not understand.

I viewed others not so much as individuals worthy of respect but as so many opportunities to gratify my own needs. I fostered false pride in my staunch personal independence and yet I craved other people's approval to make me feel worthwhile. Though I could not admit it to myself, certainly not to others, my whole outlook in life after twenty-one years was not particularly hopeful.

But that is useful only as hindsight.

All I knew in that early winter of 1959–60 was that something wonderful was happening to me and I could not understand why. Why would an attractive, bright young lady like Carol see anything in me? At the time she had several suitors, at least two of whom proposed marriage. She could have her pick and yet she wanted me. Incredible, I thought to myself as I gazed into the mirror each morning.

But she did choose me.

In later years I carefully avoided discussion of our relationship during those early days. It is fair to say that we might never have married had she not pressed her case with persistence. Not to say that our relationship was totally one-sided.

I found her very attractive, so much so it scared me. She was beautiful, intellectual, articulate, and witty. On the phone, over meals, we talked endlessly about politics, government, and new subjects I never before considered. Suddenly I was introduced to the French impressionist school and Carol's special favorite, the American member, Mary Cassatt. Carol studied art as a major at Dunbarton and as part of her thesis she copied one of Cassatt's many versions of "Mother and Child" at the National Gallery in Washington. Its glowing, misty tones of green and yellow graced the walls of our home for twenty years. Now seeing a Cassatt painting always evokes in me a mixture of pleasure and pain, of what was and might have been.

And we agreed on so many things. Politics, economics, theology (another of her areas of study), and most importantly, we shared the same political enemies, a common bond that forges strong alliances in politics, war, and apparently, marriage. (Ironically, many of those "liberal" enemies of our Republican youth are now major officials of the Reagan administration, late converts to the cause.)

Many years later, in a fit of justified bitterness, Carol accused me to my face of ". . . marrying me only because you needed a wife for your political career."

I cannot add to my considerable marital dishonesty by denying that charge completely. I did indeed see in her a person who could only be a great asset to my future. But by no means was that all I saw.

Here was a person who was kind, gentle, loving, and genuinely concerned about my personal welfare. She meant it when she told me she loved me. It had been a long time since anyone, any woman, had felt that way about me. Although at first startled and unsure of her faith in me, I definitely liked it.

We talked on the telephone a few times, saw each other at D.C. College YR functions, and dropped hints about "getting together sometime soon."

It was only a matter of a few weeks until our first "date," which I mustered enough courage to initiate. Someone on the Hill gave me two tickets to the annual presidential Christmas Tree lighting ceremony located on the Ellipse near the White House. It was so cold President Eisenhower was not there, but Carol and I were, joining the chorus of "aahhs" at the sudden sparkle of a thousand lights. We dashed into the nearby Department of Commerce building to get warm, then ran through the frosty night to O'Donnell's Seafood Restaurant at 13th and E Streets N.W.

There I did my post-adolescent best to impress Miss Dawson with my savoir faire until the wine list arrived. I never had tasted wine before, and the bottle of Blue Nun we settled on was a first for me.

My own father's alcoholism had convinced me that I should never drink and I did not until I was nineteen or twenty and in college. Then I began to have an occasional beer at the Young Republican beer busts. As their newly elected head I wanted to be "one of the boys."

After the first evening together even I realized that "something" was developing between Carol and me. I had never experienced this kind of feeling about any member of the opposite sex.

I wrestled with all this in my mind but the intellectual approach did not explain my emotional state. Maybe this was indeed what "love" was like. I missed her constantly when we were apart. I waited to hear her voice on the phone. I was happy and nervous when we were together, anxious to please her and afraid I might offend. Finally, I decided to do something about it.

Some time after New Year's 1960, I invited Carol to dine with me at the only place I could think of with some degree of privacy, the A Street S.E. house of a gay friend, Jerry. I was living a few doors away in the dingy basement of his mother's rooming house, certainly no fit scene for a romantic encounter.

Jerry was not pleased to hear my intended use of his house was for a date with "a girl, my God," as he put it, but since he worked nights, he agreed. There in his cramped basement kitchen I prepared fish sticks and some more white wine. We dined among his collection of music boxes and record players.

For several years I had collected 78 rpm phonograph records and Rudy Vallee had become one of my favorites. After our modest dinner I asked Carol to listen carefully to the lyrics of one of Rudy's better-known record hits, "S'posin'." I cranked the old RCA Victrola and out came the words:

> S'posin' I should say for you I yearn,
> Would you think I'm speaking out of turn,
> And s'posin' I declare it,
> Would you take my love and share it?
> I'm not s'posin', I'm in love with you.

When our lips met in our first kiss it was unshakable proof to me that everything—yes, everything—was going to be all right. We were in love.

Some days later, at what I considered a posh Connecticut Avenue restaurant, Ted Lewis, I asked Carol to marry me, not entirely on the spur of the moment. She accepted and we held hands under the red tablecloth, whispering about what all these irrelevant people dining around us would think if they knew what a historic event was taking place before their uncomprehending eyes.

But for the first and certainly not the last time, politics stood in our way. We were both about to embark on active roles in the 1960 election campaigns and so we decided to postpone our wedding until November 19, 1960, well after Richard Nixon would be elected President—or so we thought.

In the immediate interim, however, Carol employed her theological training from Dunbarton, unearthing an ancient church ritual which formalized engagements to be married. Before I knew it, on the Feast day of St. Elizabeth in March 1960, I found myself standing beside Carol before the altar rail of her parish church in Falls Church, Virginia. The pastor of St. James', Monsignor Heller, was asking us a series of very serious questions about our future intentions and our degree of mutual commitment. At the appropriate point, I slipped the engagement ring on her finger, containing some small diamonds from my own mother's ring.

Few of our friends had heard of a formal engagement, a rite more common to medieval European royalty than suburban Washington young conservatives. It gave me some pause, considering the explanation I received of its meaning from Father Heller, raising many of the same questions I would face again as our wedding date neared.

This was very serious business. Even if some others did not, Roman Catholics believed in the permanency of marriage. There was a finality to this event, even though I was told we could always change our minds, I sensed that this engagement pledge was almost as binding as the real thing. Almost forever, and with little chance of a way out.

Is this what I really wanted?

For one thing, I was a member of a distinct American statistical minority, even in 1960, a twenty-two-year-old male who never had a true sexual relationship with a woman. There had been many encounters with others of my own sex, though I never counted. But I was still sure that I was not a queer. I had convinced myself that I could answer that one with a firm "no."

If that were not so how could I feel as I did about Carol? These new and overwhelming sensations I felt were not fake. I was sure that the love we felt for each other would give me the strength to do what God and His church required of me. I was young but I was an adult and soon I would be a married man. My mind conjured a picture of my new duties, "I will protect and care for her and our children," I vowed. "I have the potential power to be good. To be a man. Marriage will be the very way to become the good person I have always wanted to be."

In truth I had only the vaguest notion of the general requirements of the state of holy matrimony, much less what was required of me personally.

And I only began to learn after it was already too late.

From an early age I definitely intended to be a bachelor. Marriage was not for me. Girls made me uncomfortable and the foolishness of "love" I saw as an interference with the important affairs of the world I wanted to influence. When family members inquired about my marital plans they got a firm statement of purpose. I had no intention of ever getting married. After a time Bob's bachelorhood became a given in family discussion.

Carol changed all that.

And from the first meeting at a Nixon sign-painting party, our courtship and married life, even its end, were conducted in the midst of politics. So political was our joint image that at a Lincoln Day dinner in Salisbury, Maryland, in 1961, a few months after our wedding, we were greeted by a prize remark from one of the leading Republican ladies of the day, Bertha Adkins: "Here they come folks," she boomed as we walked through the door. "The only campaign promise that was kept last year."

Indeed, "Carol and Bob" became known as a "team" in the conservative movement, on Capitol Hill where we both worked, in Maryland politics.

And we really were a team. In founding Young Americans for Freedom in 1960, in the 1964 draft Goldwater for President movement and the subsequent campaign, in my candidacies for Goldwater delegate in 1964, for the State Senate in 1970, for Congress, we worked together, advised each other, gave each other hope and encouragement. It was the kind of mutual support every married couple needs, close and understanding, doing things for each other without having to be told. From all outward appearances, we were the perfect young conservative couple with a bright future, the kind of young marrieds who reassure the older generation their fight has been worth it.

In the months after we met in November 1959, Carol and I both plunged into national youth politics at a furious pace. Both of us were active in founding a national "Youth for Nixon" with encouragement from some of the vice-president's major backers but no official sanction from the Nixon campaign organization. I served briefly as the first national chairman of the group but was replaced because of my already well-known hard line conservatism. My successor was a beautiful young lady who had been elected as national co-chairman of the College Young Republicans at the Denver convention in 1959; her name, Carol Gene Dawson. Carol was then working on Vice-President Nixon's staff and one of his aides, Charlie McWhorter, supposedly remarked about our wedding plans: "Bauman couldn't control Youth for Nixon so he married it."

While Carol toiled for Nixon against John F. Kennedy I returned to the Eastern Shore to help my friend and mentor Ted Miller in his 1960 congressional campaign. Stacks of letters tied with string attest to the agony of young lovers apart. We talked a lot by phone, as much politics as personal. We both attended the July 1960 Republican National Convention in Chicago, boosting Barry Goldwater for vice-president and distrusting Nixon's conservatism after he sold out to Nelson Rockefeller on the key platform terms. And on election night in November we watched sadly as both Dick Nixon and Ted Miller lost. "Well, let's get to work for Goldwater in 1964," I said.

In September 1960, Carol and I also participated in a series of meetings, the culmination of which occurred at Bill Buckley's family estate in Sharon, Connecticut. There Carol was one of the founders of Young Americans for Freedom, soon to become the nation's largest conservative youth group. I was at home in Maryland helping the Miller campaign and Carol, not I, was one of the first elected to the new board of directors. In those days in young conservative circles I was known as "Carol Dawson's husband."

I officially acquired that title on Saturday, November 19, 1960, when we administered each other the Sacrament of Holy Matrimony at Saint James' Church in Falls Church, Virginia, Carol's home parish. Dick Nixon, still recuperating, couldn't be there but sent a nice note. Ted Miller, with his wife, Missy, was there, as was my father, looking slightly comical in an ill-fitting rented cutaway coat, wing collar, and four-in-hand tie.

The ties were important, the rental store clerk told me. The ascot tie would be most correct "since President-elect Kennedy and his bride chose them when they were married." I instantly chose the straight four-in-hand tie instead.

Our wedding party included Carol's older sister, Nancy, as bridesmaid, and Lee Edwards was best man. Ushers included Doug Caddy, who flew down from his New York job as YAF director, Dave Franke, Bill Emerson, now a congressman from Missouri, and Christopher DelSesto, one of my Georgetown schoolmates whose father was then one of the rare Republican governors of Rhode Island.

The ceremony was celebrated by Monsignor Heller, our friend from the formal engagement, and Reverend Father John F. Harvey. Carol's father, Gene, cried more than anyone else but the wedding went off without a hitch. Carol was radiant in a flowing white gown. We drove to and from the church in a U.S. government Cadillac limousine assigned to House Republican Leader Charles Halleck of Indiana, my Capitol Hill boss.

We had a difficult time cleaning our little Nash American car soaped with "Just Married" and plastered with "Go With Nixon-Lodge" stickers in the shape of footprints. We motored to a country inn in Luray, Virginia, Carol's mother recommended because she and Gene had stayed there. The inn served only beer and light wine and then only until 10:00 P.M. We almost failed to get any champagne. So inexperienced were we both that the next day we consulted a local gynecologist to make sure we were doing things right.

But we were both in love and the newness, the mystery, was enough to infuse me with a feeling of manliness I never experienced before.

As we drove back from the honeymoon to our new apartment a car came over the hill on one of Virginia's notoriously narrow highways and headed straight for us. But for my quick swerve at least I, driving, would have been killed if not both of us. It was a nervous end to a honeymoon but nothing could upset us. We were in love, married, and setting out to change the world.

In January 1961, Carol began work as a legislative aide to newly elected Congressman Don Bruce from Indianapolis, Indiana, her hometown. I continued my work in the House Republican Cloakroom although on the bitter cold Inauguration Day of January 21, I refused to stay around to see Kennedy sworn in. I did manage to see, as I left the Capitol, the lectern go up in flames as Francis Cardinal Cushing of Boston prayed incessantly long. The smoky warning stopped him but it never fazed the graceful new President whose memorable inaugural address my partisanship prevented me from hearing.

Our love nest was a small one-bedroom walkup at 514 A Street N.E., an old Capitol Hill townhouse later converted into the Museum of African Art. At the time the first floor doubled as home and office for Maurice Rosenblatt and a group he headed, The

National Committee for an Effective Congress, one of the most liberal lobbies of its day.

At night Carol and I would lie awake and wonder what liberal skullduggery was going on beneath us.

Upstairs in our place we knew what had been going on. We both were working hard for our money, I was teaching Carol how to cook (I never fully succeeded), and studying frantically for my law exams at Georgetown.

On January 26, 1962, our first-born arrived, Edward Carroll Bauman; Edward after Ted Miller, Carroll after the Maryland Carrolls from whom Carol's mother was descended.

Suddenly I was a father.

The bond between a married couple is perhaps strongest, most fulfilled with the arrival of their first-born child. With sudden force the mystery of life becomes personal experience, filling you with a deep wonder beyond the poor power of words. "Did we really do this?" you ask at the first glimpse of the tiny human being you helped create in God's image.

Carol's labor was prolonged with Teddy. She entered the hospital early in the day. At dinner time we had been waiting all day and her physician, Dr. Holden, told me nothing looked immediate. He would call me at home. I drove across rush-hour Washington and as soon as I stepped into our apartment door the phone was ringing. A nurse told me to come back.

Again I raced across town and by the time I arrived I had become the father of a handsome baby boy. Mother and child were doing fine, I was told.

That was not quite the whole truth, unfortunately. More than a month overdue and with such a heavy weight, it had been a very difficult first birth for both mother and child. The use of forceps to assist his entry into the world had left little Ted with his right eye swollen shut. Partial surgery on Carol had been required to ease his exit. It would be several years before we realized the full extent of the damage done that January evening.

In contrast, for father, it was easy elation and joy. Peering through the thick window of the maternity nursery with my mother-in-law, Hilda, I got my first chance to meet Teddy, a slowly struggling little man with a black eye. He blinked his one good eye in a vain effort to see what the world had in store for him. Dr. Holden assured me he was a healthy baby and the eye would heal.

Whatever others may have thought I believed him to be the most beautiful child I ever saw, a rare combination of his mother's acknowledged beauty and both our brains. Waiting to see Carol I purchased a box of the best cigars for distribution the next morning in the House Republican Cloakroom. I wanted the world to share my delight.

Several hours later Carol was brought back from the recovery room and I was allowed to see her in her room. When I entered she was still under heavy sedation to ease the pain. She barely regained consciousness so that I could repeat what Dr. Holden told her earlier; it was a boy.

I held her hand tightly and suddenly I was overwhelmed with emotion. Crying softly, tears rolling down my face, I bent down over the bed and embraced Carol, who weakly acknowledged my closeness. The small hospital light above her bed shadowed her pale, tired face. She smiled as I told her she had made me the happiest person in the world, that I loved her now more than ever, that I would always love her. She slowly nodded agreement and I held her hand as she drifted back into healing sleep.

Later that night, after meeting Teddy Bauman close up when he was brought into his mother's room, I left the hospital and stepped out into the cold bracing January night air. I was armed with a renewed and firm resolve that never again would I violate Carol's trust in me. I would overcome my weakness and live as a good Catholic husband should.

I knew I must for Carol, for myself, and for that little guy up in the nursery crib.

They depended on me just as I depended so often on Carol for assistance, counsel, and love.

But the truth is, Carol could not depend on me. Her commitment to marriage was total, while I fooled myself into thinking mine was, but dared not be honest with myself.

Tentatively, during the early years of our marriage, later with increasing frequency, Carol's instincts caused her to raise the issue at the heart of our matrimonial union.

She summed up the problem in seemingly casual statements such as: "Sometimes, Bob, I get the feeling that I don't really know you that well. There seems to be a barrier between us. We talk so much about politics and other things I wish you would talk about how you feel, let me know the real you. Is there something wrong between us? Is it me?"

Of course, Carol was right. She did not know the "real me" and she must never be permitted to know. God forbid, I thought, that she should ever find out what a flawed person I am, what a terrible sham my life has become. How could I ever admit to Carol who I really was when I could not even admit that to myself. "Who and what I am" was the question that hounded me all my life. Unanswered, that question undermined our life together.

So I would glibly dismiss her inquiries with my practiced politician's response, throwing the question back at her:

"Why, what do you mean, Carol, not know me? You know me better than anyone ever has, except maybe my own mother. We share everything. There just isn't much to know."

And yet I knew, and perhaps Carol did also, that her intuitive questioning cut much too close to the truth of my inner being. She saw the inner turmoil and may have reached tentative conclusions about me I would not even permit myself.

On May 19, 1965, three-year-old Teddy was joined by a beautiful little blond sister, Eugenie Marie Bauman. "Genie" was named after her maternal grandfather, Eugene Dawson, whom she and her siblings would never know. On New Year's Eve,

1964, Gene was killed in an auto accident returning from a meeting of fellow alcoholics. He had "dried out" and embraced helping other alcoholics during the last three years of his life with a fervor. Ironically, his tragic death was caused by a drunk teenager who smashed into the rear of Gene's car. For many years afterward the sad memory of this event marred our New Year's Eves, which we usually spent quietly at home.

As our joint income increased, Carol and I moved through a series of Capitol Hill apartments until, in January 1965, we purchased a large row house at 513 A Street S.E., only two blocks from the Library of Congress. Advertised in the *Washington Post* as being "Pickwickian" in character, that better described the real estate agent, an ancient little lady named Eileen Dean, right out of Dickens. We loved the house, considered it overnight, and with Carol's mother's generous help, bought it the next day.

It was a Victorian dream house for two young conservatives. Built in the 1870s, it had a large double living room with two fireplaces and sliding doors, a formal dining room, two baths and three bedrooms, an attractive patio in the rear lined with bricks, even a small fountain. With a full basement it sold for only forty-five thousand dollars. More recently, it has changed hands for a price over a quarter of a million dollars, a commentary on ensuing inflation.

Somehow the purchase of your first home brings a special seal to a marriage and this was an occasion of hope for us. Ted and Genie would both have their own rooms, being near our jobs at the Capitol, the pace would be less hectic, and we could finally "settle down."

Becoming a homeowner brought out the domestic side of me. I followed my own father's example, repairing, redecorating, and gardening. Unlike my work in politics, here you saw results. I could cover a wall with latex paint, or plant a row of flowers and within hours or days see real accomplishments. In my little spare time I worked on the old house until it qualified for the Capitol Hill House Tour.

On October 19, 1966, on the very day thousands of Vietnam War protesters were mobbing the Pentagon, our third child and second daughter was born at Columbia Hospital. Carol's labor was induced for a Saturday morning so that Dr. Holden could get in his weekly golf date. All went well. For several days this handsome little dark-haired baby girl went nameless as Carol and I tried to come up with a proper title. She could not leave the hospital unless her name appeared on the birth certificate. Nothing seemed quite correct until, mulling it over, I thought of those protesters across the Potomac River. "Why not name her after victory in Vietnam?" I asked Carol.

Victoria Anne Bauman was baptized at St. Peter's Church on Capitol Hill a few weeks later, with a champagne brunch at home afterward. As clergy, friends and neighbors gathered to celebrate, our cock-a-poo named Shaggy, rescued from the Humane Society a year or two before, decided that she too would provide us with another birthday. Six puppies were born in the basement, our guests serving as midwives and commentators. Shaggy stole the show as little Vicky slept through most of the festivities in her honor.

Whatever qualities I lacked as a faithful husband and father, Carol more than made up in her intense maternal concern for our children. Although later years brought complaints from the children about her being aloof or difficult to get close to, her distance may have stemmed from the deep hurt experienced at my hands.

I knew how much she loved our children and as the busy young politician saving the world I was confident that no matter what I did or how late I returned, Carol would always take care of "the kids."

Her protective attitude toward all our children first manifested itself when our first-born, Teddy, came home from the hospital. We immediately discovered that he was more than just a light sleeper. The slightest noise or abrupt movement would wake him. Sometimes it would take hours in a rocking chair to get him back to sleep. Often put back into his crib he would cry again. When awake he was extremely active, rocking in the crib or playpen, always in motion.

In many ways Ted was precocious, walking at eight months and talking at nine months, but Carol insisted that something, she did not know just what, was wrong. As "first-time" parents we had a lot to learn, I kept insisting, and maybe nothing was wrong. Carol pursued her fears with Teddy's pediatrician, Dr. Charles Millwater, a portly little elf of a man who looked like a middle-aged baby. Eventually an "EKG" or brain wave test was administered to Teddy. His test chart seemed to indicate problems.

After further testing and much discussion, Dr. Millwater gave us recent medical literature describing a condition known as "minimal brain dysfunction." It was correctible, but if not diagnosed, it could be a possible source of emotional and other difficulties for a child.

That was bad news.

The good and surprising news was the discovery the dysfunction could be controlled by daily doses of amphetamines ("speed") which, if administered to an adult would produce hyperactivity, but given to a child with this problem up until the age of puberty, the drugs had just the opposite effect, calming and allowing proper muscle and mind coordination.

Carol's intuitive persistence had paid off. Overnight the administration of drugs such as Dilantin and Ritalin caused Teddy's motor control to improve immensely, his disposition to calm markedly, and he was able to sleep. But for her maternal concern he might have suffered the even greater emotional problems which often plague such children in the form of taunting by their peers or adverse reactions from teachers and parents who do not understand the cause of the hyperactivity. Fortunately, Teddy, as most do, eventually outgrew the problem.

With both of us working and now with three children, we needed help. Often Carol's mother, Hilda, would baby-sit, but finally we hired a young black lady, Francis, who kept house and took care of the children. Teddy and Genie attended the Capitol

Hill Montessori School and at a very early age learned to read and write before they entered the first grade.

But "things" never really settled down because my irresponsible though largely concealed extramarital conduct would not permit peace.

Though there was much to occupy us, politics, children, careers, Carol and I lived with an uneasy knowledge that something was wrong with our marriage. It went beyond her complaint that she did not really know me, that she could not seem to get close to me. There were the very tangible evidences of coming home late after delivering the baby-sitter, of my not feeling in the mood to have sex, of my increasing drinking.

At some point Carol fastened upon the idea that the problem was living in Washington. If we just got away from this town things would get better, she argued. It was never made clear what she wanted to escape from and how things would improve if we moved to Easton. Fate stepped in with the death of my father in 1965 and then my stepmother in 1968. Their home in Easton, which we both now claimed as our legal residence, would have to be sold to settle the estate.

There were other compelling reasons to make a drastic change in our lives. In early 1968, I quit my House legislative staff job after fifteen years to work for California Governor Ronald Reagan's presidential bid against Richard Nixon. When he inevitably lost, I tried to mend my political fences by taking the job as director of the Maryland Citizens for Nixon-Agnew, but Hubert Humphrey won the state in spite of Agnew's presence on the ticket.

After Nixon's victory I began checking around for a job with the new administration but after weeks of trying and many endorsements from friendly congressmen nothing came of it. I turned down an assistant deputy attorney generalship at the Justice Department which would have meant no active political involvement.

If my job opportunities looked bleak, Carol's prospered. Patrick Buchanan, named as President-elect Nixon's chief of communications, offered Carol a job as his deputy. The pay was good but it meant Carol had to report for work six mornings a week at 5:30 A.M. Once there she watched all the three morning network television shows, read all the major newspapers, and condensed this into a "news brief" for the President's eyes. It had to be on Nixon's Oval Office desk by 8:00 A.M.

Carol took the job and for several months in 1969 labored for the President she had once served when he was vice-president. Often her morning briefing papers would come back with Nixon's personal marginal notes: "This is excellent. Very helpful explanation. Good work!" But the hours were long, and with three children and an unemployed husband, she could not carry the whole load.

And for those very personal reasons she still wanted to leave Washington. She often talked of the Eastern Shore, of wanting to have a horse again, as she had as a young girl, of raising the children in the country away from a city full of politics and infighting. And, she might have added, away from whatever it was that generated the underlying tension that marked our marriage.

She was willing to give up a good job at the White House if only it would bring the peace of mind we both needed. In spite of all my misgivings, my foot dragging, Carol was uncharacteristically adamant about moving to Easton. And so we decided to rent our Capitol Hill house and moved "home" to a place that had never really been home to either of us.

Whether or not I wanted to admit it, during our twenty-one years of marriage Carol was right about things more often than not. Her insistence on moving away from Washington and back to the Eastern Shore produced a period of calm in our relationship even though it eventually led to my entry into public life as a candidate for the State Senate in 1970. As evidence of our tranquility Carol became pregnant in early 1971 but suffered a miscarriage. That fall she brought the good news from her doctor,

Brad Baker, that our fourth child would arrive in the spring of 1972.

For the fourth time Carol began her established routine during pregnancy, giving up the little alcohol she did drink, avoiding any medication, even aspirin, anything that might harm the unborn child. With her doctor's approval, and at her insistence, she continued riding her new horse almost until the day labor pains began. "Good exercise," I was told. In the early morning hours of May 22, 1972, I drove Carol to the Easton Memorial Hospital. Later that day James Shields Bauman came into this world, kicking and screaming lustily.

I can attest to Jimmy's noisy entrance because, for the first time, I was present when one of our children was born. Attired in white cap, gown and mask I watched as this small miracle who was our second son join the human race. The joyful sight made me wish I had shared each of the children's births with Carol, and I came away from the experience with a new and profound respect for the maternal role God assigned to the female of the species. Rarely have I ever seen an event so awesome, impressive, and at once so painful.

Little Jimmy Bauman arrived with a serious case of jaundice, just as his father had back in 1937. His yellow skin kept him in the hospital for almost two weeks until he was judged well enough to come home to Glebe House. There he was met with the adoring love of two older sisters, his mother, and grandmother. His big brother and father shared in the pride for the first native Eastern Shoreman in the Bauman family.

James Shields Bauman was named after a lineal ancestor on his mother's side (Carol's mother's maiden name was Shields), who combined more political history in his life than any ten other men of his time. The original James Shields was born May 10, 1810, in Altmore, County Tyrone, Ireland, and came to the U.S. in 1823. Before he died on June 1, 1879, he served as governor of the Oregon Territory by appointment of President James K. Polk, as well as a U.S. senator from Illinois, Minnesota, and Missouri, a combined distinction that got him into Ripley's *Believe It or Not.* He also was a general in the Union Army in both the Mexican and Civil wars cited for "gallant and meritorious conduct at the Battle of Cero Gordo, Mexico." Even though he was a Democrat, Carol and I felt he deserved some remembrance.

Each of our four children from the very first were individuals in their own right, varying widely in their characteristics and temperament.

Our oldest son, Edward (Teddy), was "his mother's little boy." Eight years old when I was first elected to public office in 1970, we hardly knew each other during his most formative years. The few precious hours I was at home often saw me preoccupied in telling Carol of my political intrigues, triumphs, and defeats, allocating Ted to the forlorn status of a little bystander who gets a kiss, a pat on the head, then ignored. I did worry that I was treating Ted in the same remote manner my own father had accorded me. Will he feel as distanced from me as I did from my father? I wondered uncomfortably.

Teddy grew to be a quiet, even shy child, still showing traces of his infant problem with physical coordination but testing in the genius range on I.Q. tests. If he wished to he could achieve high marks in school but often he chose to coast. In later years he turned to his real passion, music, establishing a successful band and teaching himself to play several instruments. His song lyrics, music compositions, and poetry are truly beautiful. Often he would spend long hours reading in every imaginable field from science and history to J.R.R. Tolkien.

Many years later than necessary Ted and I have gotten to know each other better, spending holidays and occasional meals together. So we can now qualify as friends. When Ted learned that his mother and I were to be divorced he put his arm around my shoulders and gave the greatest gift of all: "No matter what happens Dad, you're my father and I'll always love you." It was, perhaps, more than I deserved.

If the son is his mother's "little boy," Genie and Vicky were my two little princesses (a title I believe I picked up from Robert Young in his "Father Knows Best" days). A little more than two years apart in age, the two entertained and infuriated each other on a daily basis. They were usually inseparable, sharing a room, a pony for a time, a joke or a secret. One of our favorite pastimes came on evenings when I was at home, had a few drinks, and would put on the stereo a record of some Broadway show such as *Mame* or *Promises, Promises.* Taking turns the little girls, one blonde, one brunet, would swirl around the library with their father more or less leading the step. At first I held them in my arms to dance but soon they got so big they stood on my feet as I waltzed or rocked. That they were beautiful little girls goes without saying. And yet how well did I really know them?

Hindsight is much more precise. Now I know how much more I should have done as a father. Carol's devotion to our children was clear and this gave me the convenient confidence. Thus I could devote all my considerable energies to saving the state of Maryland, the United States of America, and, eventually, the world. Periodically another journalistic feature article appears describing the great difficulties of political marriages, especially in Congress where a two-year term requires constant campaigning. Of course it requires an extra measure of devotion to survive prolonged absences, constant pressure, one-parent child rearing, economic difficulties. Too often the elected official mistakenly applies the old political rule of taking his home base for granted. This allows you to make one more appearance, give one more speech, return an hour later than promised. Or many hours later. The belief in one's own indispensability produces a serious blindness toward the really important things in life, including wife and children. Soon your own family becomes another pressure group that has to be placated along with the others.

I loved my children, will always love them, and I wanted to be a good father. Long walks in the woods, snowball fights in winter, speeding on our unnamed boat on the Miles River, reading a book to one of them, ducking in the waves at Ocean City, I did cherish the time we had together. Reels of my 16-mm home movies record the antics and growth of Teddy, Genie, Vicky, and Jimmy. But once in Congress in 1973, time with my family dwindled to holidays and an annual vacation at the beach. Every weekend there seemed to be another event my staff said I could not miss lest I offend someone or some group. Often I would see my children only briefly at breakfast, returning home so late at night they would be in bed asleep. (Sometimes my oldest daughter, Genie, the night owl, would be awake to greet me.) And sometimes when I came home, I had already had too much to drink or would need a drink as soon as I walked into the house.

Were these four handsome children happy? If you asked me during much of the time I served in Congress, I could not have answered with any assurance. When Carol and I were together long enough to talk about the children, I got secondhand reports about their problems and progress, but seeing a report card every few months is not like helping with homework every night. Talks with my children tended to last as long as the ten-minute ride to school in the morning where I dropped them on my way to Washington. If something serious arose, Carol's appeals to me ("You're the father!") might or might not get a prompt response, depending on my schedule.

There was even a family joke about my absentee-father status, the story of the politician who was never home. One day the mother of the house saw father coming up the drive earlier than expected and called out from the kitchen to the kids "Children, there's your father!" In unison from the kids sitting before the television set came the response, "What channel, Mom?"

In 1973, when I was first elected to Congress, Teddy was eleven years old, nineteen when I left office in 1981. Genie was eight and sixteen, Vicky, six and fourteen, and Jimmy, one and eight. My children grew through their formative years with only the occasional presence of a father. The thousand and one little details of daily life that create and sustain relationships between parent and child escaped me. I knew every colleague in the House by sight, their foibles and strengths and yet I did not always know the names of my children's teachers. I could expound at great length on some obscure rule of the House of Representatives, but I could not tell you why a son seemed distant or a daughter burst into tears. I learned of the triumphs and tragedies of my spouse and our children secondhand, and worse, I did not realize until many years later what a mutual loss this was for us all. (One morning at breakfast, after my 1980 fall from grace, my daughter, Vicky, then fourteen, said: "You know, Dad, as bad as all this has been it was good too. If it hadn't happened we never would have known who you were.")

On weekends my congressional staff always scheduled me to attend a crab feast, bull roast, church supper or volunteer fireman's dinner. In order to keep some contact with my family I tried to take them along on these gastronomic occasions. After a time, the Bauman family contingent dwindled to one or two of the children and perhaps Carol. It didn't hurt to be seen in public as the dutiful father and many times we did have a lot of fun. If the speeches were not too long-winded, and the steamed crabs and oyster fritters done right, the event was enjoyable, especially the limitless supply of little old ladies that fawn over a congressman's young sons and daughters.

In the first few years in Congress, Carol went with me on a regular basis, driving up our baby-sitting costs astronomically until her mother moved to Easton and bailed us out repeatedly. If I was in Washington, Carol would often join me at some halfway point for an evening function at the Kent Island Arts Festival or the Southern Maryland Electrical Co-op Dinner.

The drill never seemed to vary much. Somehow I had cultivated the ability to match names and faces and people were always pleased when I addressed them by name. (For some reason many people like to punish politicians with the invariable question: "You don't remember me, do you?") I enjoyed the instant adulation upon entering the room, ladies smiling, hugging, and the men making grave comments about the state of the nation. I was treated as "the congressman"—a being apart from ordinary men. I was the one ". . . who knows what is going on in Washington and is here to tell us tonight." I went along with the game, pretending omniscience if not omnipotence. Carol at my side ("Do I look all right?"), we would wade through the crowd toward the head table, smiles on our faces, shaking hands, and patting elbows. Driving home we complained about the tiring ritual, the same old faces, the questions and comments. Almost always a member of my staff seemed to be with us for such events and this did not allow us to talk about personal matters that needed discussion. At times it seemed I spent most of my life behind the wheel or in the right front seat of a car.

Other nights Carol would already be asleep when I got home, thus mercifully avoiding any confrontation over family finances or where I had been so late. The next morning the daily grind would begin again.

In 1980, one of the less attractive Republican ladies in our area told a reporter that, "No one seemed to know Carol very well, she kept to herself."

Perhaps she did, not the least of reasons being the busy demands of raising a family alone. But with my election she did acquire a certain elevated status in the eyes of many people we dealt with, a sort of "first lady" of the congressional district. But this was still the subordinate role as it had been as I worked my way through law school and up the political ladder, always with her support.

What was lost on the Republican lady and most others was Carol's tremendous talent. Tending always to think of her as "the congressman's wife," they overlooked her estimable career as a writer, editor, and staff assistant to a congressman (Bruce of Indiana), U.S. senator (Ken Keating of New York), and, of course, to Richard Nixon, in his roles as both vice-president and President. Few people realize that Carol was the first in our family to achieve elective office. Immediately after we moved to Easton in

1969 she was urged to run for the Talbot County Republican State Central Committee and did so, leading the ticket. That was seven months before I won the State Senate seat.

Although my own life seemed to be totally submerged in politics, Carol's breadth of interests included art, theology and, of course, one of her first loves, training and riding horses, an interest she communicated to our children. Life on the Shore did allow her to pursue some of these interests even though the children came first. Soon she was writing not only for the local paper but articles in the prestigious *Maryland Horse,* the chronical of Maryland's equine breeders.

The years both of us spent in founding and promoting Young Americans for Freedom and the American Conservative Union were lost on most of the people in my congressional district, even those active in politics. We certainly made no great noise about it, preferring to stick to local matters lest we be thought of as "putting on airs."

The truth is that Carol could just as easily have been the member of Congress. Her training, experience, and solid conservative philosophy were certainly equal to mine. Yet she was raised in an era when women of all ages were impressed repeatedly in a thousand ways that they were somehow inferior to the males of the species. It was not ladylike to be pushy, aggressive, opinionated, and brash, the required stock in trade of most successful politicians. Mercifully for me, Carol lacked all of these offensive traits, perhaps to her disadvantage in our personal relationship.

Carol often gave me quiet counsel on issues before Congress and political matters. Years of active work in the conservative movement gave her an educated perspective too few congressional wives obtain. She knew most of the major players personally and kept current with the news. And perhaps because of her initial upbringing in the rough and tumble of Hoosier politics, she had a practical sense of the "good" and "bad" guys. Long after I forgot some political slight or knife in my back, Carol would recall who had done what to whom. More than once she reminded me of some double-cross just as I was about to trust the bastard again.

I found myself in the anomalous situation of being perfectly at ease discussing with her major national policy issues or my political decisions. But I could not for a minute talk easily about our family finances, children or personal problems. And, of course, I could never discuss "the problem" which remained an unspoken menace in my own mind.

To make matters worse some members of my congressional staff gave Carol to understand that in their view she was just that and no more, "the congressman's wife." Oblivious to the treatment she received for a long time, eventually I tried to change it but failed. It finally reached a point where Carol insisted upon receiving an advance copy of my weekly schedule of events so that she could at least plan what little family life we had left. She alerted my personal secretary, Nancy Howard, to our anniversary date and the birthdays of the children so that I was not completely lost to my family.

But as years passed, Carol became increasingly removed from my public political activities unless I specifically asked her to join me for some event. I often did, lest people think something was wrong with our marriage.

During our early married life, founding Young Americans for Freedom, running for State Senate, Carol and I worked closely as partners. In the 1973 House race the campaign was largely taken out of her hands and mine. Once I became a congressman it was as if we led two separate lives. That shared spirit of doing battle for the cause slipped away and at first, preoccupied with my own success, I hardly noticed the subtle and then dramatic change. It occurred slowly over a period of years, might have happened sooner, except for Carol's willingness to do all she could to help me in my work.

And yet life was certainly not all sadness for our children, whatever the difficulties suffered by their parents. A week before the election, every two years, the registered voters in Maryland's

First Congressional District would find in their mailboxes a beautiful full-color postcard from me with our family picture on it. Carol, Bob, and the four children were all there along with our pets. The smiling scene of domestic bliss was complemented by my short request that I be permitted to continue my congressional service. Often I received favorable comments, especially from women, on this biennial photo reminder. In one rural general store the cards were tacked to the wall, one after the other, as elections went by. (My goodness, how your children are growing!" "What a beautiful collie you have!")

This was not false advertising. Talking with my children in recent times they uniformly look back to the quiet of a simpler time at Glebe House and understandably wish for its return. One of my daughters insists she intends to purchase Glebe House one day and raise her own family there.

Carol and I first saw Glebe House on a spring day in 1969 just after a dark, rumbling thunderstorm. As I later learned from the rhythm of the seasons during the third of my life I lived at Glebe, we had arrived during the two weeks in May when, if the weather cooperated, every spring flower and shrub was in colorful bloom.

We drove past two brick gateposts, one with a white marble plaque marked simply "Glebe," and up a long country lane lined with a variety of trees fifty or sixty feet high, each pair neatly spaced at intervals on either side of the path. We came to another pair of brick posts and a fence covered with pungently aromatic honeysuckle. There before us, nestled in a beautifully landscaped lawn, sat a two-story wood-frame house, white with green shutters, surrounded by huge trees, one a double-topped Douglas fir rare to the area, reaching nearly a hundred feet into the sky. There were purple and white lilacs everywhere, filling the damp air with their sweet scent, red tulips, pink and white dogwood trees in bloom, snowball bushes, a row of pink tea roses bordering the gravel drive by the house. Everywhere there were leafy clouds of light green budding maples, oaks and Japanese Pawlonia, every leaf glistening with silver-gray droplets from the recent rain. Far up and behind the green leaves the sky was beginning to lighten from black to gray.

Down to our left, beyond a ring of huge English boxwoods surrounding a white dogwood in full array, we could see a sloping green lawn leading to the tidal waters of Glebe Creek framed by an enormous oak tree on its banks. There was even a small dock perfectly suited for the boat we knew we would have to acquire.

To say that we fell in love with this 1855 farmhouse is an understatement. With great good fortune we discovered that the owner, recently widowed, was willing to take back a large second mortgage with a down payment of as little as three thousand dollars. Her asking price was sixty-five thousand dollars. Although it took all the money we had and would mean we would be saddled with a monthly payment of over six hundred dollars for twenty years, we agreed. But not before Carol pressed me as to whether or not I really thought we could afford it.

Over the years we did a lot of work on Glebe House, as it was called in the Talbot County land records. It needed it but the house was an old-home-lover's dream. Research showed that the house had been built, one of three in the immediate area near Easton, by the sons of Ennals Martin, a respected physician and political leader of the early 1800s. Dr. Martin, an extensive land-owner, was also a Whig who displayed his political belief in a famous fist fight on the streets of Easton. He so thoroughly thrashed his opponent that the poor unfortunate required medical treatment which Martin, as the only physician for miles, kindly administered. When Ennals Martin died without a will in 1854, the Land Commission divided a larger thousand-acre Glebe Farm into smaller parcels for the Martin sons. (The name "Ennals" lived on during our years in the house. On cold winter nights, when the heat went on, the pipes would creak and moan. I assured our children that it was "Ennals" talking, the ghost of the owner from the past. In our Capitol Hill house our steam-heated ghost had been "Ferdinand.")

The name Glebe came from the archaic English word for "soil" or "field," but more particularly described farm land owned by a parish church for its financial support. I searched the land title of our Glebe back to the year 1800 but could find no church ownership.

The tidal saltwater creek in front of our house stretched a thousand yards across and then dwindled into a marsh to the east where on fall and winter nights thousands of Canadian geese gathered to gabble at the moon. Called "Glebe" also, the creek had been named "Fausley" after the ancestral home of Tench Tilghman, George Washington's aide-de-camp and secretary. The Tilghman place was a half mile from our house and a historical marker commemorated the former member of the Continental Congress who had dashed by horse and boat from Yorktown to Philadelphia to give the revolutionary Congress the news of General Charles Cornwallis' surrender in 1776.

In fact, Glebe Creek was crammed with history, we discovered. In the short distance of two or three miles its banks had been home to a host of memorable figures. Near its mouth is "The Rest," home of Admiral Franklin Buchanan, who commanded the Confederate ironclad *Merrimac*. On the other shore until the 1950s was a mansion called "The Villa" that housed a series of riches-to-rags financiers, one of whom came and went in a magnificent steam yacht during the 1870s. Locals became convinced the mysterious "Mr. Brady" was really a front man for the notorious New York political grafter, William Marcy "Boss" Tweed, who, it was said, escaped through "The Villa's" secret underground passage to the yacht and then to Cuba, New York authorities hard on his nautical heels.

Not far across the creek from our house is a beautiful old colonial house, "Ending of Controversy," which was home to Wenlock Christison, a famous Quaker preacher who escaped to Maryland after religious persecution in Massachusetts. And to our right, our neighbor, "Pete" Covey, lived, a possible descendant of the infamous "slave breaker" of the same name who owned

Frederick Douglass, the famous black abolitionist who was born in Talbot County in 1817.

To round out the Glebe Creek history, my mentor in politics, former Congressman Ted Miller, owned and lived at the farm to our west, "The Pines." And although Ted had died in 1967, his widow, Missy, one of the people who had given me my start in politics, became our neighbor.

Everyone needs at least one "home place" in life and Glebe House was ours. It was there, on a wide-screened porch wrapped around the front and west sides of the house, that we passed many happy hours, rocking and sipping cool drinks on summer afternoons and evenings. One could sit there and watch the late shadows slowly advance across the lawn as the creek burned to silver, gold, then orange, glimmering like liquid metal. It mattered little that the porch screens needed regular replacement because of Teddy's misguided baseballs, basketballs, and soccer balls.

The porch opened into a small but formal living room with a fireplace, a room just made for a Christmas tree and decorations. On winter afternoons the sun would stream through its French doors as the fire crackled and the kids read the Sunday funnies lying in front of the fireplace with our cat and dogs. Beyond was a wide hallway and across that "the library" we filled with bookcases and books, and there another fireplace. To the back of the house was a formal dining room with a lower ceiling than the other twelve-foot-high rooms, but it was marked by a large bow window looking out on the creek. In the very back of the house was a large kitchen with a brick fireplace and a huge picture window, also overlooking Glebe Creek.

There were four bedrooms, three baths, a summer kitchen/laundry room, workshop, three-car garage, and way upstairs, a huge attic perfect for hide-and-seek and doll houses. Out on the grounds were a grape arbor and a dog kennel. And soon a swing and a sandbox.

It was at Glebe House that I lived longer than any other place.

116

When the icy blasts of the winter wind would blow down from the northwest across the creek, its waters would freeze. Our dock would become headquarters for skating parties with woodfires in an oil drum at night, and always hot buttered rum and steaming coffee by the kitchen fireplace. While I was not a hunter myself, all around us the fields and shoreline rang with the muffled boom of shotguns during the duck and goose season. And at planting and harvesting time "Farmer" Covey's machinery clattered along our hedgerows, flushing rabbits and other small creatures our dogs would pursue but only our cat Patches seemed able to catch. Once our aging cock-a-poo Shaggy even managed, to their mutual surprise, to tree a groundhog who refused to come down for hours after the dog lost interest.

In the summer the creek always echoed with the drone of small motorboats and the eye would catch the beautiful sight of sailboats, big and small, gliding by, headed home or out beyond the Miles River Bridge to the waters of Chesapeake Bay ten miles to the west. There was swimming off the end of the dock before the sea nettles (jelly fish) arrived in June with the hot weather, and on windy days kite flying in the adjoining fields was a favorite sport. Eventually we even acquired our own seventeen-foot outboard motorboat that Teddy insisted have the most powerful motor, 135 horsepower, for water-skiing.

When I had the time I worked at a long series of home improvements, redecorating the inside, painting the outside. But on summer weekends it was the province of the father of the house to climb onto his orange-colored riding mower and cut the grass. With almost five acres this required more hours of mowing, up and down the long lane, round and round the house, then trimming and raking the sweet-smelling grass into big mounds to be hauled off. Before we got a new septic tank that area was often off-limits because of its intermittent indigestion, even though tomatoes grew best there, sometimes without being planted.

The motorboat was tied to our dock, a Ford LTD station wagon and Mercury Grand Marquis were parked near our house at the end of a half-mile tree-shaded driveway. Romping on the rolling green lawn among the boxwoods and flowers were a handsome collie named Captain Fawsley (Cappy to his many friends), and two spunky, appealing little Jack Russell terriers, Patrick and his spouse, Baby Ruth (Ruthie). The little brown and white fox hunting dogs would turn out another cute little litter of pups every six months or so. Presiding over this bucolic scene was an imperious old feline whose variegated white and gray fur coat commanded her name, Patches.

In the summer months, the cool creek provided relief and a sandbox and swing set was often filled with little people celebrating birthdays or just sleepovers. Children and teen-agers would come by car and boat to visit. Every June there would be an annual picnic for friends and political allies, filling the lawn with laughing people, sipping cool drinks and munching crab cakes and other delicacies that have made Maryland famous.

On Sunday afternoons, if father was at home, the family would gather for a big "Daddy breakfast" after Mass at Saints Peter and Paul Catholic Church, where the youngest of the children, Jimmy, sang in his beautiful treble voice in the men and boys' choir. After breakfast the children would read the funny papers and Sunday supplements and the parents sipped coffee and perused the serious sections of the *Baltimore Sun,* the *Washington Post,* and the *New York Times.* Often the father's name would appear in those very same pages, sometimes in headlines, and sometimes he would appear in editorial cartoons.

At Thanksgiving and Christmas relatives would come to visit, friends would drop in, and the father, with great ceremony and pomp beginning the night before, would clean, stuff and truss a huge turkey, twenty-five pounds or more, that would soon fill the whole house with its delicious aroma. The children would taste the stuffing to be sure it was "just right" before it disappeared into the yawning bird, especially procured from the nearby Gadow Turkey Farm. At Christmas time an Advent wreath graced the dining room table and Sunday evening would see the family gather to read prayers and Bible excerpts heralding the coming of the Christ child. A few weekends before that great event the family would honor an annual tradition by trekking to a tree farm where they invariably spent an hour in the bitter cold arguing over which was just the right tree, at least twelve feet tall, to stand in the corner by the living room fireplace. Ancient decorations preserved from previous generations would be carefully unwrapped and hung with loving care along with crude chains made of colored paper and paste, the product of the family's littlest hands. And on that long-awaited morning the smallest would be the first up to see if Santa had arrived to sip his Coke, feed the carrots to his reindeer, and leave GI Joes, Erector sets, Walkmans, frilly dresses and the like.

He always did.

And in this old house there would even be grand events.

One unseasonably warm February Sunday saw a sparkling catered social affair as the family hosted Republicans gathered in nearby Easton for one of their many interminable conferences. Elizabeth Taylor and her then current husband, Senator John Warner of Virginia, necked in our laundry room over white wine. Senator Bob Dole and his new wife were there. And Congressman John Rhodes, the Minority Leader of the House, and dozens and dozens of other senators, congressmen, and important people.

On many mornings the father of the house would be driven away in his car to Capitol Hill by one of his many staff aides, there to take his stand on the floor of Congress in defense of the principles of conservatism. With his stocky build and dapper clothes, he might even be seen that night on national television news commenting, usually acerbically, about the danger of the Panama Canal treaties, the federal deficit threat, the President's brother Billy. Or he might be flying out of Easton airport to some far place in America where he would speak or receive an award.

Cutting the grass became a rite of passage at Glebe House. When the children were younger each wanted to know when they could drive the riding mower and help Daddy cut the grass. As soon as they got a taste of the work in the hot sun they would find excuses for other activity when the weekly chore began. But once done, the manicuring of the five acres of grounds made Glebe House a fit candidate for *House Beautiful.* The job also entitled father to another few drinks (in addition to the beer consumed while mowing), to be sipped on the porch before a refreshing shower and a change into something cool, then dinner or a spin in the boat. I still cannot understand why I got more satisfaction from mowing my lawn than any legislative or political victory I might achieve. Of course, spending so much of my little time at home on a mower permitted me to avoid discussion of the important personal issues with Carol. In later years, she and our daughters were often gone on their own weekend forays at the many Eastern Shore horse shows. Prize ribbons by the hundreds soon decorated the walls of our home. Carol, the accomplished equestrienne, had successfully passed on the love of the horse to a new generation of horse nuts. In the fall and winter the Bauman ladies went fox hunting with a local private hunt, the Wye Hounds.

And each year the little Baumans would troop to the White House in Washington for the President's Christmas party for members of Congress and their families. In one photo a smiling Teddy stands before a blazing White House Christmas tree. In 1973, Pat and Dick Nixon made much over Vicky and Genie ("We used to have two little girls too but they've grown up now.") And a President named Carter telling Jimmy Bauman what an excellent choice for a first name he had made. At a summer White House picnic the Bauman daughters pronounced Amy Carter as "unimpressive" and her tree house as inadequate. It was the same evening Jimmy Bauman stepped on Rosalyn Carter's foot, accidentally, he said. The Secret Service did not wrestle him to the ground.

When I first heard him use Henry David Thoreau's phrase, the late Senator Everett McKinley Dirksen of Illinois struck a responsive chord in my brain: "The mass of men lead lives of quiet desperation." I could see Thoreau sitting up there by his quiet Walden Pond apart from the mass. I too determined to be special, that I would remain apart. But by 1980, my own life had achieved a high desperation that was anything but quiet. With all the personal and political turmoil I came to accept that "this is the way life is."

As though everything else in our lives had not been difficult enough, there was yet another problem that sapped our strength, kept us in constant anxiety, and caused repeated arguments and anger.

Throughout twenty years of marriage I steadfastly refused to heed Carol's repeated reminder that we rarely had enough income to meet our expenses, a decidedly unconservative economic approach. In the early years of our married life we both worked. As my response to her complaints about finances I turned the bills and checkbook over to her. That produced no more money but allowed a subtle shift of blame. Trying to finance living and law school, living and being a state senator, living and being a congressman, always seemed impossible. A meager sole law practice brought in very little and was abandoned when I went to Washington in 1973. The Easton merchant class came to know that eventually Senator-Congressman Bauman would pay, but the check was sometimes in the mail for an awfully long time.

Instead of dealing with our continuing economic plight I dwelt in a dreamworld that heard me repeatedly insisting to Carol that "things would work out," though they never did. As a public official I had the notion that I had to keep up "appearances" but I could not afford those "appearances." Often against Carol's better judgment economic decisions were made that were more based on future hope than current assets. So we bought Glebe House, sent our four children to the "best" school in the area, The Country School, and began a series of refinancing first mortgages and then second mortgages on the house. Anything to get cash to pay back bills. Soon I was borrowing on my signature which bankers seemed eager to allow for a member of Congress, as though the title were good collateral. Monthly house payments on Glebe grew over the years from six hundred dollars to two thousand dollars. And we were usually one, two or three months behind on bills.

The attrition on Carol was evident. It was she who had to be home all day fielding calls from irritated creditors. She went back to work, writing, selling real estate. The best I could do for her was to point to some future legal or speech fee that might come through "soon." There was no way that I could square my personal profligacy with my constant public demand for federal fiscal conservatism. The truth is all I cared about was advancing "the cause," which I confused with "me." Hardship and sacrifice might be required now but eventually it would lead to conservatism's triumph if not our personal gain. I was the one who wanted to "do good" even though I did not care if I "did well." That did not satisfy Sears, Exxon or the Maryland National Bank.

If the inherent sexual variance in my nature did not make marriage difficult enough, my lack of economic sense was the second major source of conflict. The true cost was far beyond calculation in dollars and cents. For both Carol and me it caused untold stress and contributed heavily to the eventual collapse of our marriage. Added to her tension was the conflict of having to be a sole parent during my constant absence and holding down a job at the same time.

As I unknowingly approached public exposure of my private life in the late summer of 1980, two decades of economic irresponsibility on my part came to another head. As usual I was behind on our bills and the house mortgage, and school tuition payments for four children would be due in September. Now for the first time I turned to an old and dear friend, E. Ralph Hostetter, a leading businessman and publisher of many newspapers in my district. With him as guarantor the Mercantile Safe Deposit and Trust Company of Baltimore agreed to a second mortgage loan of thirty thousand dollars. Settlement date was set for October 4, the check was in the mail, and then the Bauman scandal hit the front pages. One of the few phone calls that got through to me that day was my Easton attorney telling me the bank had stopped the loan. The check I would get in the mail was not to be cashed. (I still kept it as a souvenir of something or other.)

To make matters worse my monthly salary check from the House of Representatives, then $62,500 a year, was going in total each month to pay back loans I had borrowed on my signature through a Washington bank, a service the House Sergeant of Arms offers to congressmen in a financial squeeze. Full repayment of the loans had to be made before my term expired. Right in the middle of scandal and campaign we were left without cash income.

The day after my Tidewater Inn press conference on October 8, my political managers had sent me out campaigning to show the world that everything was going well. Carol and the children were to rest a day or two at the Ocean City home of a good friend before she joined me.

But when I got home that first night both Carol and the children who were to be there were missing. After searching the house for a note which might explain, I began to panic: I sat down in the library and began to cry, at first softly and then in uncontrollable sobs. I telephoned all over, trying to find Carol. At length the phone rang and it was my daughter Genie, calling to tell me that "Mother was terribly upset." She said that Carol had insisted that they all had to get away from Glebe House, that she could not stand it anymore. She had bundled the children, Genie, Vicky, and Jimmy, into the car and driven to Vienna, Virginia, to the home of our good friends, Trish and Brent Bozell, godparents of Genie and sister and brother-in-law of Bill Buckley.

Genie put Trish Bozell on the phone and she explained to me that Carol was all right but had been extremely agitated when she arrived. Now she was asleep and Trish said she would have her call when she awoke.

The next day Carol and the children returned. Several days

later a letter came in the mail addressed to Carol with a return envelope from Bill Buckley. Inside was a check made out to Carol for twenty thousand dollars marked "Loan" and a note to Carol saying that Bill hoped that this would help her through this time of troubles. With information from his sister, the man who a few days before had called for my resignation now stepped in to save us from personal bankruptcy in the middle of the campaign.

During the next few weeks a group of good friends from Ocean City, the major vacation resort in my district, got together and co-signed a second mortgage on our house, obtaining forty thousand dollars that allowed us to pay off several due loans and bring our personal finances into some reasonable equilibrium.

And now it was all going to end. The one remaining thing I thought I could depend on, my family, was disintegrating. Our pledge to our children that our family would stay together had lasted only a few months. I was out of Congress less than sixty days, grasping for something to hang on to in the face of repeated employment rejections, and now my wife was about to leave me.

I pleaded with Carol to reconsider and she refused, emphasizing that this was, after all, only a "trial" separation. Immediately she began to spend weeknights in Washington with her sister and brother-in-law. I was suddenly a single parent myself, with three young children to look after. My own reaction was to slip into the most profound depression I ever experienced. I simply did not have the resources to deal with this additional blow. Although I did not drink again I thought about that possibility and rejected it. I knew it would only make things worse. But I underwent what some alcoholic experts call a "dry drunk." I felt bitterly sorry for myself, pitying my situation, terribly fearful of the future, unsure that I could go on alone. I stopped eating, slept much of the time, didn't even bother to shave or dress some days. Without warning I might break into tears. This went on for at least three weeks. For some diversion I read the "Complete Works of Sir Arthur Conan

Doyle," seeking momentary escape in the cool logic of Sherlock Holmes.

Finally, somehow, I am not really sure, perhaps through prayer, reading literature about my alcoholism or attending meetings, I concluded that this was no way to spend the rest of my life. Slowly I began to realize that I had to accept things as they were. I was not in control and I could not change them. And caring for three children fortunately put a large dent in my self-pity. There was not enough time for that. They had to be driven and picked up, laundry done, meals prepared, homework helped with. In between I tried to find a job.

I also sought and got help from my weekly sessions with my latest psychiatrist, though seeking a "cure" for homosexual tendencies had to take a back seat to simple life maintenance therapy. Before I could tackle the past I had to get through one day at a time.

In April 1981 Carol moved to Washington. She presented me with the first of several drafts of a proposed separation agreement that sought custody of our three minor children. She said she wanted Genie, Vicky, and Jimmy to move to suburban Virginia with her once their school in Easton ended in June. In the fall she would enter them in schools there. I would be left alone in an empty Glebe House. None of the children wanted to leave but I knew that under Maryland law I would have no chance of obtaining even "joint custody," which Carol strongly rejected. In any such custody case the courts look to who is a "fit parent" and what the "best interest of the children" might be. In my own circumstances, alcoholic and possibly gay, no court in Maryland would have considered my plea. A contested custody case would produce more press headlines and nasty publicity for all of us. At that point I was so overwhelmed with guilt, so spiritually weak, I had no will to fight. Perhaps what was happening to me was my just punishment. One way to assuage that guilt was to acquiesce.

Painfully and painstakingly we divided up the accumulation of twenty-one years of marriage, an oil painting for you, a French bergère for me. On the appointed day in June after school ended, the movers arrived to take Carol's part of the household away. It was a hot, humid day and there had been much rain that month. I was out mowing the grass late in the afternoon when the packing was finished. Just like nothing had happened, Dad out mowing, trimming the edges, raking up piles of the sweet-smelling blades, especially the peculiar grass that grew brilliantly green down near the water's edge. It always smelled the sweetest.

What am I supposed to do on such a momentous occasion in life? I wondered. How do you react when all that is left of your world comes to an end? Losing an election, even your good name, was nothing compared to losing your wife, your children, the family you love, that loves you.

One by one Genie, Vicky, and Jimmy came over to me and said their tearful good-byes. They were as fearful and uncertain about this as I. We tried to comfort each other. Carol's mother, Hilda, came over, kissed me on the cheek, and said she would "keep in touch."

The moving van pulled away and soon Carol came out of Glebe House and without stopping got in the LTD station wagon that was now hers. Her horse trailer was attached, and in the car, our children, the dogs, and her mother. The collie, Captain, the terriers, Patrick and Baby Ruth, were going too. Only Patches the cat stayed with me.

I wanted to go over to Carol and speak to her but I was so emotionally upset I could not move. A few days before we had one last long talk, a relatively new practice for us. I had again asked her not to leave but she was determined.

"You know, it's odd," she said as we sat in the living room. "I still love you, Bob."

After a long silence she looked at me and asked: "Do you love me?"

As tears welled in my eyes I wanted with all my heart to be able to say what she wanted to hear. But there had been enough deception from me. Summoning my remaining personal integrity I told her the truth:

"In my own way, I do love you, Carol."

She understood all too well what that qualified statement meant and it was not good enough. It had never been good enough. Partial commitment is never a sufficient basis for marriage and for us it had proven disastrous.

And yet I did love her.

Carol, the children, the dogs, the car, our marriage slowly disappeared down the tree-lined lane of Glebe House, the familiar small cloud of dust from the dirt road following them behind. At the end of the lane I saw the tail lights blink as they had a million times before, but this time there would be no return, I knew. Off in the distance I could see the tower lights of our local radio station flashing red in the gathering night and I remembered what little Vicky told me about those lights. As a very small child she decided those lights were some magical signal from her father who was away in the State Senate in Annapolis. She would look out into the night and know from the glowing of the red lights that I was thinking of her, reassuring her, would protect her if she needed my help.

Standing there on the newly mowed lawn of Glebe House, the dogwood in bloom, the smell of lilacs in the evening air, roses blooming, the sun setting over Glebe Creek, a heavy knot the size of a man's fist began to grow in my chest and throat. Finally I began to cry. Grief is also a very physical experience and I was grieving.

Carol had done what she thought best. But she had also done me a great favor. For the first time in my life, I was being forced to face myself as I was.

And as each of us must, I would have to do it alone.

CHAPTER FIVE

I slept alone that night at Glebe House, Patches the cat at the foot of my bed. Earlier as I wandered through the quiet house I realized how empty life would be without the people I loved. I mentally idealized this place as home but now it was less than that. All my plans for cures, for a happy future together were gone.

But I needed some goal to keep me going, some hope to live by. Almost unconsciously I made a substitution once I knew there was no chance Carol would stay with me. It was a familiar choice, one that already dominated my personal history: more politics.

Less than twenty-four hours after Carol and the children left for their new home in the Washington suburbs I put on my candidate's best blue suit, white shirt and power tie and drove off to dine with the First District Republican Congressional Committee. The thirteen-county group of party leaders was meeting to plan for the 1982 House race, aiming to unseat the new incumbent, Congressman Dyson. The committee was dominated by my political supporters, most of whom were urging me to run for Congress again. Repeatedly we heard the political folk wisdom about my narrow 1980 loss: "If we had just one more week I think we could have won it." After all, over 187,000 people voted and 91,000 supported Bob Bauman under the most difficult circumstances. "And besides, Bob," I was told, "you're the only one who can win over Dyson."

It bolstered my battered ego to hear this from friends but I am sure we all had our doubts. Here I was, a recovering alcoholic with "homosexual tendencies," undergoing psychiatric counseling, separated from my wife, facing possible divorce, and yet I had the audacity to consider another campaign for Congress less than six months after repudiation at the polls. Dr. Kay once told me I had a resilient ego and I was about to prove it.

But first, as a modern politician, I wanted a professional reading of what people were really thinking. For the sixth time in five years Arthur Fincklestein conducted an extensive poll of a scientifically balanced cross section of First District voters. Some of the questions asked seemed brutal to me, but we had to know what people thought about Bob Bauman.

The results were astounding. I feared the worst and got the best. Asked if I had been a good congressman, 85 percent agreed; 70 percent said they definitely could vote for me again; 74 percent thought I had a good chance of winning in 1982; my approval rating overall was 60 percent favorable, the second highest of anyone mentioned except our newly elected President, Ronald Reagan with 75 percent; Dyson's rating was only 51 percent. And these very same people knew some other things about me: 47 percent believed me to be a homosexual, only 38 percent thought I was an alcoholic. Twenty percent of the people said they would never vote for me, an interesting figure since before the 1980 scandal that number had been 16 percent. Apparently I always had engendered strong opposition in a minority of people and that had not increased significantly. I remained strong with almost every voter group that supported me in the past except the tiny number who identified themselves as "liberal Republicans."

The details of the poll were explained to me and several of my former congressional and campaign aides at a meeting in a private lounge at Washington's National Airport. Afterward, hurrying to catch a plane, Art Fincklestein took me aside and said he would be back in town the following Tuesday. He wanted to talk with me alone about the poll and my 1982 plans. At the appointed time we met in the Oak Room of the Mayflower Hotel and began a two-hour conference over Arthur's succession of gin and tonics and my own summer libation, iced coffee.

For openers Art was blunt: "Bob, do you realize that a lot of people would not want to be seen with you in public in this town?"

I hadn't really considered that but conceded the point. My struggle to find employment would support it.

"I say that," Art continued in his best Jewish mother attitude, "because I do not think you should run for Congress again no matter how good that poll is. I'm talking now as a personal friend, not just a political advisor. The poll shows you could very well win the election in 1982. Many of those people still consider you to be their congressman. But I wonder if you have really considered the personal pain, the public agony, the shit that will be thrown at you. My guess is that it will be worse than you can imagine. And even if you win, will it be worth it? What will it do to your personal state of mind?" Art went on to explain how he thought the homosexual issue would be resurrected and used, how the four weeks of 1980 exposure would be dragged out into many months of ugly rehashing at my expense.

I tried to counter Arthur's arguments, telling him that nothing could be as bad as 1980, but I wondered. As I drove back to Easton I asked myself whether I did indeed need all that pain again. Was being a member of Congress so important to me that I would be willing to subject myself and my family to an extended repetition of the 1980 horror?

There were other opinions I wanted to hear and I began checking around. I talked with leaders of conservative organizations and uniformly they were encouraging. I met with my old friend, Richard Viguerie. Richard was executive director of Young Americans for Freedom when I was its national chairman and we had known each other for the twenty years since I drove him and his wife, Elaine, to the hospital for the birth of their first child, Renee, at a time when he could not afford to own a car. Now here I was sitting in his impressive office in a large office building he owned.

After my assurances that I was in the state of grace with the Church (Richard is a devout Catholic), that I had received proper counseling for my problems, that I did not approve of homosexual conduct regardless of whether a person might be homosexual, he agreed to help my campaign. Viguerie's mere presence in my campaign lent needed credibility in the eyes of other conservatives and eventually he raised more than $250,000 for the 1982 Bauman effort.

There was another source of opinion I must know if I was to have a chance to win. I got an appointment with Lyn Nofziger, then special political assistant to President Reagan. I knew Lyn by sight when he covered Capitol Hill for the Copley Press but really met him for the first time in 1974 when Governor Ronald Reagan came to campaign for me in my district. Now as I sat in the Executive Office Building across from the White House waiting to see Nofziger, my mind wandered back to my first meeting with Ronald Reagan at the 1964 Republican National Convention in San Francisco. As national chairman of Young Americans for Freedom, I had introduced him from the back of a flatbed truck outside the Cow Palace where the young conservatives, myself included, loved him. In 1968, I was a paid worker in his short presidential bid against Nixon, arranging his visit to a major political gathering near Baltimore. Nofziger had been with him then too.

By 1974, when I had been in Congress for barely a year, Governor Reagan consented to fly into my congressional district to speak at my major annual fund-raiser, the "Bob Bauman Bullroast." After a narrow victory in 1973 in the midst of Watergate, I needed help and Reagan was willing to speak without pay for a fellow conservative. I met him at Baltimore-Washington International Airport where he arrived with Nofziger and Peter Hannaford, of the firm of Hannaford and Deaver, the governor's political/public relations advisors.

When we arrived at his airport hotel suite the immaculately dressed Reagan, in tan sport coat and brown slacks, got down to shirt sleeves, savoring some chilled California white wine and fruit we had ordered for him. Nofziger was the only one present during much of the hour Reagan and I spent talking, and the governor first wanted a thorough briefing on my own congressional race and prospects.

What I wanted to discuss was Reagan's possible candidacy for the 1976 Republican presidential nomination. I urged him to run against President Ford and announce his plans as soon as possible. He said he was giving it serious thought, that a lot of groundwork would have to be done but that his mind was not yet made up. "One thing for sure, Bob," the governor told me, "if I run I'll go all out, and if I win, I'll do what must be done, even if that means I'll only have one term." He went on to elaborate, saying that as governor in Sacramento in 1967 he had to clean up the fiscal mess left by the elder Pat Brown. "Some tough things had to be done and I made up my mind we would do them even if the political fallout hurt. I told my people 'Do what's right and forget politics,' " Reagan said.

We talked of many things that evening, the nature of communism, the need for a conservative Congress, the lack of Republican leadership. He asked me questions about Jerry Ford, once he discovered I had known him for so many years, indicating that he did not know him well, but found Ford an amiable person.

Before I left the governor I again urged him to run for President as the only means to assure Republican victory in 1976. He smiled that famous tilt-head grin and said: "I'm thinking hard about it, Bob. See you tomorrow!"

After leaving Reagan that evening I coasted home on a political high. Here I was, Bob Bauman, hobnobbing with a man who might, I devoutly hoped, be President of the United States. The next day the governor arrived on the Eastern Shore by limousine and I rode with him. After a high-priced but small reception, Reagan and I appeared on cue at the bullroast before more than six thousand people, my largest crowd yet. In a light tan suit accenting his ruddy complexion, the governor wowed them. For the first time since Jack Kennedy's death I saw a crowd reaction that elates a politician's soul; when Reagan came into view people roared their approval, and as he walked along the ropes shaking hands, women and girls jumped up and down, screaming his name, reaching out to touch his hand. He smiled constantly, a mixture of "gosh-aw-gee" sincerity and personal serenity in the midst of bedlam. He didn't even seem to perspire in the humid Eastern Shore heat. Later he discovered he'd lost a cuff link to the crowd, "One of the hazards of the trade," he said, laughing.

Governor Reagan gave me a glowing tribute, speaking of my House service, my leadership in the national conservative movement and the party, predicting a great future. Then he launched into his famous "speech," which again and again produced alternating laughter, applause, and cheers from the adoring crowd. When he was finished they gave him a prolonged ovation with cheers of "We Want Reagan! We Want Reagan!" As he left the fairgrounds in a limousine I again urged him to run for President, and he flashed that famous smile. "I'll let you know, Bob. Keep up the good fight."

In the summer of 1975, after I wrote to him again urging him to run, it appeared that President Jerry Ford was rapidly getting a lock on the delegates. I called Reagan in California but he was away. A day or two later as my family and I lay on the beach in Ocean City, Maryland, at a friend's condominium, our host called down from his balcony, for all to hear, "Bob, Ronald Reagan's on the phone from California!" He was at his Santa Barbara ranch and when we talked he told me he was going to run, but the announcement would have to wait a few months for the appropriate time. "It can't be too soon for me," I told him.

Now, as I waited for Lyn Nofziger's office door to open, that all seemed light-years in the past, almost unreal. Far more unreal than once was the dream that Ronald Reagan would be the official tenant in the White House across the street.

Nofziger, true to his personal style, greeted me with tie askew and clothes rumpled. But his smile was friendly and I got right to the point. If I ran for Congress again in 1982 could I expect the President's support once I was nominated? I explained, and Lyn well understood, that it would be politically fatal to be nominated and then have the President either remain silent or refuse to back me.

After discussion of the election prospects Nofziger was clear: "My recommendation to the President would be that he support you, Bob," he said. "I'll talk with him and get you an answer as soon as I can." In a few weeks a call from Lyn informed me that the answer was a definite "yes."

I also met with Congressman Guy van der Jagt of Michigan, head of the Republican Congressional Campaign Committee, informing him of my plans to run again. He pledged his committee's full financial support that might amount to more than twenty thousand dollars. I could get part of this immediately even if I had a Republican primary challenge if the current Republican House members from Maryland would approve. There was only one, Marjorie Holt, and she refused, saying I might have a primary opponent.

Any of my doubts about my 1982 comeback plans were finally resolved by my former legislative aide, Luis Luna, who forced the issue. For months he had urged me to run, offering to manage the campaign, even though it would mean his resignation from a good Capitol Hill job and postponement of his entry into Georgetown University Law Center. He was convinced we could win, but the deadline for his entry into Georgetown was nearing in late summer 1981. He had to know. "I would rather see you back in Congress, Bob," Luis said. "I can always go to law school later."

In my second year without a drink, still with weekly psychiatric counseling sessions, I was definitely unsure that I was doing the right thing. But what else could I do for the future? I had managed to obtain some part-time consulting positions with several conservative congressmen and for the first two months of 1981 I stayed on the House payroll as a consultant by appointment of Congressman Trent Lott of Mississippi, the new Republican House Whip, a job to which I had aspired only a few months before. (For his charity toward me, Lott was blasted by one of his local newspaper editors as "immoral" and defended by another as "a good Christian." Only a few months later his Mississippi Republican House colleague, Congressman Jon Hinson, was caught by Capitol police engaged in a homosexual act with a Library of Congress employee. Lott was further embarrassed since he campaigned for Hinson's reelection after he assured Lott there was no truth to the rumors of his being gay.)

There was another reason to proceed with my race for Congress. One evening, by sheer chance, I stopped at the Monacle Restaurant on Capitol Hill, the scene of so many of my past drinking bouts. The owner, well known to the Washington elite, is Connie Villanos, a small Greek with an outgoing personality and a large heart. He told me he recently had been hunting down on the Shore near Easton at the Marine Engineers School. Did I know the president of the national union, Jesse Calhoon? I told Connie I had met Calhoon, that his union contributed to my past campaigns, but that I certainly did not know him well. I also made it clear that if the Marine Engineers needed a local attorney in Easton, I was their man and I needed the work. Within a few weeks, I met with Jesse Calhoon and shortly thereafter was hired at a respectable annual retainer as local counsel to the Marine Engineers Beneficial Association. I also was back doing legal work, as well as arranging meetings between union officials and members of Congress. This activity not only began to restore faith in myself, it gave me a small personal financial base to allow my campaign.

So, in spite of Art Fincklestein's warnings, I puffed my old ego and decided to run again.

But first there were some personal considerations that had to be dealt with. After Carol left Glebe House with the children in June 1981, the summer passed quickly. In July, Genie turned sixteen and with her new driver's license she drove Vicky and Jimmy back home to Glebe almost every weekend. In August, Vicky simply refused to stay in Virginia with Carol. After a stormy dinner session between Carol and me, refereed by Father Harvey, Vicky was allowed to come home to Glebe and start at Easton High School. I was joyful to have even one of my children with me and the two of us did quite well together, along with Genie and Jimmy's weekend visits. The children insisted on spending Thanksgiving and Christmas at Glebe, just like old times, and Carol joined us for Christmas day, although she was obviously ill at ease.

For months after she left Carol talked with me very little, mostly by phone. We saw each other rarely, corresponding by lengthy letters, which did little to dissolve our feelings or the issues between us. It took repeated redraftings of the separation agreement she proposed before I would sign it, much of my disagreement over the final disposition of our joint debts and whether I would be permitted to buy out her interest in Glebe House. I was struggling to keep up the house payments but so far had managed with my newfound consulting and legal employment. I also knew that as long as Glebe was there the children would want to return. That made it imperative for me to keep the old homestead, if only, I thought, as a spur to our reconciliation.

In October 1981, at Luis Luna's urging, I finally met with Carol at the L'Enfant Plaza Hotel bar, not far from her office at the Department of Energy. I asked her what her intentions were about the trial separation and its continuance. I said I did not want a divorce and hoped she would not seek one. We both knew that the children lived in hope we would reunite, and I said that I was continuing my sobriety, my counseling, and still hoped differences could be worked out. I also broached the delicate subject of my possible 1982 race for Congress. I pointed out that a divorce in early 1982 would be the worst possible thing for any chance I might have of winning. That would reopen all the old personal questions in a public fashion that press and opponents would make the most of.

Carol chose her words carefully and I did not push her. I came away from the meeting with the understanding that a reconciliation was still possible.

For the moment it seemed the continuation of our marriage was still a possibility, thus not a threat to my political future. Strangely, after talking to Carol, seeing and talking with her again for the first extended period of time in five months, I began to doubt whether I wanted to get back together. The well-dressed, well-groomed professional woman I met in the L'Enfant bar was not the wife I knew. Was this new Carol someone I could "handle"? That always had been my approach. I suspected it wouldn't work again. That I was thinking in such terms of control is evidence of just how far I had yet to go in my recovery.

Carol's conversation as interpreted by me was enough to convince my campaign manager, Luis Luna, that we were ready to go forward.

We scheduled my candidacy announcement for late November, after Thanksgiving. I began training for the great event like a prizefighter trying for a comeback. I had expert assistance from Luis, Art Fincklestein, who donated his services, and another volunteer, Robert Weed. Weed, a brilliant professional strategist, worked for many conservatives including Georgia Congressman Newt Gingrich, now one of the House conservative leaders, and Paul Trible, then a congressman and soon to be U.S. senator from Virginia. Weed approached me in late 1980 even before I left office saying he wanted to help simply because "the country and the Congress need you."

We planned the announcement for a rally speech before friends at the Tidewater Inn on Friday evening with a press conference the next morning. Weed and Luna figured that would give me a slight edge with the press coverage, the candidacy being the lead story and any nasty press questions remaining for the next day. Weed insisted I do something I never had done before: draft in writing and then memorize answers to the expected tough questions about my personal life and condition. I hated it but I did it, writing out in longhand responses to: "Are you a homosexual?" "Are you cured of your 'twin compulsions?' " "What's the situation with your wife and family?"

Both Weed and Luna wanted me to say I was "cured" of my alcoholism and homosexual tendencies. I flatly refused. I pointed out that although most people don't know a lot about the technicalities of homosexuality and alcoholism, it would be a lie to claim any cure since in both cases none was likely, if possible at all. And those who do know about such problems would know I was untruthful.

My proposed answer, and the one I used, was to say that anyone who knew anything about these "tendencies" knew there was no cure for alcoholism but that it could be arrested. I pointed out that I had not had a drink since May 1, 1980, and was continuing to deal with the problem with group support. As to the homosexuality, I would not deny it but note that I was continuing to receive religious and psychological counseling and "I never felt better in my life."

Through some miracle of omission, none of the large number of reporters present insisted on the issue and no one ever directly asked if I was a homosexual. At that point, had I been asked, I would have had to say truthfully that I did not know. That, after all, was what I was seeing a doctor for once a week.

My announcement speech and press conference both came off surprisingly well. The rally speech was termed "vintage Bauman" for my strong attack of Dyson's liberal voting record and his labor union campaign contributions. Newspaper and television coverage was kinder than we expected. The worst reaction came from an unusual source; for daring to aspire to return to

Congress, I was named "Asshole of the Month" by *Hustler* magazine, complete with my face superimposed on the rear end of a donkey.

But my candidacy produced an unexpected complication with William F. Buckley, Jr., who had called for my resignation in 1980. An enterprising reporter for the *Baltimore News American* wanted to know what Buckley now thought of my political plans. I told him I did not know but would find out.

When Buckley called me back the next day I informed him I was running again and he was very cordial, asking how I was feeling, whether things in my life were "going well." I said I never felt better and things were in order. Without pressing further he gave me his blessing and said "for whatever my support may be worth you can inform the press." He later confirmed this in a phone conversation with the inquisitive Baltimore reporter.

But a year later, in January 1983, *The New Yorker* magazine published several excerpts from Bill's latest book, *Overdrive,* in which our phone call was remembered much differently than I recalled it. He claimed that in 1980, after I announced my intention not to withdraw from the race, I claimed to be "cured" of alcoholism and, in his words, "any tendency to homosexuality had gone with the alcohol ..." a statement which did not even approximate what I actually said. (My words were that I suffered from the "twin compulsions of alcoholism and homosexual tendencies" but "did not consider myself to be a homosexual." I certainly did not claim I was cured, either in the 1980 press conference, when I announced again in 1981, or in my phone conversation with Bill, which he recounted for *The New Yorker.*) Buckley wrote: "I told Bob that if he thought himself cured, he should by all means do what he wants to do, and that, if it means anything, I am with him all the way." He then discoursed on the topic of curable homosexuality, comparing me to his close friend, the late Whittaker Chambers, who confessed to a five-year period of active homosexuality during the 1930s after which Buckley claimed Chambers had been "cured."

Once this Buckley statement appeared in the January 31, 1983, issue of *The New Yorker,* I was soon contacted by a reporter for *New York* magazine, eager to emphasize the apparent conflict. I gave a mild explanation that Bill must have read into my remarks what he wished to hear, but I reiterated that I did not say I was cured of homosexuality. Buckley's office, when contacted, replied through an assistant: "His understanding of [the Bauman affair] is exactly as he published it in the book."

I did not wish to publicly disagree with my friend, especially since only a few weeks after *The New Yorker* piece he had invited me as his guest at a posh reception for *National Review* Washington editor, John MacLaughlin, at the Madison Hotel. The special guest was the President of the United States, Ronald Reagan. (An insider told me that the *NR* editorial board voted on my invitation and a majority agreed I was acceptable.)

Bill and I remain good friends and he has attempted to assist me with possibilities of professional employment, for which I remain grateful. Certainly his secure place in American history does not depend on my judgment, but the courtesies he repeatedly extended to Carol and me are typical of the qualities of this man who has so greatly influenced the conservative movement and the nation. It gave me great satisfaction to see him on television at President Reagan's second inaugural standing only a few feet away from the President.

Running for Congress again in 1981–82 was a major personal mistake. Unwilling to believe Art Fincklestein when he warned me of the garbage barrage that awaited me, I just bulled ahead, my still-inflated ego and my politician's instinct telling me "you can do it again."

The key to my personal decision to run was certainly my egotistical belief that my past record and service would somehow outweigh the centuries of ignorance and prejudice surrounding the issue of homosexuality. Although the people of Maryland's First Congressional District proved themselves remarkably broadminded in their 1980 voting, I should have seen what was coming.

Art Finckelstein's prediction was right on target.

It was not easy in any sense. My former friend and top congressional aide, Ross Whealton, signed on as campaign manager for my Republican primary opponent, issuing a blast against my moral and mental health. I was, he said, "unfit" to serve in any public office.

My Republican opponent, Charles Arthur Porter Hopkins, a retired multimillionaire and former member of the Maryland legislature, had been a friend and contributor to my campaigns. "Porter" announced his candidacy for Congress in January 1982, saying he would not support me if I was nominated, that Bob Bauman was a "sick person." Having served in the army he knew that people of my ilk were not promoted to "positions of leadership" but rather "discharged for medical reasons." He later added that I was a "disgrace" to myself, my family, my party, and the state of Maryland. He somehow omitted the nation and the universe beyond.

This was only the beginning. Soon a carefully orchestrated campaign of word-of-mouth rumors began, lurid stories that popped up in various parts of the huge congressional district only hours apart on the same day; all-male sex orgies were being conducted at Glebe House; I was seen cruising for young boys in Washington and Ocean City; I had been back to the infamous Chesapeake House; I was drunk and ran my car into a ditch, and so on.

Finally, after several months of this slander, I called an old friend, Jack Shaw, a wealthy waterfront political dilettante, who often lent me his palatial home for campaign meetings. His neighbor was Paul Stokes, Hopkins' campaign chairman. I suggested a meeting with Stokes to see if we couldn't put a lid on all the garbage being thrown. "Frankly, if this keeps up," I told Shaw, "the Republican nomination for Congress will be worthless to anyone."

Before the meeting Shaw told me somewhat apologetically he was supporting Hopkins, but he, Stokes, Luis Luna, and I sat down to talk. As they say in politics, the "bottom line" was not the least bit conciliatory. Stokes, Shaw chiming in, told me they had access to unpublished 1980 "Maryland State Police investigative reports" regarding my sexual conduct. While they would "never use such things" against me, they "could not prevent others" from doing so. However, if I would withdraw from the race, they felt confident this exposure could be avoided and further, Mr. Hopkins' friends, themselves included, would be pleased to help me pay my campaign debts. The decision was mine, they said.

I was so shocked I held my tongue and soon left with Luis, telling him that this amounted to criminal extortion. After two more threatening phone calls from Jack Shaw, one just before the candidate withdrawal deadline, I became so angry I decided to discuss the matter with the Talbot County States Attorney, who called in the state police.

But even before this unpleasant event it was obvious to me that the possibility of winning the November general election after a bruising primary such as Hopkins was conducting was becoming more remote. Hopkins had to be given credit for his frankness of purpose. He repeatedly said publicly his interest was not so much in his being congressman as it was in making sure that Bob Bauman never returned to Congress. Meanwhile, the battle was tearing the Republican party ranks to shreds.

I made phone calls to Art Fincklestein and *Human Events* editor, Tom Winter, describing what was happening in the race and asking them one question: "If I win and go back to Congress can I ever expect this kind of Hopkins junk to stop? Will this go on forever, as long as I am in the public eye?" They both answered that, in spite of many variables, they thought I could expect constant public scrutiny if I was elected again, and much of it could be of the Hopkins variety.

For several days I mulled over this prospect and finally concluded it was simply not worth it to continue the campaign. Beyond the political hurtles resulting from Hopkins' destructive campaign, the personal considerations were great. I finally was getting to know my children and the possibility now existed I would be separated from them by a return to Congress. Worse, we would be subjected to brutal publicity ad infinitum. My own economic situation was not good, and I had already been forced to give up congressional consulting positions when I declared as a candidate.

Most importantly, I had to admit to myself I was not personally ready to take on a task of the magnitude this had rapidly become. I badly miscalculated the mental and spiritual corrosion that results to a human being from daily public attacks and private innuendos. The October 1980 campaign had been bad but it had been brief. Now before me there stretched the prospect of unlimited public torture.

In July, after consulting with all my key supporters, I called yet another Tidewater Inn press conference and told the world that I was bowing out of the race. I informed the large crowd of reporters I simply "no longer have the fire in my belly," that I could not and would not undergo the public trashing which Porter Hopkins was conducting against me. I detailed the meeting with Jack Shaw and Paul Stokes, the threats, the rumors, and lies. "Personal considerations are far more important than a seat in Congress if this is the way it is to be," I said.

One reporter, Dan Rodericks of the *Baltimore Sun,* noted that I appeared more relaxed and at peace than he had ever seen me. "Deeply tanned and nattily attired in a tan suit and blue shirt, Mr. Bauman looked more like a yachtsman who just stepped off a week aboard a catamaran than a disappointed office seeker. Asked what he would be doing next, he replied, 'I'm going swimming with my children this afternoon.' " And we did.

A few weeks later the Talbot County States Attorney announced he would not prosecute anyone in the Hopkins campaign, terming the threats made to me "an excess of political zeal."

When all the votes were counted in the 1982 September Republican primary election, I came within a few hundred votes of defeating Hopkins two months after I withdrew from the race and stopped campaigning. A ten-day recount showed him the winner by about a thousand votes. There is little doubt I would have won the nomination had I chosen to stay in the race but I had learned that other things in life were more important. As much as I would have loved to return, being in Congress was not at the top of my list any longer.

The unusual nature of my close defeat prompted the *Washington Times* to comment editorially:

> In his usual form, Bauman called his opponent's victory only slightly less humiliating than if it had been gained against a dead man.
>
> We think there's a message here. Voters recognized Bauman's intelligence and skill. They wanted his brand of conservatism. To many of them, his personal problems are in the past—and now of secondary importance.
>
> That's good news if it's true. Congress needs Bauman. Two years from now, it'll still need him. Because he has style, flair, and a detailed knowledge of how to make the legislative process work. That combination makes liberals deathly uncomfortable.
>
> Don't count Bob Bauman out of politics yet.

In the November election the incumbent congressman, Roy Dyson, won a second term overwhelmingly. Hopkins got only 29 percent of the vote, the lowest vote for a Republican congressional candidate in our area since 1936. On election night, Hopkins declined to comment on his crushing defeat, saying he had "more important matters" to attend to; he was bartending at an Easton charity event.

I spent the same election evening at a meeting of fellow recovering alcoholics celebrating my continued sobriety.

That I was not mentally and spiritually equipped for a brutal congressional race in 1982 was self-evident. But there was another major factor. After years of callous disregard of those I loved I was finding satisfaction in being a father. In June 1982, after nine months with Carol, my youngest son, Jimmy, then nine, decided he wanted to return to Glebe House and live with me and his sister, Vicky. To my surprise Carol agreed. In September, Jim began school at Saints Peter and Paul and rejoined the men and boys choir at our church where he sang for the two years before Carol and I separated. It was a joy to hear his beautiful treble voice singing Gregorian chant and medieval plainsong.

Our oldest daugher, Genie, who spent the year attending school in Virginia, was, at my behest, named a page in the House of Representatives by Congressman Edward J. Derwinski of Illinois, an old friend. As had her father before her, Genie loved the year-long experience and was elected student body president at Capitol Page School, my alma mater. But she started her Capitol Hill job in June 1982 only weeks before the "page scandal" made national headlines. Allegations of page-congressmen sex and possible drug use made sensational reading. Once reporters discovered Bob Bauman's daughter was a page, Genie spent several days dodging their frantic pursuit. She handled her page service with aplomb, her only major indiscretion being a comment to a local Easton reporter that she was amazed at how many congressmen did not seem to "know what was going on in Congress."

Our oldest son, Ted, away at Loyola College in Baltimore in 1980, for a long time afterward remained aloof. I would see him on weekends and at holidays but his distance may have been a needed protective device, allowing him to deal with what was undoubtedly a major trauma in the lives of all my children. Ted and I have become closer in the five years since all this happened.

All of our children are good, decent human beings. But without detailed explanation I can truthfully say my conduct and the events flowing from that conduct deeply hurt each of them. Individually, they suffered pain and anguish for which I am directly responsible. The divorce itself was terribly disruptive, especially to the youngest three children who lost their established home and the security of both parents' presence. I firmly believe it is a mistaken notion that divorce is better in many cases than maintaining a home for the children. Staying together may mean continued hurt to the parents but divorce means extending that hurt to the children. I doubt they will fully recover however long they live. All of our children have done very well in their educational achievements, well above average in their studies in spite of the turmoil in their lives. But now that I am able to read the sadness in a human's eyes, I have often been painfully aware of the high toll I exacted from my children.

And yet, in Carol's and my case, divorce probably was the only realistic answer.

That her desire for divorce came as a surprise to me is a measure of the unreality of my thinking in the months after my defeat and our separation. It was yet another compelling reason for my withdrawal from the 1982 congressional campaign.

On March 5, 1982, the unexpected news arrived in a letter from the Office of the Tribunal, the official church agency that deals with marriage. The envelope marked "Personal/Confidential" bore the seal of the Roman Catholic Diocese of Wilmington, Delaware, where our home parish in Easton is located. Over the signature of a lay attorney, a Mr. Lanphear, I was informed that my wife of twenty-one years had asked for an annulment of our marriage, an official ruling that in effect our union had been invalid from its origins. (I was later to learn that although the Catholic church strongly opposes "divorce," it grants tens of thousands of "annulments" every year in the U.S., provided sufficient grounds can be shown for this action.)

Over thirty years, I had much contact with my church, but both as a communicant and a lawyer I was struck by the breezy tone of this notice. Carol was referred to as my "former spouse" (she wasn't yet), and contradictorily, a "civil divorce proceeding" was said to be pending (it wasn't). Mr. Lanphear asked my comments on what led to "the termination of your marriage" (although it hadn't been yet). I could respond by checking the enclosed postcard if I did not wish to appear before the Tribunal or I could meet with its representative.

This was obviously a routine matter for Mr. Lanphear, but even though there was an anticlimactic quality after ten months of separation this was not a routine event in my life. Didn't any Catholic deserve somewhat better than this bureaucratic approach from his church?

I put this question to Father John Harvey by telephone and he expressed surprise. In the Archdiocese of Washington he often was involved in such proceedings and the tribunal there took a much different approach. In a similar circumstance the accused party would be telephoned and invited to meet with a tribunal representative. He would then explain what was occurring, answering the inevitable questions. Rights and responsibilities were explained as were the grounds on which the annulment was sought. Misunderstandings and bad feelings were thus minimized. And at the same time, the tribunal gained an impression of what the position of both parties would be.

I called Mr. Lanphear the next day. He was not terribly concerned about the errors of fact in his letter—"We both know what is involved here"—although he regretted any misstatements. I learned Carol already had appeared before the tribunal. Her petition for annulment was filed six months earlier. She asked that additional witnesses be called to support her case, namely Father Harvey, and my psychologist, Dr. Kay. I was told I could object to this if I wished. I did. Mr. Lanphear declined to discuss the grounds on which the petition was based but said I could find out if I chose to meet with the tribunal.

My legal background made me put in writing my questions and

I sent my response to Mr. Lanphear on April 6. And I did have many questions: If the annulment were granted what was my status in the eyes of the church? Could a marriage be annulled on the allegations of one party alone? What were the grounds of the petition? What about "due process" under canon law, what were my rights?

Two weeks later there came a much more formal document. I was now the "defendant" and Carol was the "plaintiff." I hadn't studied Common Law Pleading under Father Lucey at Georgetown Law Center for nothing. I was being served a summons by the Catholic church to appear and defend myself if I could. The grounds for this petition were stated to be Canon 1083 (1) of the Code of the Church, which states "Error regarding the person makes the marriage invalid."

I soon learned my case came within a relatively new doctrine debated in the church for years. In essence, "error of person" means that a valid marriage cannot result when one party, unbeknownst to the other, has some defect of a fundamental nature, such as being a homosexual, since such a person would be incapable of a valid consent to the marriage bond. If a person has reasonable grounds to believe that he or she is homosexual (or suffers any major defect), a moral obligation exists not to marry, since the union would be invalid *ab initio,* from the beginning. This doctrine has only been accepted relatively recently in some parts of Europe and the U.S.

Appended to my summons was a letter from Reverend Dennis G. Volmi, J.D.C., "Vice Officialis" of the tribunal. In it, Father Volmi carefully attempted to answer my several questions without being too specific: yes, an annulment could be granted even if I did not appear to contest it; any judgment made about my "conduct or character" would be a matter of the "internal record of the tribunal" only; the ultimate decision would spell out the grounds on which it was based if indeed the marriage was declared a nullity; and as for my "state of grace, that is an internal matter for your conscience and not treated in the judge's decision."

As to due process, Father Volmi assured me that I could appear, present witnesses, and appeal any decision "all the way to Rome," as Father Harvey later suggested was my right. If I chose not to appear, an appointed "Defender of the Bond" would present the case for maintaining the marriage, which was done in all cases seeking annulment.

But my concern was heightened by one statement Father Volmi made: "If an affirmative decision is granted, and all the requirements are met, the marriage is annulled and both parties are free to marry . . . The church makes no comment on your future capacity as a communicant. You are still free to receive the sacraments after a divorce provided you do not marry outside the church."

I thoroughly discussed the Volmi letter with Father Harvey, who in turn consulted a priest friend, an expert in canon law at the Catholic University of America in Washington. Thus advised I telephoned Father Volmi in Wilmington.

He was most pleasant and forthcoming in his responses, not nearly so guarded as he was in writing.

Was my understanding of the "error of person doctrine" correct? As it applied in my case our marriage might well have been invalid from the inception both because my wife had been uninformed as to a major fact concerning my personal condition, homosexuality, which also prevented me from entering into a valid marriage. "Yes, that is essentially the case," he agreed. "And so, therefore, Father," I continued, "my wife must have alleged that I am a homosexual and be able to prove that to the satisfaction of the tribunal."

"At least in part, you are correct," he said.

"But, Father," I persisted, "in your letter you said that if this divorce is granted both parties would be free to marry again. That cannot be true in my case. How would I be allowed to enter into yet another invalid marriage?" He admitted that I would have to prove that "my disability," my alleged homosexuality, had been removed before another marriage would be permitted. (I would have to prove that I was "cured," I thought to myself.) "Does the church keep a record of such potential disabilities, a sort of 'cloud on the title,' as we say in real estate law?" I wanted to know. Father explained that among the questions asked of any proposed parties to a marriage, truthful answers would elicit this information about me and the question of my capacity would be raised anew. For any valid marriage to result, such questions would have to be answered satisfactorily.

I asked: "Then your statement that 'the church makes no comment on your future capacity as a communicant' is not exactly correct, is it?" He stood by his statement. My future relationship to the church would not be impaired by any annulment decree. What that relationship was to be was up to me.

I did not appear at the tribunal hearing and posed no opposition to the Petition for Annulment. I wanted our marriage to be saved. I had undertaken religious and psychological counseling for almost two years toward that end. I so stated in a letter that I asked to be filed in the records of the tribunal.

But there was no way that I could prove that I was not a homosexual either now or when I was married twenty-one years before. What I did know was that at the time of our marriage in 1960, I did not believe myself to be homosexual and I was still not sure of that.

On the 25th day of August in the year of Our Lord 1982, the Tribunal of the Diocese of Wilmington, Delaware, an official organ of the Catholic church, Christ's church on earth, declared that Carol Dawson and Bob Bauman had never been married in the eyes of God or man. In those same eyes it declared Bob Bauman, by inference, to be a homosexual.

In some respects the annulment was anticlimactic since Carol also filed for a civil divorce in April 1982. That was granted in

June 1982 on the grounds under Maryland law of a one-year voluntary separation of both parties. We did not have to appear in court, sworn affidavits being sufficient. Of course the filing in Easton and final divorce decree were accompanied by the usual newspaper headlines, front-page stuff, since I was again running for Congress at the time.

But it was the annulment by the Catholic church which struck me with the most impact.

As long as I could remember, I fought the possibility that I was "one of them"—a homosexual! The horrible possibility twisted and disfigured my life, affected the lives of all around me, drove me from public office. I battled it with every weapon available, even the forlorn hope of an eventual "cure."

And now, without need of my presence, a priest and two laymen, none of whom I knew, sitting in a room in Wilmington, Delaware, voted to declare me a homosexual. And not just recently gay, but gay from the beginning.

As I read the judgment of the tribunal the deeper meaning of all this suddenly penetrated.

I was sitting at my law office desk in the Loyola Federal Building in Easton, the same desk I used for eight years in Congress. I kept reading and rereading the document, searching for the actual word which never appeared. And yet the paper in my hands was as sure a declaration of my homosexuality as one might ever receive in life. True, Dr. Kay told me I was probably gay and should accept the fact. Two psychiatrists hinted that was the case but offered the opinion it would take years of analysis to be sure. Even Father Harvey told me this was the likelihood, based on his extensive counseling of others with such problems.

And of course there was the lifetime of acts on my part, each countered by denial, self-deception, and a personal terror which effectively blocked acceptance.

But here lying on the desk before me was the word of Holy Mother Church Herself, my church, God's church on earth. The human beings officially charged with administering His law on earth had made up their expert minds: Bob Bauman is a homosexual.

Slowly, a peaceful resignation crept over me, not unlike the physical relaxation experienced after vigorous exercise or a taxing race. I felt the tension drain from my body.

What in God's name am I fighting this for? I asked myself.

And suddenly I was not fighting anymore.

I am what I am. Now, at last, I know what I am.

CHAPTER
SIX

I did not chose to be homosexual. I would change my sexual orientation if that were within my power.

Undoubtedly many gay people reading my statement that I would opt for heterosexuality will judge me cowardly or worse. But the price I paid for my lifelong inability to accept my sexuality, or even understand it, has been enormous in real, spiritual, and emotional terms, for me and for those I love. I definitely am not among the 90 percent of survey respondents who said they would decline to change their homosexual orientation if they could. Ironically, the same percentage of gays in the same survey said they would not recommend being gay to others.

I cannot even say with any assurance that I am "gay," in the sense that word is used now by the gay community. I am homosexual as that describes one whose sexual attraction and desire is directed toward one of his or her own sex. But "gay" denotes a term of pride which some open homosexuals apply to the totality of their existence, each accepting his or her nature as God made them, celebrating that creation, sharing their joy and knowledge of that creation with others. In this sense, "gay" expands to include spiritual, political, economic, intellectual, and social connotations far beyond the sexual dimension.

It gave me little comfort to read a few years ago that the great weight of clinical authority holds the consensus there is little conscious choice about any individual's sexuality. Dr. John Money of Johns Hopkins University, a noted authority in this area of study, says that by the time a child reaches the age of two to four years his or her sexuality is already formed. Various experts offer informed opinions on the causes of homosexuality ranging from early environmental factors to hormonal balances, brain chemistry, and even constitutional origins, i.e., "God made me that way." An admitted liberal on the subject, Judd Marmor, M.D., a respected psychoanalyst says: "There is no single cause for homosexuality. People come to it in a variety of ways. A number of recent research studies strongly suggest that many homosexuals are born with a predisposition toward such behavior which then becomes reinforced by environmental factors. In other homosexuals environmental factors seem to be more important than inborn ones." Certainly parents should not blame themselves for some perceived "failure" on their part since homosexuality likely does not flow from parental actions.

The issue of choice is the major difficulty for those who castigate gays and even for some gays themselves. They cling to the opinion that if no definite cause can be assigned to homosexuality and its associated behavior, then the individual must *choose* to be homosexual. If you are black or physically handicapped, ugly or dying of cancer, you may well be discriminated against by the prejudiced and unthinking, but you are not blamed for your condition. But the majority of non-gay people apparently view homosexuality as a manifestation of some underlying personal and moral failure involving a deliberate choice. If that be the case, they reason, then gays can be brought to account for their immoral behavior. Even Sigmund Freud, the father of modern psychoanalysis, advanced the so-called "conflict theory," that a homosexual person has at some point in his youth been forced, albeit unconsciously, to respond to some trauma or emotional conflict by choosing what Freud referred to as the "deviant" course. For Freud this involved motivation at some level even if the individual was unaware of his unconscious choice. That new sexual research is aimed at tearing down this motivational and choice theory has little impact, from my own experience, on the popular conception that homosexuals choose to be what they are and could simply stop if they wished. I repeat, I had no such choice, and I have never encountered another gay person who claims to have made such a choice, either in person or in my extensive reading on the subject. They simply "knew" instinctively what they were. And in the context of my own life, why would I want to voluntarily drift into alcoholism, torment myself internally for all the years of my existence, reject a beautiful, attractive woman as my wife, harm my children whom I love, and obliterate a career that was described as "brilliant" and "promising"?

Unacquainted with this mysterious affliction called homosexuality, most "normal" people react much as the editors of *Human Events* did when I publicly gave my support to legal protection for gay people against discrimination. They insisted, as many do, that homosexuality does involve deliberate choice; that those who indulge themselves by practicing homosexuality are guilty of moral failings, sins. Thus, having chosen to be gay, these misfits deserve no special protection from the law, only condemnation.

Of course my specific actions involved choice, although experts have assured me that at some point my conduct amounted to a compulsion I was unable to control. But the physical and intellectual urges, the attraction toward other men, this was not something I chose or would have. It was simply the way I was. It is the way I am.

With childlike simplicity I knew from an early age that I was "different." I do not mean the notion of difference my indulgent mother sought to instill in me with her insistence I was destined for some undefined greatness. My "difference" was a continuing uneasy feeling something was wrong with me and my relation to life around me. Soon I translated this into the belief there was within me some inherent flaw, something bad. Whatever this undefined spector was, it had to be hidden, denied, and fought. It was something so unique it could not be shared with anyone, not even those who loved me or that I loved. Especially not those I loved. Who can say whether this was reinforced by my father's alcoholism, my mother's death when I was eight years old, the trauma of learning in your father's drunken rage you are an adopted child?

That revelation came on a hot, sweltering summer afternoon when my father pressed me into some household duties I considered particularly onerous. I recall I was doing something in the garage while my father, who started drinking early that Saturday, was cutting the grass. I ignored or bungled several requests he made, engaging in what in our family was known as "talking back."

Impatient and growing angry, Dad selected one of a parent's ancient weapons; in a loud, threatening voice, he explained in explicit detail the physical suffering I could expect if I did not immediately clean up my act.

My response was less than satisfactory and my continued obstinacy provoked my father in a scene that will ever live in my memory.

Red-faced, sweating, and weaving from drink and the heat, he glared at me across the garage and shouted, "You know, if you don't straighten up and do what I tell you, you can just go back where you came from."

Not fully comprehending this veiled threat I stared back at him with a quizzical expression on my face.

"You know you're not my son, Bobby."

I tried to catch my breath.

His words were slurred but delivered with a clenched jaw that denoted contained anger.

"Your mother and I adopted you when you were only days old."

I felt as though I was smothering to death.

He paused, as if to allow the impact to sink in.

"You better Goddamned straighten up because if you don't you can just get the hell out of here."

I felt tears rolling down my cheeks and quickly covered my face with my hands.

What he said so unexpectedly, important as it might seem, did not immediately hit me. Only later reflection brought on total sadness and expanded self-doubt. My first impression was confirmation; no wonder no one wanted me. My own parents, my own mother, father, whoever they were, had not wanted me either.

Later that hot afternoon I remember sitting for a long time under a tree in a nearby woods considering my state in life. If the future was a mystery, now the past was also. My solitary existence, the aloneness, was complete.

My father was not an intentionally cruel man. Indeed, sober he was a mild and indulgent, if somewhat detached, father. He died of a heart attack in July 1965 after nearly four years of total sobriety, having sought help from the same groups of recovering alcoholics that eventually helped me. Among his papers I found after his death was an adoption petition describing the infant child as "destitute, unwanted, devoid of parental support and in need of care and protection." It was filed in the same Superior Court of the District of Columbia in which I was years later to appear again under even less desirable circumstances. The document's dry legalese shows me to be the bastard child of an unwed mother, born on April 4, 1937, in Bryn Mawr, Pennsylvania, a rather posh area. My real name would have been Robert Edmund Power. (What a campaign billboard: "Power for the People.")

Some might consider me to be sick. It would be a convenient explanation for a problem that otherwise requires serious thought and the challenge of old assumptions. "Sick" and "unnatural" are phrases often used to describe homosexuality. They have a superficial appeal to the unthinking. And for much of this century homosexuality found itself classified along with other phenomena under the category of "mental illness." Sigmund Freud was more kind than most, terming homosexuality a case of "arrested development." Each of us, he said, passes through a youthful phase of same-sex identification which is quickly bypassed with greater maturity.

For years gays found it convenient to accept the label of "sickness" since it provided an understandable excuse for a condition which most of society viewed as akin to leprosy. To be sick meant it was not necessarily a matter of moral laxity or fault. It also offered the hope of eventual cure. So for many reasons homosexuals had little choice but to acquiesce in their assigned medical status as sick people in need of psychiatric help.

But along the way, as gays began to realize the inferior connotation of being classified as mentally ill, they became more than uneasy. "Illness" certainly does not explain why so many well-adjusted homosexual people lead satisfactory lives of artistic, professional, and occupational achievement.

In 1973, after many years of research and debate, the American Psychiatric Association removed homosexuality from its list of diagnosed emotional disorders. Instead, the APA said it would view being gay as "different from" but not better or worse than being heterosexual. In 1975, the American Psychological Association followed suit. The groups said that being homosexual did not imply impairment in judgment, stability, reliability, or general social or vocational capabilities. In other words, some gays might have mental problems, but simply because they were gay did not prove them crazy any more than being non-gay implied sanity.

That many gay people distrust psychiatrists and their professional activities stems not only from the old definitions but the fact that psychiatric norms have tended to reflect the norms of society at large. Thus, to be sick was often defined as what people thought was sick, and in the case of gays the majority opinion was clear. That basic distrust expanded on the part of gays who encountered doctors who tried to "change" the individual gay person's orientation, often with disastrous results. In all my extensive reading I discovered no instance of a documented "cure" of homosexuality and it is my impression that none exists. It would be as easy to "cure" white or black skin pigmentation or the color of one's eyes.

A great many of the gay people I met in recent years have been under psychiatric care, especially long-term psychoanalysis, usually in proportion to how high their income might be, or the extent of their health insurance coverage.

They may have discovered, as I finally did, competent psychiatric counseling can be tremendously helpful to a gay person if devoted to life adjustment as opposed to some forlorn and misguided hope that a person's sexuality is likely to be susceptible to fundamental change.

I did not realize it at the time but Dr. John Kay did me a great favor in suggesting my own possible homosexuality after several months of treatment. I could not then accept his view and ultimately we broke off our professional association because of my refusal. Two psychiatrists and two years later, I realized I would have to accept myself as I was and begin the very difficult work of adjusting to my life. That has been the real task. But it is not unusual for a therapist to hear strong protests when he sides with a patient's homosexual tendencies, since many gays unwittingly accept society's thesis regarding their "illness."

Whether I was predisposed to homosexuality or some early environmental factors influenced me I cannot say. But at an early age I was cast into an environment that might have influenced me. After my mother's lingering death from stomach cancer on December 11, 1945, my father remarried. His new wife was a strict Catholic disciplinarian with definite ideas about what a headstrong eight-year-old boy like Bobby needed. I soon found myself at Fork Union Military Academy in "southside" Virginia about thirty-five miles from Charlottesville. A million miles from civilization, the "Fork" in its name came from the confluence of the James and Fluvanna rivers, not exactly the Blue and White Niles. The remoteness made escape impossible, especially for an eight-year-old boy in a Confederate gray uniform.

Nearly thirty-five years later I visited "FUMA," as it is still called, on a motor trip with my two daughters. By the early 1980s, unlike most boys' military schools, FUMA grew and prospered by sticking to discipline and an all-male student body. Now there are impressive new buildings and careful landscaping I did not remember. As the girls and I got out of our car we met the president of the school, Dr. Whitecarver, who, in spite of an impending trip to Europe the next day, took time to give us the campus grand tour.

Memories of three decades before came flooding back. A solitary little boy, much like Dickens' young Scrooge, off at boarding school, alone among hundreds of his contemporaries, longing for home but with no little sister Fan to rescue him.

I shuddered when I recalled the awful homesickness.

Feeling "different" and alone was nothing compared to the internal agony I experienced at military school. To this day it is difficult to describe the physical and mental anguish I was assured was "only homesickness." "You'll get over it, son," my teachers told me. "They all do."

What I felt was more than just a longing for home. I was not even sure where home was anymore. I was firmly convinced I had been utterly abandoned. The intense feeling manifested itself in a physical shortness of breath, a tightness in the chest, bodily weakness, and often, uncontrollable weeping, especially late at night.

During those initial months at FUMA the telephone was my lifeline. Its use meant I had to go to the headmaster's office after dinner each evening, our only free time period. Rural Virginia's phone system in 1947 required cranking up the operator in Palmyra (there were no dials), who eventually put me through to my father or stepmother in Washington, usually after a prolonged wait. The calls were always collect and I lived in dread Maxine would refuse to accept the charges. But once on the line I would be transported in my mind's eye away from dull gray walls, gray uniforms, and the grayness of my life. My childish conversation was filled with plans for the next trip home or the next visit by my parents to FUMA. Escape was my clear objective but Maxine would hear none of it and resignation, though long in coming, finally conquered the worst of my pain.

If the very Catholic Maxine and my straight-laced father only knew what was happening at an all-boys' military school they would have leaped into their new 1947 Chevrolet sedan and dashed down U.S. Route 29 to rescue me.

But neither they nor I knew that the education of Robert Bauman was just beginning in earnest.

First of all, there was, indeed, sex.

After the British "public school" model, an all-boys' school in 1940s America taught a great deal about sex, at least homosexuality. Although heterosexual aspects of life were discussed in endless, lurid, uninformed detail, especially by the older boys, circumstance dictated that to do anything about sex required either a solitary act or a liaison with another boy. Few if any of us knew the clinical terms to describe what happened but almost everybody did "it" in some fashion or another.

While I was terribly unsophisticated about sexual matters when I arrived at military school, FUMA was not my introduction to sex.

My "first" happened several years before, perhaps at the age of five or six, in a basement a few doors from our row house in Washington. Tommy was a well-built young lad of about twelve or thirteen, who, with little warning, coaxed me out of my play suit and provided what the current idiom describes as "head." Then and now called by the prosaic term "blow job," what he did to me felt good. For that reason, I was at a total loss to understand the major explosion when I innocently informed my mother about this wonderful adventure.

The immediate result was an incendiary confrontation between the respective parents held in our living room. I can only recall the shouted recriminations about Tommy's lack of upbringing. The poor kid was spared from reform school but not from a terrific spanking.

Thus at an early age I learned forcefully a basic axiom governing sexual matters in America; if it feels good it is almost certainly wrong.

I was only a child but the internal conflict had already begun. The encounter with Tommy and later with my fellow cadets underscored the basic contradiction in my mind. Here I was far from home and my parents, starved for love and the warmth of human contact. But while sexual activity provided a solution to my need, why did it create such a feeling of guilt?

Guilt was not something I learned from my parents or anyone in authority. I never discussed sexual matters with them. My religious training was scant up to that point. And there certainly were no books to read about all this. Why did I momentarily feel so good and then, for so long afterward, so bad?

Actually the guilt was not taught. It was absorbed. It was in the air. It came in part from the judgment of my peers, a brutal judgment especially directed at those boys who even hinted they might enjoy more than a passive role in all this. Everyone could do "it," but those who seemed too eager immediately had their manhood, or boyhood, called into serious question. If the word about you got around, you became less than a man. You were, in a harsh contemporary word, a queer.

That kind of locker-room indictment stays with the American male throughout his life. He is, and may always be, impressed with the utter depravity, sinfulness, and filth of homosexuality and all its attendant wickedness.

But, oh God, if these things were so terribly wrong, if these feelings inside me were so contemptible in Your eyes and those of Your creature, man, why was I the receptacle for this evil? It was as if I had become the victim described in the words of the Prayer to Saint Michael after the old Tridentine Low Mass, "... *Sa-*

tanam aliosque spiritus malignos, qui ad perditionem animarum pervagatur in mundo." ". . . Satan and all the other evil spirits who roam about the world seeking the ruin of souls."

This was not a matter of chance attraction to a forbidden object. This was a frightening force from deep within my being, an involuntary reaction to the sight, smell, and feel of other boys. I neither understood nor accepted it. And I came to hate myself because of the presence within me of this horrible weakness, this uncleanness of spirit over which I seemed to have no control.

So added to the loneliness was a growing but barely perceived self-loathing. Hadn't I always known that something was wrong with me? Wasn't that why God took my mom away from me? Didn't they send me away to school because I was bad? And now this strange internal desire was further confirmation of just how unworthy a person I was.

Nearly four decades later it seems easy to dramatize the thoughts of an introspective eight-year-old boy. At the time it was overpowering but not nearly so dramatic. Drama requires an audience and I was determined that no one would ever know about the turmoil going on inside. I was sure my predicament was a unique punishment designed only for me. Unable to understand it myself I could never even attempt an explanation to someone else.

I countered my dilemma with a plan that constituted the essence of simplicity. I made up my mind that I was not "queer." I heard all those denunciations of homos by my military school peers and firmly resolved I could never be considered one of such a despicable breed.

To buttress my intellectual conviction of purity, I was required to construct a whole series of mental fortifications to protect and conceal the real me, not just from the external world but from myself as well. In time the turreted, crenellated walls grew into a self-impressive battlement like the infamous Maginot Line I was to see years later on a visit to the Valley of the Marne in north-eastern France. And like that ill-conceived strategy, when the time came, my own defenses crumbled, not just in one ultimate test, but repeatedly.

It was about this time that Aunt Louise sent me that book on the life of Abraham Lincoln, which produced my plans for a future in the law and politics. Putting aside self-doubt, loneliness, low self-esteem, guilt about my sexuality, I now had a goal. I clearly recall making a conscious decision I was going to show a world that did not want me it would have to deal with me someday. I did not need anybody. If I was unloved, I would be respected. I would see to that.

Before I departed Fork Union for the last time in 1949 to return "home" to Charleston, West Virginia, like the prisoner with his familiar chains, I became accustomed to the internal isolation and loneliness. I did not know it and did not understand it, but denial of my suppressed homosexuality was becoming part of my being.

Adversity also forged some valuable assets which would stand me in good stead. I was proud of being independent, self-reliant, and at least outwardly, self-confident. I was no longer the homesick little boy on the phone. I never told anyone of my conscious decision to go it alone in life, but that personal strategy required a good front of self-assurance, even assertiveness. In verbal repartee with my military school peers I developed a youthfully cynical sense of humor. I became, if contemporary reactions are a good judge, a master of words and wisecracks, always debating, injecting my sometimes cutting opinions, seeking attention and approval. I was an early specialist in the "put-down" and that lowest form of humor, the pun. That I practiced my wit at inappropriate times was not important to me although it often drew the wrath of my teachers in class.

As I approached my twelfth year I had already been on my own for three of those years. In spite of supposed military school discipline, I had been essentially free of direct adult supervision most of the time.

That state of personal freedom vanished abruptly when I returned to Charleston where my father was now a salesman. I always viewed stepmother Maxine as an unpleasant but only intermittent presence in my young life. I saw her during vacations from school. But now we lived together on a daily basis and war was mutually declared within a matter of days after my arrival.

It was about this time that I fell madly in love with a homely little girl in my class at Sacred Heart School. Her sweet disposition made up for what she lacked in looks. I was enthralled in a case of genuine "puppy love." So deeply was I smitten that it never occurred to me that my newfound interest was at variance with my sexual experiences at military school. That was, I was convinced, just a passing phase I had outgrown.

The little girl became an obsession. After dark I would slip out of the house and walk several blocks up and down those steep South Charleston hills to her house. Under cover of night I would sit quietly on the curb across from her house staring at the upstairs window I supposed to be her room. The slightest shadow on the shade left me breathless. I imagined what it would be like to be with her in that room. When, after many weeks, I got up the courage to steal a kiss, the first time I ever kissed a girl, it was sensual bliss that shook my young being. Whenever I could I walked her home from school, carried her books, and constantly talked with her on the phone, a difficult feat since my parents had no phone and I had to bother neighbors for the use of theirs. Together we learned the meaning of what in those quaint days was called "necking."

But my feelings were definitely stronger than my young lady friend's. In spite of our limited physical contact, my constant pursuit of her, I was about to experience my first taste of what I was to hear Senator Everett McKinley Dirksen of Illinois call "the delicious agony of unrequited love."

She was really just not interested in me, an attitude she made clear.

Unfortunately, my stepmother, Maxine, was not aware of my romantic rejection.

Our house was high on a hillside, and one afternoon Maxine spied the two of us walking home from the bus stop, apparently confirmation of her worst fears.

When I got home she sat me down and delivered herself of an extensive homily on the subject of sex and the unhealthy results which flowed from it. Warnings included the distinct possibilities of mortal sin and social disease. I should stay away from my little girlfriend "for my own good." Relations with the opposite sex had to be approached with the greatest caution and often produced no good. How this unexpected theory squared with her marriage to my father was not clear, but I did not dare raise the question.

There is a possible reason for my stepmother's eccentric view of relations between the sexes. A few years later I learned she had become pregnant after she left home while still a teen-ager, producing tremendous guilt in her Catholic-trained conscience, especially since she had an abortion. She told me this sad history when I was visiting her at the Cambridge State Hospital in Maryland, where she had been confined after a nervous collapse. By then she was diagnosed as a manic depressive, a condition that electric shock treatment and drug therapy seemed to have overcome. With great difficulty she eventually recovered.

In all truthfulness, I cannot say that my stepmother's advice made any great impression on my mind or my own subsequent sexual development.

In spite of my torrid heterosexual affair at the ripe age of thirteen my interest in other boys took a significant turn in the summer of 1950. Except for the usual adolescent masturbation I had not sought or had any sexual encounters with other boys since I left military school in 1949. On the contrary, I even fooled around a little, very little, with a cute little girl in the neighborhood who came on to me. One afternoon after school, when my parents were at work, she unexpectedly stripped off her clothes and invited me to join her in bed, which, slightly numb with shock, I did.

I had never seen a girl nude before, except my own mother by accident. And I certainly did not know what was expected of me under the circumstances. Not knowing, I did not do. We hugged and kissed and that was about it. But the physical sensation was impressive enough that I experienced an involuntary ejaculation, my first, which made me question my medical condition. I knew this kind of thing could be done by hand but spontaneity was a new and troublesome experience. But I definitely liked what happened.

But I liked something else also.

Like many middle-class young Americans I was sent away for two weeks at summer camp in 1950. One night, as the cool air of the West Virginia mountains crept into our rustic cabin, my lower bunkmate quietly climbed up to my top bed in the dark. A curly headed lad with the strong hint of a manly physique, he whispered something about it being cold and couldn't he sleep with me? That prospect held great interest and although mildly shocked, I did not hesitate in agreeing, my head nodding with anticipation in the dim light.

Two macho young boys don't rush into anything which might raise questions about their manhood. We proceeded slowly, touching, hugging, nuzzling each other a bit. And very little else happened, save a little frottage before we drifted off to sleep in each other's arms.

As a small child, when I could not get to sleep at night, my mother would lie on my bed next to me, tell me stories and sing the Broadway songs she learned during her years in show business. Often I would go to sleep as she held me close, surrounded by my collection of dolls, stuffed toys and animals, the strains of "April Showers" or "Ka Ka Ka Katie" in my ears.

Sleeping with that boy at camp was the first time since her death that I could recall anyone holding my body close to theirs, willingly, and for an extended period of time. I desperately needed that feeling of human warmth and closeness. There was a certain reassurance in the thought I might be desirable to someone else.

But not everyone was fast asleep in our cabin that night.

After breakfast next morning our counselor sternly ordered all of us to gather in our cabin. His lecture went straight to the point: good little Catholic boys to not sleep together, only in their own bunks. The gravity of the situation was accentuated by the scowling presence of the camp director, a priest, standing in the cabin doorway. His silent gaze seemed to aim directly at me and my nocturnal visitor from the lower bunk. So much for cold nights and human warmth at Camp Bill Grady.

My conversion to Catholicism at age fourteen was but a few months old and here already I found myself in serious conflict with my adopted church and its unfolding doctrines. Obviously, masturbation was one thing ("An act of impurity by myself, Father"), everyone did that and confessed it weekly. But how could you ever admit, even in the confessional, what we had done; two boys together, holding and hugging each other.

For days afterward I lived in fear that not only would my parents be told their child had committed a mortal sin but that little Bobby was fatally flawed. I had visions of whippings and trips to the psychiatrist. As usual in life, the anticipation was worse than the outcome. Nothing ever was mentioned.

With Eisenhower's victory in 1952, I went to Washington to start my government service. After getting the news by phone from Congressman Ted Miller's office I blurted out to my high school principal, M. U. Zimmerman, "I'm going to Congress! I mean as a page boy."

And I really loved being in the whirl of Capitol Hill at the age of fifteen. Every morning I started classes at the Capitol Page School in the Library of Congress at 6:30 A.M. All day I ran errands for Congress with my home base the page desk on the

House floor. Democrats were human although wrong in their views. In fact, I discovered congressmen of all viewpoints were all too human. I found myself in these ornate marble halls, imposing oil portraits of the famous staring down the corridors of history at me. And on my second day on the job a Congressman from Mississippi tripped and fell on his face on the House floor. "Drunk again," one of the senior House employees muttered within my tender young earshot.

What was this?

I arrived on Capitol Hill believing members of Congress, like Abe Lincoln, were at the very least demigods. Now before my very eyes one of them was drunk, not unlike my father back home. For good or ill, members of Congress turned out to be much like the people they represented.

There was, for example, the otherwise conservative midwestern congressman who was notorious for the open bar he ran in his office, as well as the beautiful redheads on his staff. And there was the prim and prissy congressman from a western state otherwise known for its rugged cowboys. Father of several children and well regarded in his fundamentalist church, if not Washington, he seemed always to be standing at the urinal in the Members Rest Room (which the staff also used), especially when the bigger and more muscular page boys were relieving themselves.

"My, you are a big boy, aren't you?" he would say, chancing a pinch if the kid looked as if he would not object. While such an unexpected midstream encounter could cause havoc with the front of your trousers, the word got around quickly to avoid Congressman so-and-so: "He pinches!"

But who could say "no" to a congressman? Some members of Congress seemed to adopt a few of the "good-looking" page boys, even though they were not their political sponsors. This often meant invitations to dinner or a movie and whatever else I had no idea. Not being in the "good-looking" class, I contented myself with second- or third-hand accounts of events. Little of real shock value was proven except when a page ran off with the blond daughter of the Swedish Embassy air attaché later to be found in a Pennsylvania motel.

I came home one evening to find my terribly embarrassed roommate in bed with a muscular blond gentleman ten years his senior. Dropping into a Capitol Hill rooming house to visit two young male friends who worked for the House of Representatives I did not call out before I got to their bedroom door, which was open a crack. As I raised my hand to knock I saw through the slit they were locked in nude embrace on their double bed. I tiptoed away.

Just as I tiptoed away from the thoughts in my own mind concerning my sexual feelings.

Working the hours of Congress, often a ten- or twelve-hour day, studying back at the rooming house before we fell into bed, getting up before dawn for school, none of this left much time for a social life. Since there were no girl pages many of my fellow pages made contacts with local girls, picking up young tourists in town with their school group, or dating the daughters of Capitol Hill staffers or congressmen.

I had a few dates with Martha Mills, daughter of the powerful Rep. Wilbur Mills of Arkansas. (Nearly thirty years later Wilbur Mills, by then a recovering alcoholic, played an important role in getting me to stop my drinking, putting me in touch with groups that gave me the direction and willpower to deal with my own problem.) And for a time I was enamored of the daughter of Idaho Senator Herman Welker, Nan, whose father was, during the McCarthy 1954 censure session of the Senate, his chief defender and floor leader. After attending the 1956 Republican National Convention in San Francisco, where I was an assistant doorkeeper, I visited the Welkers at their home in Payette, Idaho. A rugged outdoorsman and criminal lawyer, Welker was defeated for reelection that fall by a little-known young man named Frank Church. The sleepy-eyed swaggering Welker had been suffering recurrent blackouts and the word was spread in the heavily Mormon parts of the state that the senator was a drunk. Only months after his defeat was he diagnosed as having an inoperable brain tumor from which he later died.

But the daughters of senators and congressmen, while a pleasant diversion, could not interfere with my near-total immersion in politics. I really did not need romance. At various times I lived with one, two, three page roommates. Any sexual activities were for the most part strictly onanistic and in private. When other pages were boasting of their making out over the weekend I was relating the excitement of Maryland campaign trips boosting Ted Miller's 1954 reelection.

At my senior prom I danced with my biology teacher, Naomi Ulmer, whose caustic wit was a match for my own. She was an excellent teacher but the major biological questions I needed answered remained for a much later formulation in my mind.

After a few weeks on Capitol Hill, I really needed no further proof that congressmen were human, but one evening even I was impressed at how far up the political power structure human frailty extended.

I was alone studying in my second-floor apartment on Second Street when the buzzer rang. When I opened the door there stood one of the elected leaders of the U.S. House of Representatives, a slim paper bag obviously containing a bottle of booze tucked under his arm. He immediately blanched when he saw my face because he knew me from the House floor where I often greeted him. He also knew that my recognizing him held the potential of trouble. Not only was he a party leader, he had a wife and several children and was well known nationally in his party, as well as a leader of his religious faith, the dominant religion in his district and state.

I am not sure why but I greeted him without using his name, perhaps an involuntary reflex trying to preserve what was left of his ruffled dignity. He said he was looking for "Miss Smith," I shall call her, a rather beautiful and curvaceous young Hill secretary who lived in another apartment. The gentleman had simply pushed the wrong buzzer, much to his embarrassment.

"Oh, she is in apartment number one," I cheerfully told the gentleman, trying not to look too much like a canary-swallowing cat. I pushed the right button for him and as I hastily disappeared up the stairs the lady in question flowed out of her apartment door in a cloud of chiffon dressing gown and delicate perfume.

Not all were so indiscreet as the gentleman I encountered.

Even in the early 1950s, rumors were rampant about the young Senator John F. Kennedy of Massachusetts and his romantic interests, and we all had to wait many years for proof. Coincidentally, it was in 1954 that I was interviewed for the "Inquiring Reporter" column of the old *Washington Times Herald* on the subject "Should there be girl pages?" The reporter was a wide-faced, dark-haired young lady named Jacqueline Bouvier. As usual I opposed this far too liberal departure from page tradition.

In spite of a lot of talk about the need, there was no official dormitory for the pages. So from 1953–55, when I graduated from Page School, I lived in a series of Capitol Hill rooming houses and small apartments, finally settling on Second Street N.E. on the site of what is now the Hart Senate Office Building, only half a block from the Supreme Court.

At various times I lived in different houses in this row of old Victorian buildings. In one, another page and I shared a second-floor rear apartment looking out over a small courtyard-garden typical of the Hill. On the first floor the two house owners lived, middle-aged federal workers whose dress and manners, I should have realized, were just a bit too correct and a bit too accentuated. I knew so little that their effeminate gestures, constant parade of male friends, and double-entendres meant little to my pristine teen-age mind. Somehow I never associated any of my own sexual feelings with the antics of these two queens. I knew little about homosexuality, except in a locker room sense, and the word "gay" in its current sense had yet to be invented.

When a mustachioed friend of our landlords propositioned me in the hallway, placing his arms around my waist, I uncomfortably and firmly disengaged myself, declining an honor the nature of which still puzzled me. My main reaction was one of worry. "Is there something about me that attracts such people?" I asked myself.

Not to worry too much.

Within a short while our landlords moved away and rented the first floor to a wonderfully exciting middle-aged "maiden lady" not unlike the character of "Auntie Mame." Perhaps not so flamboyant as Mame, Elizabeth Barrett Winspear was an accomplished publicist, writer, and editor who worked with authors Christopher Morley and Gaylord Hauser during her New York years. To me she quickly became just "Betty" and later, after my marriage, "Aunt Betty."

A commander in the U.S. Navy reserve, Betty traveled the world, each summer doing two weeks duty in exotic places such as Japan and Italy. Her cinderblock and board library shelves sagged with delightful authors I discovered for the first time: James Thurber, Robert Benchley, T. S. Eliot, William Faulkner, Ernest Hemingway. Undoubtedly these were sophisticated people, since I had never heard of them. And there were the cartoons and articles the weekly *New Yorker* provided.

Betty taught me a great deal about life; how to prepare chicken tarragon, choose wine, conduct one's self at table, about movies, Broadway shows and musicals, a little opera, and how to make coffee in a Silex. In return I need only talk with her, a pleasure I was eager to pursue, and sometimes fix Sunday brunch if she slept too late. Her jet black cat, acquired in Paris, named Ayrab (pronounced "A-rab"), was a constant companion except when roaming the alleys of Capitol Hill. Then Ayrab would return only if she heard the whistled Russian folktune "Meadowlands." I swallowed my innate anti-communism and learned the tune since I was often called upon to "cat-sit."

Years later Aunt Betty became a part of our family by consensus, visiting at holidays, attending my swearing in to Congress in 1973, proudly and quite truthfully telling my wife, Carol, that she had taught me to cook and iron shirts. And much about life as well.

I don't know what prompted the question but one day a year or so after I first met her Betty casually asked me, "Robert, are you queer?"

I was astonished. My reply reflected my consternation. "Why ever would you ask me such a thing?"

"I never see you dating girls," Betty said, "and I just wondered."

And it made me wonder seriously about myself. Here I was going on seventeen years old and she was quite right; I did not date girls. Had the worldly-wise Betty seen something in me that I had purposely avoided seeing in myself? Was there some telltale sign? Had she seen my roommate and me "fooling around?" Oh, God, maybe I am queer, I thought. Is that what it means if you don't date girls?

And if I was "queer" just how would I know if I was?

I tried to shut out this frightening possibility that insisted on invading my consciousness. But Betty's casual question reopened a compartment in my mind I had assumed to be firmly latched, until now.

Fifteen years later, in 1969, Aunt Betty, then living with Ayrab's successor cat in a small townhouse in Washington's Foggy Bottom, opened her eyes one morning and found her vision blurred. She noticed that her motor movements were also beginning to balk her mental commands. Tests indicated an inoperable brain tumor growing at a rapid rate.

I visited her at the Bethesda Naval Hospital as her sturdy body wasted away and her pleasant face contorted. To the end she kept up a steady stream of witty conversation, puffing her beloved Pall Malls.

Unlike my mother's 1945 funeral I could not bear to go to Betty's service, although I was an honorary pallbearer. When her last will and testament was read she had willed me two of her prize antiques, a mahogany corner cupboard, and a cherrywood dropleaf Pembroke table. She also bequeathed me the sum of three thousand dollars.

Once a researcher for the *New York Review of Books* called to ask why a lady who had been such a close friend of Christopher Morley had bequeathed a sum of money to a Maryland congressman?

When I told him the story of Aunt Betty and the page, he understood.

College years are supposed to be the time of carefree abandon. While I worked and studied hard, I was not dead to the urges of the flesh. If my constant all-consuming activities gave me a mental excuse for not dating girls I certainly did not consider myself to be "queer" as Aunt Betty had offhandedly suggested a year or two before.

But something did not seem to be working quite right.

Evidence in point: One summer during college my roommate was another former page, a brilliant student who obtained honors at Harvard and went on to become a successful New York attorney, member of Governor Rockefeller's staff, and a Reagan administration official. From his page days he had a steady girlfriend who lived in a wealthy northwest Washington neighborhood. Now, back for the summer, he invited me to go along with him and his friend who would supply a date for me. Somewhat reluctantly I agreed and was surprised when my young lady was an attractive brown-haired girl who laughed and listened to my chatter. Our foursome had dinner, went to a movie, and afterward we split. I walked my date home to the Woodner Apartments on upper 16th Street where she lived with her mother.

When we got to her apartment she invited me in, although it was almost midnight. In those long-ago days that was late for a date. She informed me that her mother wouldn't be home until the next day. "Why don't you stay awhile," she asked, smiling sweetly.

Oh, brother, I thought to myself. What do I do now? I wasn't really sure I wanted to stay but stay I did. As events progressed we found ourselves sitting quite closely on the couch, her knee touching mine, her arm resting lightly against mine, her fingers gently touching my hand, all points of wildly electric contact for me.

I guess I knew what she had in mind. I wasn't totally dense. But even in this exhilarating situation I seemed physically incapable of doing what comes naturally to most people. As if mentally straining at an emotional leash I could not quite summon up the courage, for that is what it would have required for me, to kiss the young lady. So I fell back on the wits of the budding politician and began to talk; talk about anything and everything until I exhausted my inventory and my companion.

She kept insistently turning the conversation back to the obvious subject two nineteen year olds would usually do more than just discuss. Well, talk I could do but *do* I could not.

At great length, certainly after 3:00 A.M., I begged to take my leave, though I didn't believe I really wanted to go. As I started out the door she leaned forward, closing her eyes as she did, and kissed me firmly on the lips. And for a brief moment, I kissed back. Fool that I was, I backed away, thanked her profusely for the lovely evening, and beat a hasty retreat, trying to calm my glandular reactions.

As I descended to the street in the Woodner elevator I alternated between ecstasy and self-reproach for having left the scene of a possibly beautiful accident. So elated was I by this heterosexual experience I determined to walk the entire distance from upper 16th Street N.W. to my place on Capitol Hill, perhaps thirty city blocks or more, whistling and skipping much of the way. It took me hours but at dawn I fell into bed still ecstatic. But I never pursued the matter or the young lady further. I was, perhaps, too afraid.

There were some other odd phenomena that occurred in my life without much conscious choice on my part.

I had the usual casual attraction to the "girly" magazines that were permitted in Easton during the early 1950s, leafing through their colorful pages surreptitiously at the local newsstand, every once in a while screwing up the courage to make a purchase. Those were of course pale imitations of the explicit sexual depictions the U.S. Supreme Court was eventually to rule a constitutional expression of free speech.

But some time during that same decade there appeared a small pocket-sized magazine entitled *Tomorrow's Man,* or *TM* for short. It was not like the "body building" magazines I had seen wherein bulging mountains of male flesh shone from every page. Those specimens were too grotesque to associate with any humans I ever encountered. They definitely did not appeal to me in a sexual sense.

But *TM* was different. While it made a pretense of being for body builders its pages were filled with very scantily clad young men, many of them quite muscular, but others much more natural in their physiques, "swimmers' " bodies, smooth and supple. While frontal nudity was yet to pass muster with the censors, *TM*'s near nudity was perhaps the most daring of its time. I would gaze at the photos and think, "That's what I would like to look like. Then people would respect me." And I never missed an issue of the magazine. To assuage my Catholic conscience I bought a set of barbells and weights and began to work out, for a while.

To be honest it never occurred to me that the stirrings I felt within my emotions and my groin while viewing such photos were anything but a momentary aberration, maybe a passing phase. For a time I even banished the gnawing feelings of minor guilt by the catchall phrase at my frequent confessions, "impure thoughts." As I confessed the "impure acts" rarely did the priest inquire what that meant. I just assumed the priest on the other side of the confessional screen knew I meant the great American male pastime of masturbation, a ritual that for most males has survived well-meaning parental threats of disease, insanity, and hairy palms.

I not only wanted the world to accept me, I wanted to "look good" to others. Though I did not then realize it, most desperately, I wanted to be accepted by myself.

I always had a tendency to be overweight and by the time I reached eighteen or nineteen I piled more than 160 pounds onto a short five-foot six-inch frame. I lamented my weight but did little, although eventually I tried crash diets, at one point swallowing my political pride and trying the "Rockefeller Diet," high on red meat and grapefruit. By chance a Capitol Hill secretary recommended a suburban physican who made weight reduction his specialty. Dr. Harry, as I shall call him, really specialized in pills, all sizes and colors. They were what is now known as "speed" and although they did curb your appetite, they also dried out your mouth, prevented sleep, made you constantly thirsty, and caused your emotions to stay on a roller-coaster ride. I loved them. I not only lost weight, I slept less, kept bouncing around like a rubber ball, talking constantly, even more than usual, and I always had to be doing something. But I did lose twenty pounds.

It took me more than a year of losing and gaining weight, on and off the pills and their associated highs, before I stopped. That this episode was a sure forecast of my addictive personality I had not the slightest idea.

Here I was about to turn twenty years old and had only a vague knowledge of what sex was all about. Oh, I knew God meant for men and women to marry and procreate. That was the standard by which all other sexual activity was to be judged, at least by the Catholic church. That moral dogma was reenforced by my stepmother when at age thirteen I brought home a single-pack Trojan in its bright orange wrapper that I had found lying on the street. I stupidly left it on my bedroom dresser, receiving an immediate condemnation of the possible conduct it suggested.

So I knew what was wrong. But I also knew boys at home and at military school have sex together. And girls and boys not joined in holy matrimony fool around. And even congressmen fool around. My God, who knew what Lincoln might have been doing with Ann Rutledge in the back of that country store in southern Illinois? I got the impression that whatever "standards" might be, an awful lot went on in the adult world that did not meet their "standards" or even come close.

But I encountered a life of open and unabashed homosexuality when I met someone I shall call Joe.

We were introduced by a young page from Mississippi who rented a room in Joe's rooming house. The page, a southern lad with a charming drawl, assured me Joe was "crazy but a lot of fun."

And that he was. Joe lived on Capitol Hill with his younger lover, both from a rural area of the South, both working at minor jobs for the Pentagon. Their real love, I soon discovered, was being homosexual in the big city.

Joe collected all sorts of odd objects he crammed into his row house completely furnished in period Victoriana, right down to the milk white glass fixtures on the gas lamps. The house was filled with a trove of valuable music boxes ranging in size from your hand to a small piano. There were thousands of 78 rpm phonograph records dating back to Edison and beyond, boxes of phonograph cylinders played on special machines, one with the actual voice of Teddy Roosevelt speaking about "The Strenuous Life," a favorite topic of the physical-conscious, rough-riding President. There was every conceivable kind of record player from hand cranked to stereo. There must have been at least ten player pianos, most unassembled in some state of repair. Paper piano rolls were stacked everywhere.

In other words, the place was fascinating.

And equally fascinating was the way Joe lived. A constant

stream of neighborhood young toughs, college boys, young male Hill employees, even the Metropolitan police from the local beat, dropped into his house each night, especially on the weekends. Some stayed longer than others and some stayed all night. Joe simply loved men, young and old, and having sex with them.

Joe cheerfully ran his house of openly ill-repute, making no effort to conceal his activities from his neighbors, including the church across the street. He owned, repaired, and wheeled about in three ancient Ford model A's and T's, often full of laughing young men. His snow-white-haired mother lived a few doors away where she ran her own "straight" rooming house. Mother and son seemed to fight constantly over nothing, always mending their quarrel in time for dinner, which they took together.

For a time I rented a room from Joe's mother and it was not just this proximity to Joe and his merry band that produced urgings of interest in me. There were momentary relationships with some of the young men I met at Joe's house, mostly my own age, but they never lasted more than an hour or two. No attempt was made to really know the person except in the most superficial way. Once the encounter ended we parted quickly to avoid the implications of what we did. I am sure many of the young men were as convinced as I that this was only a passing phase. Each time I would feel great guilt and head for Saturday confession at St. Peter's or St. Joseph's on Capitol Hill so I could make amends with God and be in the state of grace for Sunday Communion. I would always vow to myself and God I would never do it again. Sometimes my vow would last for weeks or even months.

"Bless me Father for I have sinned." And sinned, and sinned and sinned. In time this pattern of conduct assumed proportions experts would tell me constituted a "compulsion," an involuntary reaction to a set of given stimuli. To so define what I was doing is not an attempt to excuse myself or avoid responsibility for my actions. But I was actually able to convince myself that what was happening was transient in nature, not a deep-seated problem. I knew something was wrong but I was just as certain I could not be a queer. That possibility was too horrible to contemplate, much less accept.

And then one lively summer evening about dusk it happened for the first time.

It was 1957 or 1958, I had a few months of blessed relief from college, and I was out for an evening of fun. As I came down the steps from my rooming house near the Supreme Court I saw a dark-haired young sailor in navy whites walking toward me. He had a duffle bag over his shoulder and a smile on his face.

He stopped and asked directions to the main route to Baltimore. He had just come in from Norfolk on the train at nearby Union Station and, short on money, he said, wanted to hitch a ride home the rest of the way. (The old "short on money" routine which I was too green to recognize.)

I told him truthfully it was easier to give him a ride to a good hitchhiking spot than try to explain it and my trusty 1932 Packard was parked nearby. (I had purchased this automotive beauty a few years before for the sum of five hundred dollars, naming it "Lou Henry," after Herbert Hoover's wife.)

I cannot to this day explain what happened next.

Something occurred between this young sailor and myself, some undefined understanding we both accepted. Without words we knew what was going to happen. The mere thought made my head dizzy, my heart beat wildly as if it would burst. After a moment, both faces masked in solemnity, eyes searching for some sign of disapproval or danger, he smiled again, making plain he had more on his mind than a ride to Baltimore. It was a couple of hours later before I let him out of "Lou Henry" at the entrance to the Baltimore-Washington Parkway.

For the first time in my life I had picked up a guy (or he, me), a man I did not know. Drained but emotionally satisfied, I realized I almost enjoyed the terror that I had felt in my heart, the fear of rejection, even the possibility of violence. I risked all that for what? Just for the chance to go to bed with an attractive young man?

I momentarily considered but rejected the possibility I was sick. This young sailor wanted to do what we did and he did not seem sick to me. Indeed, he was an exceedingly healthy young man. I could swear to that.

Whatever was wrong with me, I did know that it had to stop, not because of any peril, but because the danger was far exceeded by the immorality of my conduct.

I hastened to confession the very next day.

In spite of this first-of-a-kind encounter during my college years, 1955–59, I really had no time or desire for emotional relationships with anyone. My aim was to get through Georgetown University's School of Foreign Service with reasonably good grades so I could be admitted to the university's law school. Any remaining passion was spent on my Capitol Hill job and politics. Time for fleeting sexual encounters was brief and usually with someone I knew from my neighbor Joe's wide acquaintance. I did not date girls, reasoning that would come in time.

I consciously avoided learning about homosexuality because I did not want to know. And in those distant days of the fifties, sex was not the lead story in every publication from the *Reader's Digest* to the *Homelitic Review* as it is today. Somehow I did manage to spot and read all the small items in the press about some unfortunate caught in a compromising homosexual situation such as the western preacher who might be viewed as an incipient Jerry Falwell of yesteryear. The Reverend's radio show and fundraising quickly dried up when stories got out that he and several male aides engaged in more than religious experiences together. And why did I tuck away in my files, where I recently found it, a copy of an October 1964 issue of *Time,* folded open to the page on which appears the sensational story of President Lyndon Johnson's top White House aide, Walter Jenkins, having been arrested while having sex with a man in the restroom of the Washington YMCA? At the time nervous liberals feared the Jenkins scandal might tip the election to Barry Goldwater! Jenkins, Catholic, married, father of several children, quietly disappeared from the scene, was taken care of by the Johnson establishment in Texas. It turned out he had been arrested for the same charge several years before but the Washington police file was covered up after intervention from higher government powers.

I vaguely recall thinking as I read the Jenkins article in 1964 (*Time* only gave me a few lines in 1980): "What must that poor soul be feeling now that he is exposed? What had his life been like all these years?" I did not dwell on those questions because the answer would have come too close for my own comfort.

Undoubtedly it is difficult for anyone to understand or believe that a boy, a man who suspects himself to be homosexual, can practice life-long self-deception, can actually convince himself that a major element of his personality is simply untrue. It can be and is done hundreds of thousands of times each day. Someone recently referred to me as "an admitted homosexual," but that was not an accurate description during most of my life. I admitted nothing, especially to myself. Long after public exposure I was still fighting this acceptance. And to some extent, I must admit I still have difficulty with that acceptance. I lived most of my life with an internal dread I dared not address though it was always felt. Not given to deep introspection and self-examination, I was startled a year or so ago when I encountered the quote attributed to Socrates: "A life unexamined is a life unlived." By this measure I lived hardly at all. I blotted out my doubts, my actions, submerging myself in the excitement of politics where compliments, victories, and deference helped reassure me I was a good person. Rather than accept myself as I was, I fought for symbols and abstractions promising greater glory and meaning to my life. If I could save the world I might avoid having to save myself.

My homosexual encounters were an aberration that plagued me but I would overcome this by sheer force of will. What I really needed was someone I could love, who would love me. That was what I was searching for. An end to the aching loneliness and empty feeling inside.

And then I met Carol.

On the evening of November 18, 1960, the eve of our wedding day, we had a rehearsal and dinner. I had a few drinks with the men but it did not really qualify as a bachelor party. I already had moved into our new apartment on A Street near the Capitol and when I came home on this last night alone, this last as a single person, I could not get to sleep. It was more than the usual prenuptial nerves. I was deeply troubled.

Well after midnight I dressed and went out into the dark, damp streets. I walked to the Capitol, the familiar dome illuminated in the mists. I thought of Carol and I, one night months before, walking through the silent building, footsteps echoing on the marble, silent statues of the great seeming to watch as we passed. We sat in the darkened House Chamber, in the front row of members' seats, only a small light over the American flag behind the Speaker's chair glowing. We talked, whispered, of many things, our dreams of the future, our love for each other. In the soft quiet of the big room there were sounds, creakings, rustles, memories of the past.

I realized that night just how lucky I was to find a person like Carol to share my life. It was not only our common interests but her goodness I imperfectly thought would help to make me whole.

Now on the eve of our wedding I had serious doubts that I was worthy of her. What would she think, this good Catholic young lady, if she knew of some of my past actions? I conjured a picture in my mind of some nameless figure who would rise up in church the next morning, some specter from my past, responding to Monsignor Heller when he intoned that traditional request that anyone having an objection to this union "should speak now or forever hold your peace."

Maybe I should be the one to cry out at that crucial point.

And as I returned to restless sleep in our new home I wondered what I would do even then if some appealing young man came out of the dark and smiled at me. I got down on my knees beside our bed and prayed that God would deliver me of this curse; that the next day would bring the beginning of a new and different life. As I drifted off to sleep I convinced myself that with God's help and this good person about to be my wife I would become the good person I always wanted to be.

In the early years of our marriage I usually managed to adhere to the better path I desired. Encounters with other men were few. Although I started out as a relative novice in heterosexual experience I found our physical relationship to be pleasing and reassuring. Perhaps I was proving to myself that I was normal. Maybe all I needed was to prove my manhood in the traditional American way. My love for Carol grew as her sweetness and solicitous concern gave me a needed feeling of being wanted for the first time since the death of my mother.

And yet, when a handsome, well-built young man came into view on the street or at a party I might experience an undeniable mental and physical reaction signaling that within me the worst still lurked.

When it happened, as inevitably it did, it was always the same. The encounters were furtive, brief, with no attempt to know the person or even his name. Usually I was the aggressor seeking some sort of symbolic possession of the physical attributes I recognized in the other person. His body's form, muscular development, facial features all had to appeal to me. And if that right combination was found I knew it instantly. In having sex with this person I was somehow adding to my own being, trying to fill in the enormous gaps, strengthen the weaknesses I knew afflicted me. I was seeking what one psychologist calls "complementarity," a certain elusive fulfillment that only such an act with another man could produce in me. The momentary gratification of another's acceptance, of being valued for myself, of a conquest over someone I deemed in my mind's eye to be more perfect and attractive than I was; all this produced exhilaration.

Years later only the closest professional probing brought me to

185

the realization of just how alone, how inferior I felt during most of my life. My near self-hypnosis allowed me to believe my carefully constructed exterior facade of a bright, brash, opinionated young politician. But beneath the surface I drove myself to prove, to others, to myself, that I was a worthwhile human being. But I did not believe it for a minute, as much as I wanted to.

In May 1963, I faced a tough week of law exams at Georgetown. Customarily I tried to keep up with my night law studies on a daily basis, reading and briefing cases in my spare time late at night or in the Cloakroom when the House was not in session. This week I had crammed hours for the exams. When at last they were over I felt I had done well. As often happened my elation translated itself into lessened inhibitions.

It was warm for early May and driving home after the last exam I felt the fresh night air, hinting at spring, on my face. I suddenly wanted to wind down and just "let go."

As I drove the short distance from the law school to Capitol Hill I stopped for a red light. On the curb were two muscular young men thumbing a ride. One approached the open car window and asked for a lift. Impulsively, without even considering the inherent danger of letting not just one, but two strangers into my car, I told them to "hop in."

"Where are you headed?" I asked, a slight tingle in my body.

"Down near the navy yard," was the reply.

"Isn't there a queer bar down there somewhere?" the other asked.

The implications of that question were plain. Instead of a sudden chill of fear, I seemed to tremble at the possibilities.

I was mildly concerned my questioner thought I was a homosexual, that there was something identifying in my appearance, but I reasoned maybe they were interested themselves in such a place.

In a few short blocks we easily established they were indeed interested in sex of an immediate and homosexual nature, that they did not have "a place to go," but they knew an appropriate spot down near the Anacostia River next to the Naval Air Station where they were in service.

I stupidly drove them to the suggested place, a dark stretch of river front concealed by a grassy bank. I followed them when they got out of the car and without warning one of them wheeled on me, delivering a tremendous blow to the left side of my face that staggered me, knocking me to the ground. As I lay pinioned to the ground, the two looted my pockets, emptied my wallet, and threw it on the ground.

Convinced I had nothing else of value, they let me get up. It was then I put my hand to the point of contact on my face, now numb with pain. A wave of fear swept over me as my fingers, suddenly sticky with my own blood, slipped into what seemed like an enormous hole in my cheek. My teeth had apparently cut through on impact, creating an opening big enough for a finger to go through. As my head began to throb I felt my mouth filling with blood.

The two forced me to drive them back to the vicinity of the marine barracks, where they jumped out and ran. They need not have been concerned about pursuit by me. I was weak, in semi-shock, slowly realizing my predicament. I could never have identified them since the violence erased any memory of their faces.

I had gone off to law school for an exam a few hours before, was now only a few minutes late in returning home to Carol, but I had a gaping hole in my face, was bleeding profusely, with no idea of what sort of medical help I might need.

Carol stared in horror as I came in the door, rushing to help. I stumbled to the bathroom and was shocked myself at the size of the rip in my face. It was obvious that stitches would be required to sew up the wound and that meant finding a doctor or hospital emergency room.

In summary what I told Carol was a lie but in its bare essentials true enough; I picked up a hitchhiker who demanded money, and when refused, he hit me and left the car.

We drove to Capitol Hill Hospital where I got emergency treatment, several stitches, antibiotics, and tetanus shots. "It's pointless to file a police report," I told Carol, "because I could never identify him anyway."

Within a day a serious infection ensued and my face swelled up like a balloon. Only massive doses of penicillin saved me from far more serious consequences, my doctor later told me. As it was I was in bed three days, all the while terrorized that Carol would want to know more.

God only knows what Carol really thought. After her initial questions she fell silent on the subject and never brought it up again. Throughout the ordeal her focus was concern for me and my recovery. My own selfish goal was to conceal the truth. Looking back it is difficult to believe the degree of insanity marking my own self-deception and that I tried to impose on my wife. At some point surely I was not the only one engaged in self-deception.

After we bought our own home on A Street S.E. in 1964 my strange conduct began to draw Carol's serious attention. With two, then three young children, our maid, Frances, often baby-sat for us when politics or social life required a night out. Afterward taking Frances home only ten blocks away often took me an hour or more. "Where were you? What were you doing? Why did it take you so long?" All legitimate questions.

And, of course, I could never truthfully answer.

There was no specific destination. My pattern never varied much. I drove around aimlessly hunting, looking for some young man, about my age, walking the street late at night, headed home or out looking for similar adventure.

Often I aborted my nocturnal travel, overcome with the enormity of what I was doing, fearful of Carol's reaction. I would go home, hopeful Carol was asleep, thus avoiding a confrontation. If she did ask I mumbled something about "stopping for gas." Nobody stopped for that much gas. At first she avoided pressing me, perhaps fearful of what she would discover.

One evening, driving home by myself, I picked up a hitchhiker who immediately placed his left hand on my leg. His intent needed no elaboration and I drove him to the ACU office in response to his statement that he had "no place to go."

As we stepped into the darkened office the young man underwent an instantaneous Jekyll-Hyde transformation. What had been a most accommodating gentleman suddenly became a snarling animal with a menacing switchblade knife in his hand. Adrenaline pumping, I managed to convince him there was no money in the office, that people lived upstairs and might hear any noise. I gave him what little money I had. All the while my heart was pounding, my mouth dry, my head dizzy. At last he shoved the knife to my throat. "All right, queer, take me to your home and we'll see what you have there."

Belatedly I thought of Carol and the children, determined I would never take him to our house. I had to escape this nightmare. My panic cleared long enough to recall that the nearby Coronet Hotel was open all night with a desk clerk on duty near the street-level entrance. I drove there, jammed the car to the curb, jumped out, and sprinted into the hotel. I vaulted over the desk into the arms of the shocked desk clerk, screaming "Call the police."

There was no need. My would-be assailant fled the scene on foot, but it was a long time before I screwed up my courage enough to get back into my car and drive shakily home.

Then there was the disastrous day when Carol called me at the Cloakroom to relay an anguished call she got from our housekeeper, Frances, who, she said, was near tears. It seemed that Teddy and his neighbor–best friend, Nicky, then four years old, were playing in our basement recreation room when an ominous silence warned Frances. She found them leafing through a couple of all-male nude magazines I thought I had carefully concealed. The boys thought this was hugely funny but Frances, a devout churchgoer, reacted in horror, producing the call to Carol.

I got home first so Carol never saw the offending "literature."

Somehow I was never able to explain the utility of these publications, but I don't recall being forced to do so.

Another nail had been driven into the coffin of our marriage.

Perhaps worst of all, for purposes of temptation, our Capitol Hill home was only two blocks from the house of Joe the Queen. Although I was not a regular visitor it was the same old neighborhood. I would see Joe zip by in his Model A Ford loaded with laughing young men. Infrequently I would meet some of his ever-changing circle of friends.

In a perverse twist I rationalized the doctrine of the Catholic church to aid and abet my sexual appetite. "Good Catholics" believe the only acceptable form of birth control is the rhythm method. Based on the daily female body temperature, the degree variation allows a usually accurate prediction of days on which ovulation occurs and pregnancy might result. Practically this means half of each month is off limits for intercourse in order to avoid pregnancy. When my adventures happened it was usually during those two weeks each month.

How could any normal and moral human being do what I did?

How could anyone, however callous, repeatedly be unfaithful to one's spouse, lying, evading responsibility, breaking solemn vows?

I have described how it could be done. Why I did it is the serious question.

And I have no answer, even to this day.

I do not know.

In many ways I was driven by a force over which I seemed to have little control. Of course my choice was conscious and deliberate. It could have been altered. But some compulsion drove me, blotting out all I had learned, diminishing in importance all that was most dear and important. I seemed willing to risk my marriage, my wife and children, even life itself. I might easily have become the subject of one of those brief, puzzling newspaper accounts in which some prominent figure, a man, is found dead in his auto after having given a ride to a young man of indeterminate description. One promising young Maryland official suffered just such a fate and a protective press was careful never to explain too fully.

Here I was a young man achieving one career success after another, yet willing to gamble everything for an instant of physical release with a person I did not even know. I engaged in acts, which, if exposed, would destroy all I worked for and harm those I loved.

And yet I felt compelled to act as I did. Some inner force drove me and repeatedly pursuing this insane conduct made it more difficult to resist each time I was tempted again.

Most amazing was my failure to consider asking for help. Each time I would feel shame, remorse, and guilt. That tough trio of emotions gnawed at me constantly. I prayed for deliverance, went to confession, always at a church where the priest would not know me. Sometimes I would go for weeks, even months, without incident, and then something would set me off; a period of depression, an event that brought elation. Setback or triumph, there was no set pattern of causation each time but repetition seemed inevitable.

How Carol must have suffered in those dark and sleepless hours waiting for me to come home. Then only to hear lame excuses and denials. The anguish of fear and not knowing was surely worse than the truth. Yet I gave little consideration to Carol's pain. My primary concern became keeping the truth from her. Fortunately for the success of my deception hers was not a demanding personality. She often suffered in silence, unable to change the situation, not understanding what caused it.

But if she did not fully comprehend the dilemma Carol thought she might have found a solution. Gently at first, then more insistently, she began suggesting we should leave Washington and move back to Easton.

In 1964, I finally graduated from Georgetown Law Center. During 1965, I struggled repeatedly and on the third (and under bar rules, the last) time I passed the Maryland Bar Examination.

In June 1965, Carol stood in the old Maryland Court of Appeals Chamber as I was sworn in as a member of the bar. Now I could go home and practice. Hadn't that been what all the work and study was about? It would be 1968 before she finally got her wish and we moved to Easton.

During the 1968 presidential campaign I agreed to serve as paid executive director of the Citizens for Nixon-Agnew. I set up headquarters in the old Emerson Hotel in Baltimore. Weekends I would return to Washington where Carol and our three children were still living.

Away from Carol, alone many evenings, there were two more indicators of future trouble.

I never drank anything but beer and white wine, and of the two, beer had the preferential edge. I drank too much beer. Married in 1960 at a trim 145 pounds, I was edging up over 165, and beer was a large part of the expansion. When I dined at the Polynesian Restaurant in the Emerson my habit of downing Heineken's caused the Chinese maitre d' to call me "Mr. Green Beer." Soon I was drinking to get that familiar "buzz."

The second flag was my encounter with what is now called a "gay bar." Rumor had it there were bars catering exclusively to homosexual men. I even stepped into one in Washington one night only to meet another member of the Young Americans for Freedom board of directors. Both of us feigned confusion and beat a hasty retreat. In Baltimore I learned there was such a bar only a block from the Emerson Hotel, called "Eddie's," after its owner. It was located in a side alley off Charles Street, its small entrance dramatically under a lone street lamp.

For a few nights I nervously "cased the joint" trying to get up enough nerve to go in, but an inexplicable fear gripped my heart. Having talked with others about their first encounter with a gay bar there emerges a Rubicon-crossing pattern about this momentous step. Picking up a guy who is thumbing a ride is one thing. But the conscious choice of entering a gay bar is, for many, in a very real sense, an admission of a sexual status they would rather deny.

I finally overcame my fear of whatever it was, perhaps being recognized (though I reasoned I was far from home), and once inside found it to be a most ordinary place. The clientele was of all ages and descriptions and did not appear to be homosexual, or at least to my untutored eyes. I was in that quaint stage of attitudinal development which amusingly believes you can spot a gay person by his or her appearance. (In fact, when I returned to the hotel after that first visit I kept peering into the mirror to compare my face with those I had seen. If I am like them, I thought, could anyone tell by looking?)

I went back to the bar a few times but nothing happened, although I did run into a local Baltimore City Republican official I knew slightly. Neither of us acknowledged the implication of the meeting.

Once we moved back to Easton in 1969 there was little opportunity for any sexual contact. But there was some. Walking down a sunny street one day a handsome, dark-haired young man came toward me, our eyes met, and we both knew what the visual contact meant. He stopped and used the timeworn gambit: "Do you have the time?" What happened did not take much time.

Although I was careful once I was elected to the State Senate it meant I was away from home intermittently for ninety days each year. I definitely began drinking too much. When the Maryland Inn bar closed for the night I would weave up to my room, often passing an attractive young blond maintenance man who always smiled and spoke cheerfully. One night he cheerfully followed me to my room. In the cold morning light he was gone but my hangover lingered on.

In print these recollections sound as if I were totally promiscuous. In fact such events were few and far between. But they were happening with much greater regularity when I had the opportunity.

One incident during my State Senate career bears retelling, even though it received little notice.

On the last night of one of the ninety-day sessions the annual glut of last-minute legislation was as bad as usual. It is the time, as the State House saying goes, "when the snakes come out."

There was one bill I determined was not going to crawl through. Proposed by a liberal Democratic Delegate from Baltimore, Maryland, Maclyn McCarty, the bill would have made illegal discrimination by renters in the city of Baltimore. I discovered the ban on discrimination extended not only to racial, ethnic, and religious bias, but also sexual preference as a grounds for refusal to rent. Anyone claiming such discrimination could sue the allegedly offending landlord. When McCarty heard I opposed the bill he came to me, bending down next to my desk on the busy Senate floor amid the rush for midnight adjournment.

He pleaded for me not to object to the bill's consideration, a power any one senator had to kill last-minute matters, but to go ahead and vote against it on record. He pointed out the bill only applied to Baltimore city, would not affect my own rural area, that it had the backing of city officials.

"Am I correct it would force a landlord to rent to a homosexual a room in a private home?" I asked. Admitting that, McCarty said people should at least have a right to a place to live. "Wouldn't a homeowner be forced to rent to someone who engages in immoral conduct in that home?" I asked further. He replied that "immoral conduct" was a matter of broad interpretation; anyone could be evicted if he violated the homeowner's rights or the law. "Who are we to decide what constitutes moral conduct?" he asked.

"Just don't bring up the bill," I told him firmly, "or I will be forced to object to its consideration." At midnight the bill died along with many others.

Maybe this was my way of fighting the dread threat of homosexuality even as I was fighting within myself without acknowledging the battle existed. That my ignorance hurt others I did not

even consider. It was not one of my best legislative hours. It justi-
fies nothing that now, more than a decade later, the current Baltimore City Council still refuses to pass an ordinance banning
discrimination in employment against gays or lesbians as of this
writing, futher evidence of the persistence of prejudice and ignorance that once afflicted me.

When the Bauman scandal appeared on the front pages in 1980
a predominant theme of the sordid story was hypocrisy. Here was
a leading conservative congressman who preached on "family
issues," supported the right to life and staunchly opposed abortion, had even sponsored anti-pornography bills. Now he had
been caught, as the old saying applies here all too well, "with his
pants down." It was alleged I was "aligned foursquare with the
Moral Majority and the New Right and all the fundamentalist
groups that have been holding up the Bible and holding back the
tide. . . ." That from *Washington Post* columnist Judy Mann.

Whatever the validity of the hypocrisy charge, in truth I was
not exactly a leader of the Moral Majority or the New Right. My
votes and my actions were based on what I believed to be right
and I did not coordinate or clear them with anyone. What especially seemed to offend was the tone and manner of my personal
public style. I was too "righteous," Bill Buckley wrote, suggesting
I cultivated "an Elmer Gantry–like quality." (I read Sinclair
Lewis' book afterward and was offended by the comparison. But I
understood the allusion.)

For the news media it was just a short jump to a conclusion
that was demonstrably untrue, that my career had been marked
by gay-baiting, that I had publicly condemned homosexuality
and gays, that I was "a leader of the anti-gay faction" in Congress, as columnist Jimmy Breslin wrote. The charges were never
followed by any direct quotations, however, for good reason. I
never made any such statements.

Fearful of my own sexuality, still trying to maintain the inner
sham, I studiously avoided the "gay issue." This avoidance was
not difficult because the issue rarely came before Congress in any

form that required my comment or vote. On roll call votes on the gay issue I twice voted against homosexuals receiving equality of treatment under the law that all American citizens deserve. These votes came in 1977 and 1980 when my friend and colleague from Georgia, the late Congressman Larry McDonald, offered his amendment to the Legal Services Corporation authorization bill. The amendment would have banned ". . . legal assistance for any litigation which seeks to adjudicate the legalization of homosexuality." Although there was no debate in 1977 on the amendment, my own interpretation was very close to that which eventually became the government's position when the McDonald language became law, that the amendment did not bar legal civil cases which do not seek to adjudicate the legalization of homosexuality nor does it prevent an attorney from defending a client who claims discrimination based on his or her sexual orientation. In any case the client would have to qualify under poverty standards, showing that an attorney could not be hired privately because of lack of funds. The amendment clearly did prevent government-paid lawyers from representing indigent gay clients seeking to legalize homosexual acts or mount constitutional challenges to consensual sodomy laws. And that is and remains as it should be in my view. Government and the taxpayers have no obligation to expend funds to aid in legal battles against laws governing homosexuality, heterosexuality or any other sexuality. Indeed, I did not support the existence of a Legal Services Corporation at all, believing this was not a proper role for the federal government. But surely if such a federal program was to exist, in equity no person who is qualified to receive assistance should be denied help on the arbitrary grounds of sexual orientation. My votes were wrong.

Perhaps more serious hyprocrisy was my co-sponsorship of the "Family Protection Act" first introduced in the House and Senate in 1977 by then Congressman (now Senator) Steve Symms of Idaho and Senator Paul Laxalt of Nevada. This omnibus legislation included the entire conservative domestic agenda on issues affecting "morality" in general and the American family in particular. It was first called to my attention by my legislative assistant, Ronald Docksai, a brilliant young man who was himself national chairman of Young Americans for Freedom and now serves Senator Orrin Hatch of Utah as staff director of the U.S. Senate Committee on Labor and Human Resources. A devout Catholic, Ron told me the new bill was co-sponsored by all the leading congressional conservatives. It contained such laudable proposals as tax credits for private and parochial school tuition, prayer in schools, tax credits for home care for elderly relatives and parents, protection of the right to life, and much more. What I did not know (and if I had it would probably not have made any difference) was that the bill allowed overt discrimination against gays and lesbians based on their sexuality, sanctioning government-protected exclusion of gay people from employment, housing, and other areas.

How wrong I was in taking these stands was to be forcefully driven home to me in a few years as I myself felt the sting of economic discrimination because of my own belatedly accepted sexuality. I was wrong in my votes and in my co-sponsorship of the bill, but the price I have since paid for knowledge has been high, appropriately so, many would say. I could not accept my own sexuality and I acted in public consistent with my religious and moral beliefs, even if my private life was totally inconsistent.

While I avoided public comment on the issue of homosexuality, I addressed the subject in several letters to constituents who asked me to support gay rights legislation. My responses were drafted by my legislative assistant, Ronald Docksai, and rewritten by me. Fortunately they have been preserved as a good example of my state of mind on the issue when I was forced to address it publicly. What I said was an accurate summary of the conservative Catholic doctrine on the matter. Hinting at my libertarian attitude on private conduct, I said "I generally favor a weakening of those [governmental] measures restrictive of individual behavior when no harm is incurred by citizens or society."

197

I even managed to bring in "states rights," noting that most laws governing sexual behavior were state statutes which the federal Congress should not usually overturn without strong reasons. But the core of my argument went to the gay life style: "I do not accept the premise that homosexuality, like obscenity or drug consumption, is not inherently wrong but only that citizens like myself do not like or understand it . . . Certainly I could not approve of these practices . . . Personally speaking I believe that homosexuals are in need of treatment and cure . . ." In another letter I went further: "I certainly share your support for civil rights . . . At the same time, I cannot support legislation which would 'guarantee' jobs to citizens who were denied these jobs by other citizens believing that homosexuality is a perversion of nature. I subscribe to this view. I would not want my children taught or influenced by gay people if this could be avoided . . ."

Rereading those letters now I can still call myself a political conservative but I have learned the bitter lessons of discrimination against gays. And yet in the transformation of my own thinking I believe there is a lesson for all conservatives.

I have not become a convert to "bleeding-heart liberalism" but I know the party of Abraham Lincoln is too often viewed by potential supporters as rigid and uncompromising on issues involving the human condition. As a dedicated conservative, I found comfort and simplicity in abstract principles and ancient, valid doctrines. Statistics, bar graphs, and tables could be hauled out to illustrate a point about welfare costs, Soviet military growth, or crime. It was always easier to advocate a clampdown on "welfare cheaters" than to envision a squalid country shack where some black mother's children would have less to eat if stricter "aid to dependent children" rules were imposed from Washington. To rail against foreign aid was easier than visiting, as I once did, the mud-floored, tin-roofed hovels that pass for homes in the barrios of Managua. To look closely at why communism appeals to impoverished people whose children are dying of hunger in their arms does involve possible reconsideration of pat slogans about free enterprise and capitalism.

It was easy for me to write the laws and let others enforce them, to make the exhortations and let others explain. As Bill Buckley wrote of me: "It should never be supposed that sinners cannot effectively rail against sin, else there would be total silence everywhere." And I was not silent.

But how much more could be done by government leaders who wed a reasonable conservatism with a humane approach? If tenderness and compassion are to be desired in individual lives, how much greater their need in collective application? Blacks, the poor, the mentally defective, the handicapped, drug addicts, yes, even homosexuals, are all human beings created in His image. Which of us knows with certainty that fate will not cast us into a position in which we will need the understanding and compassion of our fellow men?

"Humane conservatism" is not an inherent contradiction in terms. Reasonably defined and applied by future political leaders it could provide an extended course for the change in direction Ronald Reagan has properly given America. But it would require the politicians to de-emphasize the papal "we" and a renewed exaltation of "the people" in the best traditions of Jefferson and Lincoln.

CHAPTER
SEVEN

Too many years ago to count, the late Hollywood actor, William Powell, starred in a then racy film entitled *The Senator Was Indiscreet*. As the title suggests, the debonair, suave Powell was cast as a respected member of the United States Senate, but one with a decided penchant for young ladies, all of whose names and curricula vitae he kept in a little black book. Which disappears. And thereby hangs the tale.

I never saw this film but I am eternally indebted to my friend, William Rusher, publisher of the *National Review*, for informing me about this masterpiece. He did so, ironically, on August 27, 1965, at a Washington testimonial dinner in my honor on the last day I served as national chairman of Young Americans for Freedom. Gathered at the Shoreham Hotel was a stellar group of young and older conservatives willing to speak in my behalf, including Congressman John Ashbrook, Rusher, Brent Bozell, Lee Edwards, Marylin Manion, and Tom Charles Huston, my successor as YAF chairman. The officiating clergy for the evening was Reverend Father John F. Harvey, O.S.F.S.

Rusher used the Powell film to illustrate what he said was my great political prowess at working out deals, handling situations in YAF, winning elections, and disposing of opponents before they knew what hit them. And unlike the indiscreet senator of movie fame, Rusher hoped I did not keep a diary since it might reveal "what happened at Chicago."

"Not Chicago," the senator said, crestfallen.

"Yes, Senator," his nervous aide said.

"And what about that evening in New York City?" the senator asked hesitatingly.

"That too is in the book," the aide said.

"And that weekend in Miami. Is that all in there too?" the senator said, sinking down into his chair with a look of abject defeat.

"It's all there, Senator, I am afraid!" the aide says.

Of course, this infamous diary had fallen into the hands of an unfriendly member of the press and the senator faces political, if not personal, ruination.

As for Bauman, Rusher said, he hoped that no one would ever find out what really happened in all those YAF board meetings and national conventions "in New York, Washington, Fort Lauderdale, and elsewhere."

Over the years I came to live in terror but not because of any diary. I constantly denied my homosexuality but continued to engage in conduct I knew had to be concealed lest my life crash down around me. This congressman was more than "indiscreet," courting discovery at every turn as I careened toward the inevitable end.

Armchair psychiatrists, and even qualified experts, described my nocturnal conduct prior to my downfall as "a cry for help." An old friend, former YAF national chairman and now national chairman of the American Conservative Union, David Keene, told ABC television's "20/20," "Bauman obviously wanted to be found out. Why else would a well-known member of Congress pay repeated visits to a gay bar, get drunk, and solicit sex from male prostitutes?"

Why, indeed?

But long before any public revelation came the repeated

brushes with private discovery. Looking back now I can see numerous instances when my conduct, which I thought carefully discreet, was really designed to reveal to someone, anyone, what was happening to me. Perhaps my unconscious conclusion was that someone else must deal with the chaos of my life because I was rapidly reaching the point at which I could not do it myself.

Over the years of our marriage there were few instances in which Carol and I directly confronted my sexual problem. But the hints became louder. Added to the unusual absences, the tardy returns at night, there were the photos of nude men. It was almost as if I wanted to be found out. After her initial anger at this scandalous material I was so overwhelmed at the prospect of what she might do I broke down and wept, tearfully asking her forgiveness of "this weakness of mine," a phrase that went undefined. Admitting to "a problem," I told her I felt it was under control, that I did not want anything to destroy our marriage and our family. I remember it was evening, late, we were sitting on our bed in night clothes, the only time of the day we often had to talk about anything, and I began sobbing that "this terrible thing" would not happen again. Carol took me in her arms and told me gently things would work out somehow. And I prayed God they would.

It was in 1978–79 that my health began to give me problems of an acute but mysterious nature. On the way to Sunday mass a sudden tightness in my chest caused me to turn the car around, drive home, get into bed, and call the doctor. When he returned my call hours later the symptoms had abated and he suggested it was just "tension and anxiety." "Slow down," he said.

Next I began to experience excruciating lower back pains, then upper back pains. Often it would be so bad I could not sleep at night. The slightest turn would wake me and I could not get back to sleep. An extensive series of X-rays showed nothing wrong pathologically with my back or nerve system. I was given prescriptions for powerful pain-killers, muscle relaxants, tranquilizers, and the like. I even wore a neck brace for a while, especially during the long hours while driving my car, a time when the pain was worst. Repeated hot compresses and physical therapy at the office of the U.S. Capitol physician provided only momentary relief. It got so bad that at times, sitting on the House floor during session, I could barely rise from my seat to make a point of order or ask a question.

But Dr. Freeman Carey, the Capitol physician, and several specialists from Bethesda Naval Hospital could find nothing that would cause such pain.

Finally, when the back pain seemed to subside, I began to suffer lower abdominal pains and stomach upsets. A complete series of abdominal tests and X-rays again showed no cause and eventually this too abated.

In early 1979 when I had my annual physical examination Dr. Carey noted that I had reached a peak weight, 185 pounds piled onto a medium frame only five feet six and one-half inches tall. I was a bloated pig. My clothes did not fit, I was puffing up stairs, and I looked like hell. Although tests showed my heart to be sound, my blood pressure was high and rising. Dr. Carey sent me to Bethesda Naval Hospital for more tests, including the famous stress test on the moving belt.

At last Doctor Carey called me in for the test results. He asked me a series of questions based on long years of Capitol Hill experience. I assured him I did not smoke and never had, a plus. But did I drink alcohol excessively? "Not me," I lied without hesitation. "About how many drinks do you have each evening, Congressman?" Dr. Carey asked. "Oh, maybe one or two, perhaps three at the most," I lied some more. And he must have known better.

Dr. Carey patiently explained his opinion that I was at a physical crossroads in my life. At forty-two, I had a sound and healthy body that showed no obvious signs of major problems. But he said, "You are greatly overweight and obviously under a lot of stress. Both of those factors are probably playing a large part in your back and other painful conditions." In his quiet bedside manner, he looked at me and said: "If you wish to live out your normal life expectancy you will have to make some major changes in your life style right now. Limit your diet, lose weight, start regular exercise, possibly jogging, and limit the intake of alcoholic drinks." He handed me a small booklet which elaborated on these themes and wished me well. "If you have any questions, just call me," he added.

I had a lot of questions in my mind, all right, but they did not pertain only to my physical state. One who always thought he had a high degree of certitude suddenly really began to doubt himself and many of the things around him. These growing questions were unleashed unexpectedly by a paperback book Carol brought with us to the beach at Ocean City in the summer of 1979. Authored by Gail Sheehy, *Passages* sought to describe the "mid-life crisis" through which modern men and women pass, using case studies. Much of what I read came too close to allow me comfort. From the symptoms described in the book I began to realize what a mess my own life had become. I never finished the book but it started me thinking as I sat there in my beach chair, my fat stomach hanging over my bathing suit.

It finally began to dawn on me I could not go on living as I had been. Something had to give.

In the winter of 1979–80 my drinking became worse. One Saturday evening I drove into Washington to attend the annual awards banquet of the American Enterprise Institute, honoring Milton Freidman. I got there late and was only able to throw down two drinks before the bar closed and dinner began. Fortunately wine flowed at dinner and afterward I was invited by Melvin Laird, former congressman and Nixon's defense secretary, to a party in the *Reader's Digest* suite at the Hilton Hotel where the dinner was held. By then I was feeling "no pain." I wanted to leave the roomful of stuffy politicians and journalists, to go out and meet some young man, to really have fun. I did, and I kept on drinking. About two or three in the morning I found myself driving along U.S. Route 50, between Washington and Annapolis, headed back home to Easton. But I also found myself asleep at the wheel, waking with a start as I heard the crunch of gravel on the road shoulder under my tires. It was not too late. I swerved the steering wheel to the left and instead of careening down a hundred-foot embankment to my probable death, the right front wheel went up over a guardrail. But the car continued along the guardrail for another hundred feet.

I sobered up in a hurry, quickly discovering my car (with Maryland "Congress 1" license plates) was going nowhere. A motorist called the state police as I requested and I was later ferried home by the troopers. Not a word ever appeared in the press, and I am, in retrospect, not grateful for that fact. Had I been treated as the drunk driver I was it would have forced me to face what I was doing to myself and others. But I was destined for a further fall.

A few months later, one evening when I was drinking, I stopped at the infamous Chesapeake House, and though nothing happened, on the way out I picked up a couple of gay publications lying on the bar near the door. I absentmindedly slipped the magazines under the front seat on the driver's side, intending to remove them later. I never had to.

The next day, a Saturday, I stayed at home in Easton. For some reason, I am not sure why, Carol asked to use my car. Either her station wagon was having problems or was low on gas. She drove into Easton on some errand and was home a little while later.

But as soon as I saw her stricken face, her desperate air, I knew something was wrong. Something terrible. Rarely had I seen her so agitated before. With growing panic I realized that I left the male magazines in the car and that might be the cause of Carol's state. Had she dropped her keys, her gloves, something, and reached under the seat?

"What's the matter?" was my way of trying to show concern but not wanting to know the true answer. And I said to Carol, my own nervousness evident, "What's the matter?"

I do not recall her response. I know that at first she did not want to talk at all. She apparently went upstairs and called Father John Harvey, because shortly she came down saying she must go to Washington to talk with the priest, immediately. Then my fear was confirmed. I begged her to wait until the next day, to calm down, but she insisted on going. "I have to talk to someone," she said with desperation. I insisted I would go with her, as though being with her could somehow erase what had happened. Perhaps I thought I could talk her out of telling Father. I don't remember much about the drive through that cold, damp January night in 1980, but I knew all the pretending was over. For both of us.

When we arrived at St. Francis de Sales Seminary we talked with Father Harvey for a short time, long enough to confirm what had happened. Then Father asked to talk with Carol by herself, for what seemed an eternity. After several hours, it now being quite late, he emerged from the room. He told me he believed a "very serious situation" existed in our marriage. He would like to talk with me about it, but not this evening. He suggested next Monday, two days hence, and we made a date for lunch.

How I got through the weekend I do not know. How did Carol survive? Now more than five years later I have shut out the horror although a certain numbness still lingers. Suddenly I was no longer the master of my own fate (if ever I had been). My life rested in the hands of my wife and a little Irish priest.

Although I knew Father Harvey had written extensively on theological matters (he and Carol often talked about them), I was ignorant of the fact that John Harvey had become one of the most respected American Catholic experts on the subject of the church and homosexuality. He acted as advisor to the National Conference of Catholic Bishops helping draft their 1973 statement on the pastoral counseling of homosexuals. He also conducted regular retreats, counseling Catholic priests, brothers, and nuns who suffered with personal problems of a homosexual nature. His writings on the topic were extensive and his humane, understanding treatment of the issue from the traditional church viewpoint gained him respect from both sides, though his view was fundamentally uncompromising.

It was a very cold, clear, sunny January day when Father Harvey and I met in the Members Dining Room of the House of Representatives for our initial talk. We sat by a frosted window although I could gaze across the Capitol Plaza to the Library of Congress and my old alma mater, Capitol Page School. People, bundled against the biting cold, were scurrying along emitting puffs of steamy breath. It was a view I had seen a thousand times, and yet I knew everything was different. Nothing would ever be the same again.

Father and I talked in low conspiratorial tones. Generally he related what Carol told him about the magazine incident but also her suspicions over the years, the incidents, the problems, my drinking, the debts. All the "little things" I tried to suppress, to ignore for years, had grown into an unsightly pile of emotional refuse both Carol and I must deal with though I was not ready to admit that. Father made clear our talk was only preliminary, that he needed to hear my side at length before he could give advice. He suggested, and I agreed, we meet that evening at the seminary where he lived, the same place Carol and I visited him the Saturday before.

As we left the dining room, greeting other members of Congress, shaking hands, being introduced by my colleagues to their luncheon guests, I thought what their reaction might have been had they known the nature and topic of my talk with Father. What an item for "The Ear" column in the *Post*. But maybe now, I mused, it will never come to that. Maybe we can work it out.

That evening, while my staff member, Kevin Sard, waited in the reception room, John Harvey and I sat in a small institutionally furnished parlor used for just such counseling sessions. Father's tight-eyed, smiling Gaelic visage beamed empathy as he sat across from me and said simply, "Now, Bob, why don't you tell me what's on your mind and I'll listen."

And for the next two hours there was little that Father could do but listen. Haltingly at first, then in a torrent of repressed emotion and memories, I poured out the story of the Bob Bauman nobody knew. The story you now know.

Months later Father confided that it was terribly painful for him to learn that in more than four decades of life I had never discussed any of this with another human being.

At length I was drained. Father Harvey suggested what I told him be considered as my confession. He put on his vestments and gave me absolution for my sins. His response throughout was compassionate, understanding, without condemnation.

It was obvious from what I told Father that my comprehension of my sexual problems was limited in many respects. So Father gave me several clinical and spiritual books regarding homosexuality. We agreed to meet within a week and I gave my permission for him to discuss my words with Carol to the extent he judged it helpful. I made it clear that my objective was to save our marriage, if that was possible.

I left St. Francis de Sales Seminary with a physical and spiritual feeling, as though a great weight was lifted from my shoulders. At long last I had shared this terrible burden with another person who understood. Father Harvey assured me the vengeful God of wrath I fashioned in my mind was, on the contrary, a loving, caring, and forgiving God who accepted me as I was. I doubted this assertion, since I could not accept myself, but at least I now had hope. I had unburdened myself of my sin before man and God and I was forgiven. Now I could go about setting things right. I could live my faith, save my marriage, my family, and my soul.

One factor which loomed large in our discussion was the role alcohol played in my sexual activities. Father Harvey had only to listen to correctly assess how I used drinking as a catalyst for sexual conduct. He directed me to his friend, a clinical psychologist, John Kay, Ph.D., in suburban Maryland. Kay, he told me, specialized in problems of alcoholism as well as homosexuality. He also counseled students and taught at a Washington area university. I began regular appointments with Dr. Kay almost immediately and he also met with Carol.

I avidly read all the books Father Harvey gave me; accounts of Catholic gays who said they kicked the habit; experts arguing that homosexuality is a mental illness, moral depravity, simply a problem of rampant self-will, and even an unchangeable human trait to be accepted and made the best of. And I asked for and got more books, rapidly depleting Father's extensive library.

Dr. Kay had difficulty breaking down my pride to reach the point at which I would consider the possibility of my being an alcoholic. I kept repeating I did not drink that much, I could stop any time and had done so, that complete abstinence was just not necessary in my case. Kay conducted various basic psychological tests and one conclusion he shared with me: "In all my thirty years or more of practice I have never seen a more self-contained, isolated, and alone individual than you," he said.

For three months, from February to May 1980, Dr. Kay kept chipping away at my considerable reserve, allowing me to slowly realize the tremendous turmoil in my life, how abnormal my view of reality was, what havoc I caused for myself and those around me. If there was any comfort from all this it was my gradual realization that what I was describing was not my agony alone, that many others suffered from similar compulsions and problems. There was hope of recovery.

But first things first, Kay said, and he strongly urged me to associate myself with established groups that deal with alcoholism in a self-help setting. This I resisted, not only because of my pride, but because of the fearful possibility I might be recognized, a concern that never bothered me when I was doing my nightly cruising. And all the while I was seeing Dr. Kay I kept drinking, tapering off for a while, switching from the "hard stuff" to beer and wine. But none of these home remedies, which I was to discover are quite common at this stage of concern about alcoholism, seemed to help. I still got drunk and I periodically found myself out cruising again. I simply could not and would not accept my alcoholism or my sexuality. But by seeking professional help I no longer could claim the defense of ignorance about what I was doing.

Now I knew, but that did not stop me, not yet, anyway.

Dr. Kay's quiet, gentle approach, his deep probing, focused on the problem at hand—my alcoholic drinking. There would be time enough later to talk about sexuality in depth, but first I had to sober up and that meant no more alcohol ever again.

"You mean I can never even have a glass of white or red wine at dinner?" I asked incredulously.

"Never again," he insisted.

I did not want to hear it. But gradually I began to learn from the twice-weekly sessions just how unmanageable my life had become, how important drinking was in my life. How I needed it to calm down, to keep going, to avoid the truth.

Although my ignorance hid it from me I had been drifting into alcoholism for years. The dictionary defines "alcoholism" as "a diseased condition due to the excessive use of alcoholic beverages." That simple definition is more than I then knew about the problem. Had anyone asked me, one thing I knew for certain, I was not an alcoholic by any definition.

Like most Americans I absorbed unconsciously all the myths surrounding alcoholism, then employed them in my mind to assure myself I had no problem. After all, alcoholics were those dirty stumblebums nodding off on street corners, a bag-wrapped bottle in their hand. I couldn't be an alcoholic because I never drank before 5:00 P.M. I was just a "social drinker." I never drank much more than beer (at first), further proof of my nonalcoholism. And if I did drink it was usually on weekends. Besides, I was too young to be an alcoholic. And, of course, the real clincher: I knew I was not an alcoholic because I could quit drinking any time I wanted to stop. It was to take me time and lots of counseling before I realized the vast majority of America's nearly twenty-two million alcoholics are, to all outward appearances, "ordinary people" with decent jobs, maintaining their families, and "getting along," although usually with a great deal of difficulty caused by their drinking.

The mixed reality of life and motion pictures provided my own first recollection of drinking alcohol. In the 1940s, when my musician father worked at the Earl Theater in Washington, it was obligatory (he thought) to have an annual series of Christmas parties for the boys in the band. (Our little row house was so small that one big party would have been an overload.) My dad, who eventually understood and overcame his own alcoholism, would invariably get drunk at these parties which he tried to film, his hobby being the making of 16-mm home movies. The early part of the film would be acceptable enough but toward the end of the reel somebody else would hold the camera. There Dad would be, weaving as he walked, swaying back and forth on some lady's lap, his face and nose red, his puffy eyes half closed. And in some of these same films, at that very point, little Bobby Bauman moves into the camera's view, dressed in pajamas, all of four or five years old, rubbing his sleepy eyes. All the drinking musicians, their wives, and girlfriends make a fuss over me and I am rewarded with a tiny shot glass full of beer. It may well be that my first drink is recorded in living Kodak color. And there is good old Dad pouring.

Over the years my father's alcoholic behavior impressed me sufficiently that I made a conscious decision never to drink. I acquired a strong antipathy toward alcohol which grew in direct proportion to my father's increased drinking as his own life became more difficult. My mother's death, a not always happy second marriage, economic decline, and disappointments all pushed him to the point where he would start drinking early in the day, drink on the job, and fall into bed drunk. His chosen poison was a cheap sherry wine labeled Thunderbird but affectionately called "sneaky pete" by my father. The empties could always be found under the front seat of his car.

In the last few years before his death in 1965 my father faced the awful reality of his alcoholism, associated himself on a regular basis with other recovering alcoholics in groups devoted to their common welfare, and became quite active in helping others who suffered from the problem. Coincidentally, Carol's father, Gene Dawson, followed a similar path, living his last few years in complete and active sobriety, helping others as he had been helped.

Save for my own youthful encounter with beer in a shot glass, I never took a drink until I was almost through college, about the time I entered Georgetown Law Center, my twenty-second year, when I was elected president of the university Young Republicans. Consciously aware I was waiving my life's rule against drinking, I reasoned a sociable beer now and then with the other students would not really be a problem. It made me "one of the boys," and the slight buzz helped me overcome my inhibitions. My quick wit seemed to speed up a bit, my jokes seemed more amusing, life seemed lighter and, should I say, gayer. My first glass of wine celebrated my first date with Carol, though I did not let her know what ground I was breaking. ("Ah, yes, Blue Nun seems like a good label to me. A bottle for two, please, waiter.") That was December 1959.

But until the end of my drinking in 1980 I did not think for a moment I drank "too much" or that alcohol really was a problem for me. In the early years of our marriage I did not drink a great deal and for a long time I drank nothing but beer and less frequently, wine, usually only with meals. Within a few years I graduated to gin and tonic in the warm-weather months, although gin invariably gave me a headache. Next came bourbon and ginger ale; the fuzzy bubbles seemed to get me high faster. (Early Times was my bourbon because that is what I recalled my father drank. Eventually I graduated to that smooth sour mash "George Dickel.") Somewhere in all this bibulousness my firm resolve not to drink was conveniently forgotten.

My first memories of drinking to produce a psychological state of mind, that euphoric "high" we alcoholics seek, dates from the early 1960s when Carol and I would attend Capitol Hill parties staged by our young conservative friends. Drinks once spaced at one each half hour began to follow one right after another. I looked forward to that sensation of tightness in the brain and around the eyes, that buzz, that allowed me to cruise awhile when I drove the baby-sitter home instead of coming right back to Carol and her reproachful gaze.

And I began to get drunk when I drank. Before I had been able to "hold my liquor," but now I found it difficult to walk that straight line. And there were occasional "hangovers," nothing serious, you understand, but a noticeable physical disability that caused morning-after discomfort. Thus was I introduced to Alka-Seltzer. By the time I took my seat in the Maryland State Senate in January 1971, drinking might have become, I began to consider, a bit of a problem. Now and then I would consciously decide to stop drinking for several days, once or twice for several weeks, but I could "never stay stopped." Oh, it was not that I *needed* to drink, I just wanted to, and so I resumed. Usually I told myself I stopped doing it "to lose weight."

During the ninety-day sessions in Annapolis my hotel room in the ancient Maryland Inn was just an elevator ride away from the basement bar. But when you are a state senator you need never buy a drink for yourself. There are always parties, dinners, and receptions every evening at which lobbyists ply you with unlimited free drinks. You could drink all night and never have to pay, and too often I began to do so. The late night that handsome blond maintenance man accompanied me back to my room I was so drunk I could hardly walk.

But such heavy drinking episodes were the exception, I told myself. Besides, as I looked around at my fellow legislators, everyone drank. Surely my conduct differed little from the norm, at least the Maryland General Assembly norm.

One thing I was quite sure of was that drinking, at least openly excessive drinking, did not mix well with political success. My churchgoing constituents might imbibe a little themselves but temperance was important. There were plenty of cocktail parties to attend in the line of my political duty but State Senator Fred Malkus' narrow loss to me in the 1973 special congressional election taught me a lesson. If you are going to be in politics you must drink moderately, leave it alone entirely, or conceal it. At various times I had tried all three and finally settled on the latter course. Fortunately for me, unfortunately for Malkus, his reputation was as a heavy drinker, too heavy, or he might have gone to Congress.

Soon, perhaps in the middle 1970s, I reached the predictable point where I did not get that high as quickly. I had to drink more to achieve the same reaction. That high became ever more elusive. Just when the third or fourth or fifth drink would produce that effusive feeling of well-being and relaxation, the sensation would slip away and I would have to keep on drinking. My drinking had to be affecting at least Carol because I recall she began to quietly suggest at some point in a social evening, "Bob, don't you think you've had enough to drink?" Usually the answer was an irritated, "No, dear!" I began to down a drink or two in the kitchen before Carol and I would go out to a party (careful that she not see me) so that I could lay down "a base" of booze for the evening. At a Washington reception or an Eastern Shore party I would skillfully rotate from one bar to another, confident I could thus double my intake without anyone noticing how many trips to the bar I made.

There were many times at home, a bar, a party, when I would quietly repair to a corner and intellectually consider whether or not I was getting drunk. I would accept the fact my head was dizzy, I had consumed an unspecified number of drinks, that I might be acting less than sober. I would try and get "outside myself" and examine whether my motor control was impaired, whether I was slurring my words, whether anyone else was likely to realize maybe I had too much. Always I concluded this internal debate in favor of myself. That is to say, I would convince myself I was "j'es fine" (as Pogo used to say) and order another drink to celebrate having passed my own rigorous test for personal sobriety. That is how the drug called ethyl alcohol works on the brain.

I was never a "morning drinker" and it was very rare for me to drink at lunch. There were practical reasons. I just had too many responsibilities during the day. I could not impair my reason or ability when the fate of the world, or at least the Congress, rested on my shoulders.

But evenings, and those few weekends at home, away from the public eye, especially those who might be voters, I did overindulge. Lee and Anne Edwards were guests overnight at Glebe House, old friends from the YAF years, and Teddy's godfather in Lee's case. We invited some close friends for dinner. The last thing I remember was pouring stingers after dinner, a lethal mixture of white crème de menthe and brandy over ice. I fell down once and when I awoke it was dawn. But I was not in bed. I was lying flat on my back on the floor of the library, staring up at the ceiling.

My hangover was so painfully intense that I could not get out of bed to bid the Edwards good-bye later that Sunday afternoon.

Now I began to insist on driving home after having too much to drink at a party, often brushing Carol out of the way and getting in the driver's seat. Summer vacations with friends at Ocean City turned into one long week of drunken evenings and nursing hangovers on the beach the next day. Even after wives would abandon us at some club, my several associates would stay 'til closing and then have nightcaps when we got home.

It was during my summer beach drinking in the late 1970s that I switched to ice cold vodka on the rocks as my favorite libation. Two or three of these would mainline right to my brain and I would be on the way to a full evening of alcoholic fun. One night I made a pass at a handsome, tanned young man who was assigned to drive me home (Carol had long since left the party). For my pains the thoroughly heterosexual lad opened my vacation apartment door and threw me in face first. "What was all that noise about last night, Dad?" the kids wanted to know the next morning as my head throbbed. Frankly, I could not exactly remember, but I knew I had done something wrong, experienced an unguarded moment in the wrong place. But when nothing happened I erased the incident from my already dim memory. I later learned at least one friend did not miss the implication of my conduct but preferred to ignore it. ("He was just drunk," he reasoned.)

By 1978, I was definitely drinking far too much and yet I was unable to realize it. In the classic phrase, "my life was becoming unmanageable." Our family economic situation was getting desperate. Carol had gone to work selling real estate in an attempt to make ends meet, the pressure of my daily schedule never seemed to lessen, and I added the post of ACU national chairman to my growing roster of duties.

If I did not have an engagement or meeting in the evening after the House adjourned I would go to my office, finish my paper work and phone calls while drinking a bourbon or two, and then go to dinner, usually at the Monacle, a favorite Capitol Hill watering hole. My companions might include a member of my congressional staff, usually one who lived in Easton and could later drive me home, plus one or two of the House floor staff members, Ron Lasch or Don Anderson, my rules committee aide, John Scruggs, and often, the minority staff director of the Rules Committee, J. L. Cullen.

We would rehash the day's floor battles, talk Hill gossip and politics, and generally relax. But we, or at least I, would also drink.

I would start with two or three vodka martinis with olives and olive juice (very important). During dinner I would have several glasses of wine, maybe half a bottle if there were only two of us. After dinner I would have three or more Irish coffees ("Heavy on the whiskey, please"). Then I turned to the lethal stingers on the rocks once again. All this consumption of alcohol would occur in the space of three hours or less.

I would then get into my car and either drive home to Easton, if I was not with a staff member, or on other occasions with growing frequency, to a gay bar where I would drink still more.

There were times when I did not get home to Easton until three or four in the morning, have to get up at 7:00 A.M., shower and shave and get back to the Capitol, eighty-five miles away, by 9:30 A.M.

There were nights when I did not come home at all, holing up drunk in a downtown Washington motel, often with some trick I picked up from the streets or in a bar.

And yet, if anyone told me of the insanity of what I was doing to myself, my wife, and family, I would undoubtedly have protested that they were wrong. I could control myself and my life. I was certainly not an alcoholic, and I had proven that often by stopping my drinking.

I really knew nothing about alcoholism except that I was not one of them, either.

Denial is one of the classic symptoms of the alcoholic and I practiced it almost until the end. For me drinking and the euphoric high it temporarily produced was an escape from a reality I no longer wanted to face, could no longer deal with using my own meager internal resources. Of course I just drank more and more and increasingly I would begin hiccoughing, lose motor control, vomit, slur my speech, generally make an ass of myself. But I was not an alcoholic.

It seemed necessary for me to drink to do what I increasingly found it necessary to do—go out and pick up young men for sex. I needed the "courage" of the bottle to go against everything I had been taught, to betray my wife, and dishonor my family. And being under the influence helped to wipe away the reality of who I was, that I might easily be recognized, that I could even wind up dead in an alley somewhere in downtown Washington just as many others in similar circumstances have done.

The insanity of my conduct is crystal clear to me now but then it was impossible for me to see, hard as that might be to believe. It rarely if ever occurred to me I was courting disaster every second I continued. That alcohol was playing a large part in my downhill slide escaped me completely. Theories about alcoholism as a disease, a genetic predisposition, a psychological addiction, all were unknown to me. I just knew I wasn't in that category. I could manage my own life. I had no idea that I was a drug addict, addicted to a drug, etherlike and hypnotic, a sedative compound C_2H_5OH, on which I was regularly overdosing.

No one can offer conclusive evidence about what causes alcoholism in a given individual. Recent studies indicate it may result from heredity, or even chemical imbalances in the brain and body that block normal assimilation of ethyl alcohol, creating a dependence on it. But most alcoholics drink to relieve tensions and worries, to escape from the reality of their lives. Thus alcohol becomes a substitute for maturity and the ability to cope with the world around you. For the person who has a low opinion of himself, poor self-esteem, drinking momentarily helps him create the mythical person he wants the world to think he is.

Many alcoholics seem to have a tremendously inflated ego, whatever they truly may feel inside themselves. We all know the drunk, sober or not, who is insensitive, impervious to others, pompous and self-centered, plowing unthinkingly through life bent on doing what he wants to do, whatever the cost to others (and often himself). Such a person may be prideful, arrogant, domineering, aggressive, attention-seeking, opinionated, stubborn and impatient. (Does it begin to sound as though I am describing someone I know?)

Sigmund Freud advanced the opinion that such a person, one whom we would call "egotistical," is in many ways infantile in his conduct. In his priceless phrase, such a person can be described as "His Majesty the Baby." Like the infant when first born, the alcoholic is the ruler of all he surveys, tolerates frustration poorly, and must do everything in a hurry. Often such a person harbors the childish attitude that he has some special role in life that sets him apart from mere mortals. This status confers special rights; his success and victory only confirm this special status. Conversely, such a person deals poorly with defeat, thinking of himself as being unstoppable.

One can easily see how such a personality would resort to the abuse of alcohol allowing the instantaneous creation of a personal condition in which he can believe himself to be king, unable to be stopped by anyone or anything.

Long before my own alcoholism developed I decided I was someone special in this life. Eventually I came to believe I had been conferred some exceptional role to be played out, in this case in the forum of politics and government. Certainly my own feeling of inadequacy does not detract from the correctness of many of the principles which I espoused but often part of the motivation for good acts stems from less worthy causes.

And alcohol helped me to escape from my undeserved success because deep inside I knew that there was something dreadfully wrong with me as a person. There was this fatal flaw that prevented me from being the husband and father I wanted to be. At bottom, in those darkest recesses of the mind, I knew that I was less than a man. And for that terrible offense I had to either escape or be punished. In drinking I tried escape and thereby assured punishment.

I needed the "courage" drinking gave me. How else could I relax the moral and philosophical strictures by which I was said to live, by which I said others must live. So fundamental was the conflict I felt that at times it manifested itself in physical ways. As my car wove through the darkened streets of the nation's capital city, now and then running a red light, the alcoholic haze would lift from my brain long enough to force consideration of what I was doing. A powerful physical sensation would come over me, convulsing my body, shaking my limbs, my hands trembling as they tightly gripped the steering wheel. My jaw would twitch, my teeth chatter, and the condition would even impair my speech until I could "get hold" of myself. I needed that drink. And yet another.

On such nights my objective would be a visit to the "meat rack" on New York Avenue N.W., near 13th Street, that seedy strip of gay bars, porno book stores, fast food chains, and young

male prostitutes, "hustlers." I would be part of the passing automotive scene as varied as those who seek companionship, including Cadillacs, Mercedes, and transport of lesser glory.

There I would be, driving my big blue Mercury bearing license
plates with the Maryland State Seal and the legend, "Member of
Congress 1." My head throbbing from the drinks, I would edge
up to the curb and, without the need of words, a nod of the head
would cause a young man to jump in, eager to seek my momentary and monetary company, providing the price was right. On
more than one occasion members of the Washington Metropolitan Police witnessed this little vignette. Long before my public
downfall they were not unaware of the nocturnal habits of the
gentleman from Maryland. Almost from the start, whenever that
might have been, they knew.

From February 1980 until the end of April, I continued to fight
the assessment that I was an alcoholic. And finally there came the
night when I could no longer deny my alcoholism.

It was Thursday night, May 1, and the House had adjourned
for the traditional long weekend. I finished my office work and
went to the Monacle with J. L. Cullen and John Scruggs. For a
month or more I had cut back on my drinking, a noticeable
change that brought comments from my dinner associates. My
own office staff began to ask questions about my appointments
with Father Harvey and Dr. Kay.

I cannot remember what set me off that evening of May Day
but I know I started out dinner with my old friend the vodka
martini, a drink I had not dared in several weeks.

I do recall getting more and more drunk as dinner progressed.
The question became, should I drive home to Easton or would I
head downtown. I don't remember much about the rest of the
evening except that I consumed a great deal of alcohol. At some
point I checked into one of Washington's poshest hotels, the
Madison. I then went out on the prowl, picked up a young man,
ironically named "Ted," and brought him back to the hotel. Each
suite of the Madison has a well-stocked "honor system" bar al-

lowing you to drink as much as you like. The amount is then billed to you. I recall we drank a lot. So much that I passed out and nothing happened between us. When I woke up the next morning I was nearly disabled by the hangover. I crawled to the bathroom on my hands and knees and vomited repeatedly. And when my head cleared enough to allow some logical thinking I remembered I had been with someone the night before.

When I checked my wallet the cash was gone. So was my wedding ring, a gold band that Carol gave me inscribed with our initials. My gold pocket watch survived only because I placed it in my side coat pocket rather than on the dresser. And when I finally pulled myself together and struggled downstairs, I did not have the slightest idea where my car was. I could not remember anything about where I parked it. I slowly circled several streets and finally called the D.C. police after the Madison doorman assured me that it was not in their garage. Almost two hours later I discovered my car across the street about a block away.

Fortunately I had scheduled a morning appointment with Dr. Kay that very day. I drove to his office early and waited in the parking lot, my head throbbing, my stomach in turmoil. Most of all my mind was scared and confused. I was about to accept the idea that I was an alcoholic, that I must do something quickly. I had suffered my first prolonged "blackout."

The moment Kay saw me, he asked, "What's happened to you, Bob? What's wrong?"

I immediately poured out as much as I could remember of the story of the ghastly night before, concluding meekly with the statement, "Doctor, I think I am an alcoholic. I need help. You were right."

Kay, who for almost three months had been trying to get me to attend meetings of groups dealing with alcoholism, saw the time had come. He flipped open his address book, looked up a phone number, and dialed. On the other end of the line was the famous "Buck D.," a Washington-area alcoholism counselor and recovered alcoholic himself. Within half an hour he would meet me for lunch at the Holiday Inn in Bethesda. We would go from there. That night I attended my first meeting with Wilbur Mills, my former colleague from Arkansas. I had not seen Mills since his highly publicized escapades with the infamous Fanne Fox, a strip-tease dancer at the Silver Slipper on Washington's 14th Street. For the next several months Wilbur and Buck acted as my sponsors, making sure I was in good shape and attended meetings.

The date of my Madison Hotel adventure was May 1, 1980, and, thank God, I have not had a drink since.

In spite of all my problems the summer of 1980 was one of life's high plateaus.

I had stopped drinking. For the first time in nineteen years of marriage Carol and I were learning to open up, to talk with each other. Our family life seemed to improve markedly. Emotionally and spiritually I was beginning to feel the effects Dr. Kay predicted after thirty or more days of abstinence from alcohol. He and Father Harvey were giving me the counsel and support I long needed. I was starting to learn something about who and what I was. More than once I egotistically thought to myself, My God, if I have accomplished all this while suffering these disabilities, how much more can I do now that I have stopped drinking and face my problems? Little did I know how far I had to go. But "drying-out" euphoria is not unusual for recovering alcoholics.

Others seemed to notice a change as well.

Mary Russell, writing in the *Washington Post,* said:

> Until this Congress Democrats brushed [Bauman] off as bothersome and pesky but not significant enough to make them change their ways . . . Now that assessment is changing. Bauman is winning some votes. He is branching out, taking an interest in more substantive issues . . . A Democratic vote counter said, "It used to be we could tell Democrats coming on to the floor for a vote it was a 'Bauman amendment' and we would get an automatic 'No' vote. Now they want to

know what the amendment is about . . ." Freshman Republican Newt Gingrich of Georgia says many of the new Republicans look more to Bauman for leadership than they do the elected leaders . . . "Bauman is the real leader of the opposition party," Gingrich said.

Another reporter asked me what gave me the most pleasure and wrote, "Oddly, Bauman says what gave him the most satisfaction this year was when he helped [Speaker] O'Neill out of a procedural bind on the cargo preference bill. Afterward O'Neill came up to him and thanked him. 'When you fight with someone all the time it is nice once in a while to be able to help the guy,' says Bauman."

In an article entitled "Congress's 'New Right' Makes Its Mark," *U.S. News and World Report* featured me along with Senators Orrin Hatch of Utah and Richard Lugar of Indiana, Congressmen Jack Kemp of New York and Phil Crane of Illinois as ". . . among the five most effective young legislators, exerting influence beyond their numbers . . . true movers and shakers." The article said: "Robert Bauman . . . has a mastery of House rules and parliamentary procedure that frequently gives him a leg up on his colleagues . . . This would have less effect on the House if the Republican lawmaker were a man of timid or uncertain views . . . But Bauman . . . is deadly serious about being the House's resident whistle blower. Anytime the House is in session America is in danger."

Perhaps Allen Ehrenhalt of the *Washington Star* best captured the change in a Sunday feature on June 8, 1980:

> Some of Robert E. Bauman's House colleagues think he may have turned the corner last week in a long march from mischief to party leadership.
> The Maryland Republican was in his familiar place on the floor all week, arguing, objecting, and using the rules to cause confusion on the Democratic side of the aisle.
> But when the argument was over he had not just drawn the few customary drops of Democratic blood, but had forced

a direct vote on President Carter's oil import fee, which Speaker O'Neill had vowed would remain bottled up in the Rules Committee forever.

Bauman's speeches and maneuvering so impressed his friend Henry J. Hyde that Hyde promptly withdrew from the contest for Republican House Whip and decided to endorse him. "He's the de facto leader already," Hyde admitted later. "We might as well give him the title."

The article noted "Some House Democrats have long believed that Bauman not only enjoys embarrassing them, but that he enjoys it more than winning on a substantive issue. Now some of them are not so sure."

In the same article, Congressman David Stockman of Michigan told Ehrenhalt: "The rough edges are coming off. Bob can still be abrasive but he does things with some polish now. His penchant for attacking moderate Republicans has diminished. He's gotten self-conscious about his image."

Ehrenhalt concluded: "All sides concede that as a debater and master of the House rules Bauman has few peers in either party. Two weeks ago he engaged House Majority Leader Jim Wright in a debate on foreign aid that reminded some of those present of House floor debate in an era when oratory really counted . . . On other occasions, Bauman has been deliberately and carefully entertaining, a response to earlier press accounts that he was a rigid ideologue with no sense of humor."

The headline on the article: "The 'New' Rep. Bauman Is Picking Up Clout."

Within a matter of months *Congressional Quarterly* weighed in with an article on House conservatives entitled "Bauman and Company" and I appeared on ABC's "Good Morning America" and "The Today Show" on NBC. My political career seemed to be soaring. Earlier in 1980 I declined to run for the Republican nomination for U.S. Senate from Maryland. But I let everyone hang in suspense to the last minute, then staged a major press conference at the State House in Annapolis, a move which had all the earmarks of a Senate race. I decided not to run because it would have meant a highly costly fight in the Republican primary against the incumbent U.S. Senator Charles "Mac" Mathias, finishing his second term. I believe I could have defeated Mathias among the small number of conservative Republican primary voters, but the general election in 1980 would have been most difficult to win, especially if the Republican party was split by the primary contest. Then too I did not want to give up a sure House seat. And it did not escape my thinking that the personal problems I was having, although they were at last being addressed, would not help in any race for public office, much less my first try for the U.S. Senate.

As I passed the thirty-, then sixty-day marks without a drink I began to feel a new confidence. In the May 1980 Maryland primary election I was as usual unopposed but Carol, at the request of Maryland Reagan campaign chairman, Don Devine, filed as a delegate to the Detroit national convention. She and two other Reagan delegates I picked won by wide margins, Carol leading the ticket. When the Maryland State Republican Convention was held in June, I was chosen again for a delegate-at-large slot but a complicated political deal suggested by Republican National Committeewoman, Louise Gore, made politicians and journalists alike gasp. With the likelihood that Ronald Reagan was going to win the nomination (he had won the Maryland primary already), Louise properly pointed out it was time for true "party unity," the kind that had escaped us in Maryland for so long. And so, named as co-chairmen of the Maryland delegation to Detroit was Congressman Bob Bauman, on the Right, and Senator Mac Mathias, on the Left. The *Baltimore Sun* promptly dubbed us Maryland's political "odd couple," noting the wide differences in our policy views. I personally saw it as enhancement of my own political standing, a moderating of my image, and a chance for future cooperation should I run in a statewide race. But most seasoned observers could hardly believe we were able to pull it off. As I said to Mac Mathias in the smoke-filled hotel room where the deal was closed, "If you can do it, so can I."

When we got to Detroit for the convention we had a grand time. My oldest daughter Genie joined us as a Maryland delegation page, I was co-chairman and a delegate, and Carol was a delegate as well. Senator Mathias, probably not all that comfortable with so many conservatives, all but disappeared and let me run the delegation show. I presided over caucuses, served as press spokesman, even phoned back to Washington where within six hours my congressional staff produced enough Baltimore Oriole baseball hats for the entire Maryland contingent. I sat in the delegation chairman's seat on the convention floor, right next to the red phone hooking me into the Reagan communications trailer outside Cobo Hall. My credentials were all in order as they never had been before. Tuesday, July 15, when I returned to my hotel to change for the evening convention session I found a message, "Call Ronald Reagan's suite at the Renaissance Plaza." When I checked in with Reagan aide Bill Timmons he told me Reagan wanted to see me the next morning with a small group of key supporters to discuss his vice-presidential running mate.

Within an hour another call came from Senator Jesse Helms at the North Carolina delegation's motel halfway across Detroit. Jesse said he was being urged to run for vice-president by conservatives. He wanted me there to discuss this since I would have to help him if he did.

The next morning, Wednesday, July 16, I met in Reagan's suite along with House Minority Leader Bob Michel of Illinois, Senator Strom Thurmond of South Carolina, Senator John Tower of Texas, Governor Pete duPont of Delaware, Timmons, Lyn Nofziger, Michael Deaver, and Reagan. The July 28, 1980 issue of *Time* records a photo of this august group.

Reagan told us he was considering former President Jerry Ford as a possible running mate and asked our reaction. I was startled. One by one the assembled leaders told him what a great idea. I was last, sitting at Reagan's left, and by the time my turn came I was for once too intimidated to tell him I thought it was a stupid idea. It would infuriate many hard-line conservatives who would never forgive Ford's picking Nelson Rockefeller as vice-president in 1975. I mumbled something about it "might be a good idea" if there was no "constitutional problem," but I also warned Reagan that Senator Helms ought to be consulted before this was decided.

At the meeting later that afternoon in Senator Helms' suite I found Howard Phillips of the Conservative Caucus loudly advocating the senator run for vice-president with no holds barred as a protest. Conservatives had made Ronald Reagan possible and we should tolerate no Jerry Ford on the ticket, he argued. Phyllis Schlafly urged caution, close to my own view which I now firmly stated: Ronald Reagan was our candidate and conservatives should do nothing to hurt him, including causing unnecessary party disunity.

Before my arrival Senator Helms had already placed a telephone call to Reagan to discuss the vice-presidential issue and I told the group I had also urged Reagan at our morning meeting to call Helms. As we talked the phone rang. It was Reagan calling. Helms turned to me and said, "Bob, you take the call. If I talk with him he's going to ask me to commit to not running for vice-president and I don't want to do that yet." The honest Helms then left the room "so you can tell him I am not here."

I picked up the phone and relayed to Reagan what had been going on since our morning meeting. "Bob," he said, "since we talked I've decided it will be George Bush. I hope you agree. Please tell Senator Helms I need his support on this and have him call me as soon as he can." I told Reagan I was not sure how well this was going to sit with the assembled conservatives but we would discuss it immediately and Senator Helms would call him back. "Frankly, Governor," I told him, "I think you've made a good choice."

In the ensuing talk the consensus of those present was that Helms should be placed in nomination as a token move allowing him to have his say before the convention. I was delegated by Helms to go outside the suite where a crush of newsmen, TV cameras and microphones had assembled. At an otherwise uneventful convention the press smelled a right-wing revolt and as usual wanted blood. In my statement I did nothing to discourage this thought, knowing it would add to the suspense of Helms' nomination and withdrawal. ABC's Sam Donaldson especially wanted to know if we were going to fight Bush. "We'll see," I fibbed.

As soon as the other conservative troops cleared out of the room I talked with Tom Ellis, the shrewd North Carolina lawyer who has served for many years as Senator Helms' political manager. We agreed the best thing for Jesse would be his nomination for vice-president, then a dignified withdrawal speech calling for party unity. We could offer this to the Reagan camp as a unity move and at the same time give the senator, the leading party conservative, a chance to stake a clear claim by the Right on the party, the campaign, and the hoped-for Reagan presidency.

Shortly afterward I called Reagan but talked with Bill Timmons, outlining the Helms plan. He told me he would have to get Reagan's approval and would get back to me.

The deal was confirmed as Senator Helms and I were called off the convention floor that evening while Congressman Guy van der Jagt of Michigan made one of the more ballyhooed and less impressive keynote speeches ever heard at a national convention. Timmons told me the details were all cleared and I then put Senator Helms on the phone, who chatted with Reagan as though no deal had ever been required. Both of them were sweetness and light. The confrontation of a convention vote on Jesse Helms vs. George Bush was avoided.

I thought to myself, Bauman, you must be getting old. How in hell did you ever manage not only to avoid a good fight with the liberals, but even help engineer peace?

Maybe it was true; I was mellowing.

When I got back to the Maryland delegation on the convention floor the rumor had started I was one of the leaders in a revolt against George Bush, a very popular man with the more moderate Marylanders. I denied it but then, a few minutes later, I was accosted by Helms' manager, Tom Ellis. It was a replay of Kansas City four years before.

"Bob," Tom said, "we want you to nominate Jesse for vice-president. You've been in on this all during the discussions with Reagan. When Maryland's name is called for nominations for vice-president, state that you have a nomination."

I agreed and later that evening as I went up to the rostrum to be introduced by the convention chairman, Rep. John Rhodes of Arizona, my House leader, the Maryland delegation gave me a standing cheer. They now knew and approved the terms of the Reagan-Helms deal.

It was, by all accounts, a good speech; at least my most important critic, Carol, said so. And Senator Helms' withdrawal was both dignified and appropriately conservative.

I had not only done my job, we had a glorious week in Detroit nominating the man we had been told could never win that nomination. Our daughter Genie had a wonderful time as a page at the convention. (In 1984 she was elected a Maryland Reagan delegate in her own right.)

We flew back to Maryland early on Saturday, tired but happy.

A few weeks after our return from the Detroit convention our youngest three children, Genie, Vicky, and Jimmy and I left for a week's vacation at Ocean City, Maryland. We would return just after Labor Day when my 1980 reelection campaign would formally begin.

The beach had always been a favorite of mine and of the children, but never Carol's. She preferred some place cooler. But also she knew in the past the beach meant drinking for me and unpleasantness for her. I was no longer drinking and yet, for the first time, she declined to come with us, saying she would stay at home, visit her mother, ride her horses, and rest. I guess I should have known something was amiss but Carol was insistent this was not the case. In my general good feeling I was not about to doubt her assurances.

It was a historic visit to Ocean City for me; the first time in years when beach time would not mean booze time. No more drinking all night and recovering all day. Genie, Vicky, Jimmy, and I had a wonderful week doing things together and my oldest son, Teddy, joined us for the weekend with his current young lady friend. I took a beautiful snapshot of our four children during that 1980 vacation, showing each of them smiling or mugging in characteristic ways. Teddy's mildly shy smile plays around the edges of his bearded lips. Genie has that wide politician's grin under her fashionable straw hat. Vicky is clowning around with her dark head tilted at a playful angle. And little Jimmy proudly displays a sweet ear-to-ear smile aimed right into the camera.

It would be a long time before these handsome young children of Carol and Bob Bauman would be able to smile in just that way again for my camera. If they will ever be able to.

A few days later in Washington two agents of the FBI called on me.

CHAPTER
EIGHT

*I*t seems so long ago and yet so near, that fifth day of September 1973, when I was sworn in as a member of the U.S. House of Representatives. The chaplain prayed, the journal was read and approved, and then the Speaker of the House, Carl Albert of Oklahoma, asked that the member-elect from the state of Maryland present himself at the Bar of the House. Escorted by other Maryland congressmen and Jerry Ford, the House Republican Leader, I moved the few steps to the Well where I raised my right hand at the Speaker's command. After all those years as a page and staff member, all those countless hours of watching and listening, now, for the first time a Speaker of the House was addressing me as a co-equal. Up in the Family Gallery, Carol, Ted, Genie, Vicky, and little Jimmy were watching. Hundreds of my political supporters filled the public galleries, bused in from Maryland.

"Do you solemnly swear that you will support and defend the Constitution of the United States against all enemies, foreign and domestic; that you will bear true faith and allegiance to the same; that you take this obligation freely, without mental reservation or purpose of evasion, and that you will well and faithfully discharge the duties of the office on which you are about to enter, so help you, God?"

In a firm, loud voice I replied, "I do."

In the galleries, on the House Floor, there was what seemed to my prejudiced ears louder and more enthusiastic applause than is traditional. I turned toward my family above me with a wide schoolboy grin, bowing to them; then toward the men and women who were now my "colleagues," acknowledging their applause.

But the applause has faded into the imperceptible distance now and I am prompted to paraphrase Mark Antony in his eulogy for Caesar: The evil that public men do lives after them; the good is oft interred with their defeat. Especially when that defeat comes in the midst of scandal. I like to think, indeed, I know, that I did many good things in my private and public life but I also know how most remember me. The last words of Tennessee Williams' *Memoirs* reflect his status as another soul tortured by alcoholism and homosexuality: "After all, high station in life is earned by the gallantry with which appalling experiences are survived with grace."

How graceful has been my survival I leave for others to judge. In many and profound ways life since 1980 has been easier than four decades of self-deception and isolation in the closet of my mind. My new life has brought so many unexpected problems but opportunities as well. In the darkest hours of my despair well-meaning friends kept telling me "life presents no adversity from which some good does not come." Then I silently gritted my teeth thinking these people could not possibly understand my personal pain. What possible good could there be? But they were right.

It was probably imperative I suffer this emotional trauma to shock me into reality. If I had continued down my insane path I would surely have killed myself by accident or design. Even though I ceased drinking in May 1980, my persistent inability to accept my sexuality would have probably led to drugs or back to alcohol. If I was to be able to live life I had to confront the truth.

Before the deluge of headlines, stories, and jokes engulfed me, sweeping me to inevitable political defeat, I actually believed I was equipped to deal with the situation. Hadn't I always been able to handle everything? Hadn't I voluntarily placed myself in the care of expert counselors and associated myself with proven groups helping those who shared my problems? What I did not realize was I had then only shuffled the first few steps in a journey to understanding that will never be completed in this lifetime.

What seemed to rankle most about the Bauman affair was "hypocrisy," that I pretended, they said, to exalt attitudes, beliefs, and principles that in retrospect the world knew I never could have possessed.

This harsh judgment was fast in coming and the sources were not always dispassionate and totally objective in their reasoning. Although some of the most sympathetic comments came from members of the gay community, some in this group, quite understandably, were also the most violent in reaction against me. My alcoholism, my psychiatric assistance, my refusal to accept my sexuality, all were cited as evidence of my duplicity even after exposure. But the main thrust of the charge was, as one gay writer put it, I had been "an important spokesperson against the very life style he has been a part of, albeit on the most vulgar side of gay life." But the same charge echoed repeatedly from non-gays as well. Peter Kumpa, a writer for the *Baltimore Sun,* offered his opinion that: "His personal tragedy is that he is now trapped by the often cruel standards that he set for others in the political arena. By the standards of the part of America he despised, Bauman's personal life would not matter." Similarly, on the right, Bill Buckley reminded the world that Bauman "ordained standards of conduct which he himself transgressed." An unnamed aide to a U.S. senator expressed what was said to be a common Capitol Hill view: "This couldn't have happened to a nicer guy. Bob was not at all compassionate to his colleagues on the floor of the House. He could be merciless and vicious. He upbraided people for their own failings."

But it was these very qualities of tenacity and relentless pursuit of principle that gained me applause and a following, a place in the Congress and the conservative movement. Others held similar, even more extreme views, left and right, but they inspired no animosity because of their passive attitude. One writer offered his opinion that each of us is entitled to our own views but we have no right to impose them on anyone else, adding, "Bauman is paying the penalty for a lifetime of ignoring that touchstone of human wisdom." A gay leader said: "Bauman needs to realize that people who disagree with him can also have reached their decisions with prayer and they can also believe they are right with God and are willing to be judged by Him." Now I cannot totally disagree.

What is missed here in this relativistic approach is the truth that there are immutable standards by which our lives must be ordered. Whether one believes that "God," some "higher power" or "natural law" imposes such standards is inconsequential. While there can be a wide variation in the application of life's basic principles, to say everything is "gray" and "there are no black and white issues" is to beg the wisdom of the ages. Further, that I transgressed those standards surely makes me guilty of hypocrisy but it in no way makes those standards less worthy of belief or adherence.

I have been asked: "Surely you must have realized what you were doing when you committed these acts. Didn't you feel a constant conflict between your public persona and what you were doing in private?"

The answer has to be, "Yes!" I felt the conflict in the most damaging way, but not at a fully conscious level. That is why alcohol was so useful, so attractive. Rather than focus my mind on what I was doing I literally suspended reason, ignoring the conflict between my self-imposed political, moral standards and my personal actions. I did not want to consider, to even think about the validity of what I did. I shut out the questions in order simply to act. I was, I learned eventually, in the grips of compulsion, an irresistible impulse to perform acts contrary to my will.

For a great part of my life I indulged in an intellectual practice known as "compartmentalization." Like the unsinkable H.M.S. *Titanic,* my mind constructed impregnable steel-plated compartments, also designed to prevent my sinking. The great difference in the dark recesses of my personal vessel was that it must never be known in one compartment what was happening in the next. And like the famous White Star ocean liner (a ship which obsessed me to the point I collected every book about it I could find), I too was doomed to destruction.

Such compartmentalization allowed me to act in a flagrantly irrational manner in one part of my private life while at the same time permitting me to believe my considerable political accomplishments outweighed the evil I might do. I followed impulses the validity of which I did not care to consider. It is small wonder ultimately others would see much of my life as hypocrisy.

Oddly, it was not so much the walls I constructed within me that gave me strength but rather the focal points of activity within each of the strictly segregated areas of my life.

In one compartment was politics, the very *raison d'être* of my life. Here I exalted principle, feverishly manufacturing the false self-esteem I so desperately needed. And I was good at it. Carol told me: "When you are away in Washington in my imagination I see you having a ball, really eating it up. After all, it's what you really like to do. There's no denying it; you're good at it. It all adds to my admiration and pride in you." From a different viewpoint Henry David Thoreau once said: "If anything ails a man so that he does not perform his functions, if he has a pain in his bowels even ... he forthwith sets about reforming the world." How much more reform could I accomplish drawing on my well of pain? I was not just a foot soldier of the conservative movement, I became one of its "forceful, articulate leaders." As the acclaim became greater I began to believe my political works were far more important than my secret life. Soon politics would overshadow my family, my wife. This focal point of politics literally held me together, kept my life from flying apart. For a person who believed himself to be worthless, it was my one source of virtue.

In the other compartment was my homosexual activity. Here I

drew the self-validation I thought I needed as a human being, as a man. Part of my low self-esteem was my poor physical self-image and so I sought after imagined physical perfection in other men, as though I could somehow share their strength and beauty, covering my own perceived ugliness. The man I wanted was always the same: young, almost boyish in appearance, slender with a "swimmer's build"; but his physique would have strong, well-defined muscles, broad shoulders, a slim waist, big biceps with prominent veins in the forearms, a flat, well-defined chest and chisled abdomen. In other words, I would settle for Michelangelo's *David*. And he must have dark curly or long hair, dark eyes, a ruggedly handsome face, never "pretty" but roughly appealing, almost with an air of danger. It was the "me" I wanted.

If I could not be the person I wanted to be then I would possess, if only for a moment, a person who was the physical embodiment of all the attributes I was so acutely aware I lacked. That I was deficient stems from my earliest memories of life. As a child I was described as "cute" and "a darling baby." But as I grew into puberty, especially after my mother died, I saw in the mirror an ungainly, plump, and hopelessly unattractive boy. I had no interest in "sports" and I just knew girls would reject me. At one point as a teen-ager I went on a series of "crash diets" supervised by a pill-pushing doctor who handed out amphetamines like the Easter bunny drops jelly beans. I actually managed to get down to 145 pounds when Carol and I were married in 1960. In 1978, I had piled 185 pounds onto a five foot six and one-half-inch frame. (Today I weigh in at around 145 and have been working out for three years with free weights using the "Gold's Gym" routine.)

It occurs to me now, so many years later, that in seeking this idealized person, this "other me," I might have been attempting to love myself, seeking some sort of self-validation by proxy. I can only speculate what this lack of self-love produced in my mind and attitude toward life. The French philosopher Blaise Pascal long ago said that self-contempt produces in a man "the most unjust and criminal passions imaginable, for he conceives a mortal hatred against the truth which blames him and convinces him of his faults." And Eric Hoffer echoed him when he wrote: "Self-righteousness is a loud din raised to drown the voice of guilt within us." If I truly "despised" anyone, it was not others, but myself.

Of course one of the controlling emotions of my life was a terrifying loneliness, which Dr. Kay identified with his first battery of tests. His judgment: "You are one of the loneliest, most isolated people I have encountered in all my years of practice." Like the old Bolsheviks Stalin sent to purge trials, there were times I felt, like Nikolai Bukharin, "isolated from everything that constitutes the essence of life." But how could it have been otherwise? I did not dare permit another human being into my walled-off compound. I was isolated, banished into this lifelong internal exile, seeking help was out of the question. I might be found out. How many times was Carol to say, "I don't feel that I really know you, Bob." I could speak from my heart about politics to eighteen thousand cheering people in Madison Square Garden but I could not speak from my heart to my own wife about the truly momentous things in my life—what should have been our life.

If I could not allow others to share my dark secret I also must go further and convince myself that I was not homosexual. My thoughts were as those of James Joyce in his *Portrait of the Artist as a Young Man:* "His soul sickened at the thought of a torpid snaky life feeding itself out of the tender marrow of his life and fattening upon the slime of lust. O why was that so? O why?"

I had to keep this disturbing possibility at bay. Even the smallest notion was rejected, every slip rationalized, every act followed by sincere and deep contrition. If only I could escape from these unclean attractions, this desire that arose without warning, the "impure thoughts" the devil uses to cloud men's minds. These distractions threatened my very being. So I repressed them, refused to consider them logically, avoided the chance to gain the knowledge I needed to understand my life. Had it been a suspected disease, a physical injury, I would have sought a competent doctor or specialist asking for advice and help. But what was happening to me, I was certain, was virtually unique. There was no way I could ever reveal it to another human being. The shame would have been too great, the obloquy too devastating. And so I made them inevitable. Of course this approach only made everything worse—far worse—because deep within me there grew a dangerous enemy I could neither face nor escape. I lived in a state of chronic dread that I eventually came to believe was the lot of mankind.

I prayed to God to deliver me from whatever this thing was that gripped me and made me "different." I knew I could not be insane, but there was this one part of my life I seemed unable to control. Later I discovered this strong but ill-defined feeling at an early age of being "different" is one of the common traits of gay men. I simply did not blend into life around me, could not understand why at home and out in the world I seemed never to "fit in."

I have spoken repeatedly of my "low self-esteem," the "low opinion of myself" that haunted me. Understand that this nagging specter was at a near subconscious level. In early 1980 when Dr. Kay gently began to raise this issue it came as a distinct surprise to me. His first observations were fairly casual: "You know, you really don't seem to like yourself very much, do you?" Of course my first reaction was incredulity. On the contrary, I was very proud of my achievements as a public servant, husband, and father. I dragged out my humble origins, underscoring how much further I had come than my own father or his forebears.

"Then why do you always put yourself down in all our conversations?" Dr. Kay demanded. "Don't you realize you constantly make small, almost casual remarks, which, taken together, seem to indicate you think yourself to be nearly worthless in the eyes of others." That did give me pause.

Of course, the doctor was correct. This was not just the practiced politician's self-deprecation. This verbal self-flagellation signified only the surface vapors of a subconscious cauldron of simmering self-doubt, self-hatred, ultimately, self-destruction. Not too far below the brash and blustery exterior of Bob Bauman was a vague but gnawing belief that I was a miserable being who, once exposed, would be justifiably hated by all. Toward the end, when election returns confirmed yet another winning margin, a small voice in my mind's depths quietly whispered, "You know they would not vote for you if they knew what you were really like, don't you?" How in God's name could I ever let Carol, or anyone, even myself, really know what I was like, what the problem was? If she knew she too would reject me just as I rejected myself. What else could she possibly do?

In a desperate effort to create my illusion of self-esteem I adopted conservative politics with a fervor amounting to neurotic escape. It would be my refuge from the unacceptable inner reality. Always incomplete and insecure I had no inner resources from which to generate self-assurance. I passionately needed something outside me to hold on to and I found it in my books about Lincoln, Taft, the Republican party. If I felt I was a failure internally, a bad person, then that bred an extravagant audacity that made me seek out the impossible. This was one way to conceal my perceived shortcomings. If I failed at grand tasks no one, particularly myself, would hold me nearly so accountable as if I failed at the mundane. Why not reach for the stars? And suddenly, miraculously, I was touching them.

This is not to denegrate my many solid achievements. But being brilliant and talented in my chosen field allowed me to escape the judgment of my own ego. The late John Ashbrook used to often quip about various people: "Deep down you know he's shallow." In my case, deep down I knew I was nothing.

One gay leader wrote of me: "Bob Bauman's hypocrisy is bad enough, but it becomes tragic when you realize that it is a hypocrisy borne of self-hatred and fear. We can only pity the Bob Baumans of the world. They are more terrible figures when they have the power and influence, as Bauman did, to cause incredible suffering among people who should be their brothers and sisters."

That this concept of low self-esteem is almost universal among gay men who have fought acceptance of their true sexuality makes my own personal agony no more bearable. I have come to envy those younger gays who, as times and minds become more open, avoid the suffering of self-hatred so many endured. In my own life the consequences have been many and devastating.

Always there was the guilt, total, enormous, the feeling of culpability and remorse for some indefinable offense, for just existing. If I was indeed as bad as I thought, then I must be the guilty party. I must eventually pay the price, accept the punishment for my inadequacy. One conservative publication righteously offered the gratuitous opinion that ". . . he brought scandal upon himself and his family . . . and has never exhibited any real remorse for his actions or acknowledged in any convincing way that he believed they were sinful, or even wrong." How easy it is to pass judgment on others; I have done it thousands of times.

In Allen Drury's classic 1959 novel, *Advise and Consent,* which was about Congress and the ways of Washington, Senator Brigham Anderson of Utah, an attractive, principled conservative, husband and father, takes his stand against a presidential nominee for secretary of state in whose past is hidden a direct association with communism. This past is unknown to most but armed with this knowledge the senator cannot permit himself to vote for the nominee who seeks to keep his past hidden. As part of that cover-up, in retaliation Senator Anderson's wartime homosexual liaison with a young man in Hawaii is about to be exposed in order to discredit him. As he sits at his Senate office desk on a bright Sunday afternoon he calmly goes about his last tasks before he holds a gun to his head and commits suicide. I can fully empathize with Drury's "Brig Anderson" as he scrawls on Senate stationery bearing his name, in a large irregular hand that was far from his usual script, two words: "I'm sorry."

And he was sorry, with a sorrow deeper than words could convey; sorry for himself, sorry for his family, sorry for the boy [in Hawaii], sorry for all his friends and his country and the world and for all the things in human living for which there are no answers and from which there is no escape. And not the least of these, he knew now, were a man's weakness and a man's strength, for each in its time he had obeyed the commands of both, and together they had brought him down."

Yes, I am sorry for what I have done wrong, for the suffering I caused my wife, my children, for the discredit I brought upon others and upon my principles. I have experienced a sorrow, a remorse so profound and overpowering I had to put it aside in order to continue to exist, lest, like Brigham Anderson, I destroy myself. Perhaps for some of my old friends that would have been a more comforting solution.

Allen Drury observes about the demise of Senator Brig Anderson:

> As it was, he was the ideal sacrifice to ease the conscience of them all. The ruthless and the righteous could rejoice equally, for one could say, "See? He stood in our way." And the other could say, "See? He broke the rules." And they could join hands together and dance around his bier.

No, nothing could remove the feeling that much of my life was a living lie; nothing but exposure and expiation. And that profound guilt was reenforced and intensified by the fact that I freely embraced the Roman Catholic faith.

If my life seemed a labyrinth of contradictions none is so difficult to reconcile as the gross disparity between my personal conduct and the requirements of my chosen religion. It is a reconciliation I may never be able to effect.

But it was my faith that helped me through some of the darkest days of my life. As John Fortunato wrote in his inspiring *Embracing the Exile* (New York: Seabury Press, 1982), I too feel a compelling need to heal the deep gash that separates my faith from my sexuality. I suspect I will never achieve the feeling of wholeness as a person I seek, gain the inner peace, until this is finally done.

Though I am not nearly so spiritual as I would like to be I must hold firmly to the idea that without a belief in God, or some higher power in life, denied the possibility of ultimate salvation for my soul, I would suffer a double condemnation, earthly and eternal. Yet I must repeat, there is no more difficult reconciliation to attempt than the teachings of the Catholic church and the inherent sexual nature of a gay person.

The true paradox lies in the fact that the gay, more than the non-gay person, desperately needs a greater dimension of spirituality simply in order to survive.

In light of my life's history it may seem difficult to believe religion always meant a great deal to me. From a very young age I took formal religion to heart and have yet to abandon it.

In 1949, while I was away at school, my father, trained as a musician but forced to become a salesman, was transferred by the Sonotone hearing aid company from Washington, D.C., to Charleston, West Virginia, where he was made a district manager. His business territory encompassed most of this remote state and there could not have been a worse time to go into those mountains. John L. Lewis had just led his United Mine Workers out on what was to become one of the longest and most costly labor disputes in American history. My father's business did not prosper, the hard-of-hearing West Virginians stayed deaf, and the Bauman family tuition money for another year at Fork Union Military Academy ran out.

In September 1949, I began the sixth grade at Sacred Heart Elementary School in Charleston, only a block from the broad flow of the Kanawha River and a few blocks from the gold-domed state capitol building.

As did my philosophical hero, Edmund Burke, I believe "man is by his constitution a religious animal" but I did not know that then. Maxine, my stepmother, was a Roman Catholic but she did not pressure me to embrace the faith. I was raised an indifferent

Methodist, the nominal religion of my late mother, and my dad was a baptized but nonpracticing Lutheran. As a child he was told by his mother not to walk directly past a Catholic church lest the demons pop out and get him.

At Sacred Heart for the first time I was exposed to the beauty of the Mass ritual. In religion class I learned this was Christ's one true church on earth; He had founded it for all of us. I even joined the children's choir where I sang Gregorian chant and became the pet of the choir director, Sister Mary Angeline, a bubbly Franciscan nun who encouraged me to embrace the faith with the same fervor with which I sang a Mozart gloria or a Gounod kyrie.

My sense of history and developing conservatism drew me to Catholicism but, ever the reactionary, it was a violent attack on the church that made up my mind. My father had been attending a Presbyterian church headed by a local version of the yet unknown Billy Graham. Dad had been told at the Charleston Kiwanis Club it was good business to attend Reverend Joe Overmeyer's church. And so one Sunday I found myself sitting in the pew of a solemn tan and maroon church, its innate dignity broken only by the glowing neon yellow cross above the choir's heads at the back of the sanctuary.

The Reverend Joe chose that morning to denounce the Roman Catholic church, the pope, and all associated idolatry with a matchless passion. This infuriated me, especially since I was at school with Catholics and knew they were not as portrayed by this narrowminded Protestant minister.

It was not long after that I asked and received permission from my father to begin instructions in the Catholic faith. On Easter eve, Holy Saturday, 1950, at the age of fourteen, I was baptized a Catholic "... *in nomine Patris, et Filii, et Spiritus Sancti, Amen.*" The saintly old German Capuchin priest who gave me my instructions, Father Boniface Weckmann, uttered the ritual words, poured the holy water, then smiled and said to me, "Now you're a Mick."

As in the case of my adopted Republicanism I became a convert with all the zeal such free choice entails.

In the years to come my youthful decision to embrace the faith was to bring me great comfort and solace. But it was also to engender within me the deepest possible sense of guilt and despair.

The faith I embraced was a vengeful religion whose God was a God of strict requirements, perfect conduct, and, for those who failed to live by its standards, His church gave assurances of eternal damnation. Nowhere have I seen it better described, my early view of Catholicism, than in the third chapter of James Joyce's *A Portrait of the Artist as a Young Man*. There Joyce employs the words of the priest, Father Arnall, a member of the Society of Jesus, who conducts a retreat for male students. He describes the position of the church on sin, the results of sin, Hell, and that dark region's every torment; exterior darkness, the awful stench, a fire constantly burning but that does not destroy, the intensity of suffering, the numbers of the damned, the company of devils, thoughts of past sins and the awful eternal knowledge of the denial of God's beauty and presence. "Every word of it was for him. Against his sin, foul and secret, the whole wrath of God was aimed. The preacher's knife had probed deeply into his diseased conscience and he felt now that his soul was festering in sin."

When I entered the Georgetown University School of Foreign Service in the fall of 1955, it was only another part of the life's plan I formulated at the time I read *Abraham Lincoln's World*. To be a success, I reasoned, I needed a solid grounding in political science, economics, and the law. The nation's oldest Catholic institution of higher learning, founded in 1789, offered not only a good education but academic prestige as well. And as a convert to Catholicism I felt comfortable with the knowledge I would be learning from teachers whose views would be doctrinally correct.

Or so I thought.

The late Professor Carroll Quigley, Ph.D., was a fixture at G.U. long before my arrival in 1955. He taught required freshman courses in "development of civilization," was a noted historian, author and Democratic party intellectual activist. He was also outspoken, opinionated, and never wrong. Ironically, one of his books formulating a theory of world economic domination by an international business/banking/political elite was fashioned into an article of their faith by the leaders of the right-wing John Birch Society, much to Quigley's chagrin.

One night I listened impassively as Dr. Quigley held forth in his broad Bostonian accent interspersed with a maddening clearing of his post-nasal passages, his hallmark. Suddenly my lethargy was jolted by the realization Quigley, a Catholic himself, was telling us the pope of Rome, Christ's vicar on earth, was not infallible in matters of faith and morals. I now listened intently as he said by the time some doctrinal issue was proclaimed *ex cathedra,* from the Chair of Peter, as a matter of faith, the subject would have been hashed over for years if not centuries by countless cardinals, bishops, and theologians. The final result was a simple committee product, not a God-inspired revelation funneled through the lips of the pontiff by heaven. "If you want to believe that's divine inspiration," Quigley sniffed, "that's your business."

My hand shot up, question at the ready, my own divine inspiration pumping. Surely I recalled Father Boniface explaining all about papal infallibility during my instructions to become a Catholic. It was risky questioning Quigley and his reply was a short restatement of his position, allowing no quarter for this freshman upstart.

But this classroom heresy so scandalized me I took the matter directly to Father Lee Bradley, S.J., my theology professor, at our next class. Bradley tried to dismiss the matter as inconsequential but he soon realized I was genuinely upset. Pressed, he suggested I put down my concern in writing and send it to the head of the theology department, which I immediately did. Weeks went by and finally I was called before a panel of Jesuit priests, questioned about my letter and what I had heard, then dismissed. A few days later a statement was read in all religion classes restating the traditional Catholic doctrine on papal infallibility but also noting that the views of teachers at G.U. were their own and not always those of the university or the church. Professor Quigley's name was never mentioned.

Like the crusader of old I listened with smug satisfaction to the statement, thinking, I have protected the faith.

I also got a grade of C minus in Development of Civilization I.

In retrospect I must say I earned it. It was so easy to protect the faith, even if one was incapable of practicing it in every respect.

By now homosexuality has passed through the shock value stage of public discussion and has become a cliché for TV talk shows and even the Broadway musical stage. To paraphrase Bill Buckley, "The crime that dare not speak its name is rapidly becoming the crime that won't shut up." But only recently it was taboo.

Wasn't I a voluntary member of the Roman Catholic church? A convert? Didn't I know the church steadfastly maintained a well-defined position on the responsibility for such individual actions?

Though I never once heard the topic of homosexuality addressed from a pulpit, indeed there has been a clear Catholic position on the morality of this problem. As currently stated it is no sin to *be* a homosexual, but to commit ". . . solitary or homosexual acts is forbidden all men because of nature's purpose of procreation is absolutely defeated by such acts . . . no exception to this general law of nature is possible." So wrote Reverend Father Thomas J. Higgins, S.J., in *Man as Man,* a standard text in Catholic ethics in 1949.

In August 1982, a young reporter for the *Washington Post,* John Feinstein, wrote a Sunday front-page feature about me prompting many phone calls and letters from those who sympathized with my predicament: a ruined political career, an uncertain future. One of the questions he asked was whether I "considered homosexuality to be sinful."

Exercising the politician's traditional prerogative of evasion I replied that the question "cut too close to the quick" for me to hazard an answer at that point in my life.

The church has had no such hesitancy in responding to the same question for the past twelve centuries. And in that time the church's position has not changed essentially since it was first refined by Saint Thomas Aquinas. Yet in more than eleven years of study in the Catholic educational system I never once heard the topic of homosexuality mentioned.

As a young boy I assumed that God's attitude toward sexual "deviation" was not too different from what I heard articulated in the gym and locker room; such people were "queers" and "faggots." The *Baltimore Catechism* told me their conduct constituted mortal sins, those acts "which displease God the most" and "makes the sinner deserve Hell." To engage in such an act, then die without a valid confession and absolution from a priest meant consignment forever to James Joyce's eternal damnation, denial of the Beatific Vision of God from which all happiness flows.

Indeed, I once firmly believed *to be a homosexual* was a mortal sin, a position held until comparatively recently by some Catholic theologians and still believed by many fundamentalist Christian sects. Tempered by modern psychological findings the church no longer automatically condemns 10 percent of its membership or the human race to eternal perdition, but its teaching regarding homosexual acts is clear: homosexual relationships are contrary to God's will as revealed in Scripture as well as humanly destructive to those who engage in such conduct. For the true homosexual, Father John Harvey's recommendation to me is the church's official position: complete abstinence from sexual relations and the practice of chastity until death.

Although I have many times heard the Catholic argument which rationalizes the existence of evil, I find it difficult to believe a loving God would create, or permit to exist, if you will, millions of human beings who, because of their inherent nature are condemned to live a life devoid of the human contact and the physical expression true love entails.

In 1976, John J. McNeill, S.J., a psychotherapist and theologian, received church permission to publish a small volume entitled *The Church and the Homosexual.* (Kansas City: Sheed, Andrews and McMeel, 1976). Almost immediately the permission was withdrawn and the book is now a collector's item. In it he states:

> Homosexuality is not, as commonly supposed, a kind of conduct, but a psychological condition. It is important to understand that the genuine homosexual condition, or inversion, as it is often termed, is something for which the subject can in no way be held responsible. In itself it is morally neutral.

Father McNeill, who has since been banned by his superiors from speaking or writing about homosexuality, also observed that the church teaches a homosexual should avoid all close contact with women since this might lead to a marriage which could not be valid. Similarly, close male friendships were also discouraged for they might lead to an occasion of sin. Pastoral advice even included admonitions against gays entering occupations which might include close contact with other men or boys—teaching, the military, and religious life itself. While this teaching has been relaxed somewhat in recent years, it is still prevalent.

Father McNeill summed up the despair of many Christian gays, saying:

> Cut off, then, from all deep and affectionate female and male friendship, the homosexual is literally condemned to a living Hell of isolation and loneliness . . . and such life is not urged temporarily but must be sustained until death under threat of possible eternal damnation.

In my own experience I have encountered many gays who feel that the church position on homosexuality destroys any possibility of self-worth or dignity in the minds of Christian gays. They speak of themselves ruefully as "recovering Catholics" and ask simply: "How can you have any value if the essence of your being is but an expression of the effects of sin in the world? We are told that our very existence constitutes a contradiction of the divine will for man." Others are far harsher, calling the Catholic church "the foremost oppressor of gays in the world."

While I do not share this angry reaction, I understand it. I do not believe God intends to reject gays or condemn them by their nature to Hell. But the constant rejection of gays by many of the human beings who administer God's church is enough to produce such frustration. For every understanding priest or nun who tries to reach out to the gay community there is a bishop who cracks down, preventing the contact with the church that gays so greatly need and that so many desire.

Typical of this type of hierarchical thinking was the successful effort of Washington, D.C.'s, Archbishop James A. Hickey (a political liberal on most other issues) to have their religious orders reassign away from Washington Sister Jeannine Gramick and Reverend Robert Nugent, co-founders of the "New Ways Ministry." Both were instrumental in the ministry to Washington-area gays which gained national notice because of its willingness to "state but then debate" the church's position on the issue of homosexuality. Hickey said he found them "ambiguous and unclear with regard to the morality of homosexual activity."

The widespread growth of gay church groups in many religious denominations in recent years seems to prove gays do not wish to leave the church. Gay Catholics have "Dignity," Episcopalians "Integrity," and similar groups exist in many other Christian faiths, as well as Jewish and nonsectarian churches, such as the all-gay "Metropolitan Community Church" now established in many major cities. This developing movement is an expression of what Canadian Catholic theologian Gregory Baum describes as the gay's need to say: "God made me this way and I must affirm what God has done."

I am all too aware the great majority of people who know little of homosexuality fear and loathe it if they consider it at all. But to the gay himself, trying to deal with his human condition, it is often a matter of intense interest and preoccupation, especially in the area of religion.

The Catholic church's stand on homosexuality is much like the philosophic basis of heterosexuality in our society. While heterosexuality will always be the orientation and preference of the vast majority of people, society has built up a whole host of restraints and bulwarks to intensify this majority preference. From our earliest days we are told that "sex" is not for fun, variety, or purely erotic purposes. Society outwardly agrees with the basic church position that sex is to be confined to those who officially sanctify their affection and accept the social commitments which go with this contract.

That millions of married and unmarried men and women do adhere to this supposed optimum condition for "having sex" makes the firmness of its hold on the popular mentality no less important. The rule may rapidly be becoming the exception but it is still exalted as the rule.

But what of those millions of gay people who by their very nature cannot mentally or physically relate to this rule? One recent response, other than outright hostility to social mores and the church, has been an expanding gay challenge to the authenticity of the church position.

The 1981 American Book Award went to gay Yale history professor John Boswell for his *Christianity, Social Tolerance and Homosexuality* (Chicago: University of Chicago Press, 1980) in which he used scholarship to question not only the church's position on the gay issue but the traditional interpretations of the biblical texts used to justify that position. My friend, Father John Harvey, has strongly disputed many of Boswell's conclusions in a similarly scholarly article.

Both Boswell and a former Jesuit priest, Malachi Martin, author of *The Decline and Fall of the Roman Church* (New York: Putnam, 1981), document the extensive incidence of homosexuality among popes, bishops, and the Catholic clergy throughout history. Although it receives little public notice and discussion homosexuality among current Catholic clergy is well known to observers and widespread by my own knowledge. Some have estimated that perhaps 30 percent of present priests and brothers are homosexual and one Boston priest suggested that the figure for current seminarians is closer to 80 percent, at least in his area.

From my own first-hand experience I know frequent retreats and counseling sessions are held throughout the country for Catholic religious who are gay. Many of them suffer from alcoholism as well. I was told of a leading East Coast priest who will carry to his grave a bullet lodged in his body received during one of his many evenings cruising for young male companions. A priest of my acquaintance regularly leaves his New England parish for weekday evenings in New York's Times Square area where he acquires handsome young males who spend the night with him. More than once he has run into other priests from his area bent upon similar concerns and once it was the bishop's personal assistant. It was hardly a well-kept secret that one of the late Princes of the American church had similar tastes although they were exercised with greater discretion during his lifetime.

In an article in *The Christopher Street Reader* (1981) entitled "A Cruel God: The Gay Challenge to the Catholic Church," former seminarian Tim Dlugos describes a New Year's party at a suburban Washington, D.C., parish rectory (the pastor was away) at which Catholic priests and seminarians, all of them gay, gathered to celebrate the holiday. Writes Dlugos:

> I recall one distinguished seminary rector talking about his fear that the young gardner he had been forced to fire would blab about their affair. It sounded like a bad French novel until I realized that each of the men in the room—and there were at least seventy, from seminarians to retired *monsignori*—could face the same kind of threat to their careers and reputations any day. They move in a world as clandestine as those of gay diplomats or gay Hollywood stars.

Or, he might have added, gay congressmen, politicians, and government officials.

Nor is this phenomenon of gay clergy confined to one religious denomination. I sat on the beach in Delaware one recent summer day with no less than seven gay clergy of a leading Protestant church, including the bishop of a major city there with his lover of twenty years.

Obviously, for a young Catholic boy, unsure of his sexuality (or perhaps sure he is gay) struggling with the problem of self-worth, the priesthood offers a supposedly perfect way out of life's dilemma. Author Dlugos quotes Reverend Paul Shanley of Boston, who had been commissioned by the late Humberto Cardinal Madeiros to minister to the area's "sexual minorities" (an assignment later withdrawn because he was too successful) as follows: "If you're eighteen, gay, and Catholic, what's in store for you? You're told that God is going to hate you, society's going to hate you, the church is going to hate you. Your own mother will hate you if she finds out. But if you become a priest you don't have to get married. God will love you, society will love you, the church will love you. And, of course, your mother will love you. If Catholics knew what we know about gay priests and seminarians the church would be decimated."

None of this argues in favor of the misguided thesis that having been persecuted for so long by those who control the institution gays should abandon formal religion. I firmly believe increased spirituality for gays is an essential element in answering the unique and painful demands imposed upon the homosexual.

At the same time my own church, the Catholic church, and all religious institutions have a special obligation to thoroughly reexamine their position toward homosexuals if the existence and purpose of the church is to have any true meaning.

My own position with my adopted church is ambivalent at best. I remain a Catholic but I doubt I have the right to partake of Holy Communion if the doctrine of the church excludes those who are homosexuals. That it does not is some comfort. But I know that if I pursue my homosexuality, seeking out another person I find attractive to share my life and love, a male, then I should not avail myself of the sacrament of the Eucharist. Of course I am already cut off from the sacraments of Holy Orders and Marriage because of my sexuality. Conceivably, I could be denied the final sacrament of life, what used to be called extreme unction, at the time of my death if the church officials deemed me to be living a life of sin, although this is rarely done anymore. One well-known personage to suffer this indignity was the late F. Scott Fitzgerald, who was denied burial in the consecrated ground of a Catholic cemetery in Maryland because of what church officials of his day believed to be his sinful life. (Recently his grave was blessed by a priest with church approval.)

Of course, the answer to my seeming dilemma given by "the church" is to repent my sin, confess, and receive the sacrament of reconciliation; "go and sin no more." I am then to live the life of chastity and sexual abstinence recommended for gays, lesbians, nuns, and priests, only the last two of which truly can be said to enter voluntarily into their status.

Sorrowfully this recommended course of action comes at a time when intimacy and love finally have come to mean much to me, both concepts I hardly considered much less understood for most of my life.

Bishop Walter F. Sullivan of the diocese of Richmond, Virginia, has been one of the more compassionate and understanding clerics in the American Catholic church. In 1983, he wrote an introduction to *A Challenge to Love* in which he restated the traditional church teaching regarding homosexuality but added:

Yet, we cannot remain satisfied that, once we have clearly articulated the official church position on homosexuality, nothing else remains to be done in the area of pastoral care for homosexual people and education on the topic for the larger community . . . This is especially true where the teaching of the church itself has been presented in such a way that it has been the source or occasion of some of the pain and alienation that many homosexual Catholics experience. We cannot overlook those injustices including rejection, hostility, or indifference on the part of Christians, that have resulted in a denial of respect or of full participation in the community for homosexual people. We must examine our own hearts and consciences and know that each of us stands in real need of conversion in this area.

What then does one do when, after a lifetime of communion, however imperfect, with his church, one suddenly finds himself declared by that church to be in a status denying him access to some of the sacraments because of his nature, and to others if he indulges that nature?

The temptation is to rationalize one's condition and to continue to act as if nothing has changed externally. A Catholic convert friend of long standing asked me whether I took communion. I replied the clear church doctrine was I could not engage in homosexual acts and also remain in the state of grace, thus eligible for the sacrament of the Holy Eucharist. His reply: "If you love Jesus and believe in God why not simply remove the middle men of the church and partake in the ritual without all this worry about your status?" Easier said than done, especially for one who tries to maintain some respect for the magisterium, the teaching authority of the church. I am not quite comfortable with the theory annunciated by Reverend Andrew M. Greeley in his book *How to Save the Catholic Church* (1985), in which he reports a common current attitude to be: "As long as you define yourself as Catholic, no one is going to throw you out of the church or refuse the sacraments to you, regardless of what you do in your bedroom or what reservations you have on doctrinal matters. Make your peace with God and don't worry about the pope or the bishops."

How much simpler it would be if the church could be put aside "just like that" when found inconvenient. But a religious institution so expendable would obviously not be worth worrying about. And I am aware some of the gravest sins are those of the intellect, often producing free will run rampant. In the very book Bill

Buckley obliquely recommended by his comparison of me to *Elmer Gantry*, Sinclair Lewis describes the forlorn character of the Reverend Frank Shallard, a Methodist minister who loses his faith in that church and momentarily considers the possibility of becoming a Catholic. And yet Shallard is not entirely comfortable with the doctrines of the Catholic church either. Consulting a young priest Shallard asks if one can be a Catholic and not accept all the church's doctrines and Lewis has his "Father Matthew Smeesby" reply:

> Shallard, you can't understand the authority and reasonableness of the church. You're not ready to. You think too much of your puerile powers of reasoning. You haven't enough divine humility to comprehend the ages of wisdom that have gone into building up this fortress and you can stand outside the walls, one pitifully lonely figure, blowing the trumpet of your egotism and demanding of the sentry, "Take me to your commander. I am graciously inclined to assist him. Only he must understand that I think the granite walls are pasteboard, and I get tired of them." Man, if you were a prostitute or a murderer and came to me saying "Can I be saved?" I'd cry "Yes!" and give my life to helping you. But you're obsessed by a worse crime than murder—pride of intellect. And yet you haven't such an awfully overpowering intellect to be proud of, and I'm not sure but that's the worst crime of all! Good-day!

I do not expect the Catholic church to modify substantially its teachings regarding homosexual acts. It might indeed do much more to consider and address the basic dilemma which says a man's very nature prohibits him for life from pursuing his nature's dictates in seeking love and companionship. To simply love the homosexual and hate his acts is akin to lamenting the state of the mentally insane but saying, by all means keep them locked away where they will do no harm to themselves or others. Except in the case of the gay person the individual, in order to attain eternal salvation, is told he must voluntarily isolate himself from not only others, but himself. If that is the only available solution the human beings who administer the church and God's doctrines have to offer, then there need be no Hell after death. For homosexuals the consequent suffering here on earth will do quite well, thank you.

I mentioned to a Jewish friend I had reached the conclusion that whether there was a Hell or not, the suffering here on earth certainly equaled if not exceeded any possible suffering the afterlife might offer. "My God," he replied, "you're becoming a Jew."

In my drinking days I would sometimes get high and listen to a Deutsche Grammophon recording of Charles François Gounod's "Misse Solemnelle Ste-Cecile." Gounod gave up his studies for the priesthood in order to compose opera and religious music, a favor to me. I would turn up the volume, lie down on the carpet between the speakers, and let my blood alcohol level affect my brain, transporting me to Notre Dame de Paris, Mont Saint Michel or Chartres. Especially appealing was the closing hymn for Emperor Napoleon III, "Domine salva fac," a powerful anthem asking salvation for the ruler and his people.

In 1855, about the time he composed the Cecilian mass, Gounod wrote to his mother: "Always pray that my weaknesses of all kinds and my ill fortune may be transformed into strength and lightness of heart and understanding."

But sometimes lightness of heart and understanding is difficult to come by. In 1981 my then eleven-year-old son, Jim, knowing of my choir experience as a boy, suggested I apply to become a member of the men's and boys' choir at our Easton church. Jim had been singing with the group for three years, taking great pride in his music. "We could be the only father-and-son team in the choir," he said enthusiastically. So I talked with the choir director and after a silence of several weeks, although he said he would get back to me, I called him. "Well, Bob," he said, "I thought about it and this is a small town, and you have had a difficult time, and this is a men's and boys' choir, you know?"

Yes, I knew. His was a reaction that was becoming all too familiar.

Henry Adams in his *Education* wrote of the tremendous awe inspired in him by the electric dynamo he saw at the 1890 Paris Exposition. It reminded him of nothing so much as the unseen but forceful power of the Virgin of Chartres which so influenced the world. His book on Chartres and the cathedrals of France demonstrates his boundless love for these earthly symbols of the love of God and respect for His will. To Adams, and for me, there is sure but indefinable unity and relationship between that dynamo and the Virgin.

I have to believe there is a higher power. Few are fully privileged to understand His will for us but if I am to make any sense out of my existence I have to believe. But I have come to believe that the merciful God of my understanding is that power, not man.

CHAPTER
NINE

I must have a fat file in the archives of the *Baltimore Sun.*

One editorial appeared on August 4, 1983, under the title, "Seeking a Private Redemption." It begins: " 'This above all: to thine own self be true,' counseled Shakespeare's Polonius." (You will recall Polonius was the character in *Hamlet* who unwisely hid behind a column and a drapery and had the consequent misfortune to be stabbed in the arras.)

The *Sun* continued: "It has taken time and much pain, but former Eastern Shore Congressman Robert Bauman seems finally to have reached that truth. Once an able if self-righteous spokesman for conservative causes, Mr. Bauman stood before an American Bar Association panel on homosexual rights to declare: Yes, I am gay.... Mr. Bauman's declaration in Atlanta did more than assert public principles, however. He seemed mainly to be expressing a form of redemption, some new level of understanding and a coming to terms with all that happened to him after 1980 ... Since then his political career and marriage have ended, his law practice has declined, and potential employers have regularly turned him away in varying accents of hostility, indifference or embarrassment. Those were the visible wounds left by a lifetime of deception and self-hatred. If he has now made peace with himself we can only wish him well."

A few months later I gave an interview to Dorothy Collin of

the *Chicago Tribune* who came to Glebe House where we talked for a long time. Her thoughts in part: "The new Bob Bauman is like a man caught on an island between two shores. Back where he came from, former conservative friends and associates either sigh in private, saying things like, 'Bob has become the Elephant Man of politics,' or castigate him in public . . . On the other shore is the gay rights movement . . . [his] views on almost everything were considered anathema to those gays who had even heard of him . . . a national gay leader said: 'Whom will he influence? Liberals won't listen to him and conservatives have written him off.' . . . Ironically, some conservatives and gays agree that Bauman, who seemingly has lost almost everything, is in search of something that will give him back his place in public life he has sought ever since he was a boy. A gay observer said: 'He obviously went through a lot of soul-searching, but I'm not sure he found his soul. My impression is that he is searching for a cause.' And a conservative said: 'I think he is trying to find himself and find a place in public life once again. He loves this country. He is searching for his place in it!' "

Indeed, I have done a lot of searching in the past five years, not so much for a return to public activity, although I tried that for a while, but rather for some sort of personal peace. But that odyssey has led me in some strange and new pastures. It has included the writing of this book, countless press stories, appearances on Cable News Network's "Firing Line," the "Phil Donahue Show," and a life story on ABC's "20/20."

My treatment at the hands of the gay community has been curious. After less than flattering comments at the time of my 1980 problems, eventually I was welcomed by some. In 1983, Dan Bradley (the former head of the Legal Services Corporation under President Carter, who resigned that post and announced he is gay) called me on the phone. He wanted to know if I would consider appearing before the annual meeting of the American Bar Association in Atlanta to endorse extension of the 1964 Civil Rights Act to gays and lesbians. Having experienced employment

---

259

discrimination myself, Dan's request struck me at a vulnerable, frustrated moment and I agreed. My Atlanta speech was greeted with much national news coverage and the ABA's rejection of a gay rights resolution by a narrow vote. (The same outcome in 1985.)

For a while after the ABA appearance I was paraded around the country by a few gay leaders, speaking to gays of my experiences. The reaction of individual gays was friendly, sympathetic, and understanding. Many of those who had been married and were fathers particularly identified with my plight, they told me. Younger gays surprised me with praise for being a "role model" for them, showing the possibility that gay people can serve in government. Gays with conservative political views told me they were relieved finally to have any openly gay conservative spokesman: "I'm tired of all gay leaders mouthing the liberal line, aligning themselves with all sorts of crazy groups on the Left." It was a repeated refrain.

But I quickly found my unwillingness to change most of my conservative views limited my usefulness to many gay "leaders," as they saw it. It was not enough for me to admit being gay, I had to repudiate conservatism and embrace not just my fellow man, but the liberal agenda as well. Steven Endine, then national executive director of the Gay Rights National Lobby (GRNL), proposed to me that his group hire me as their Capitol Hill lobbyist. Endine managed to wring maximum publicity out of this arrangement, including an article in *People* magazine built around my proposed GRNL activity. Then he told me my paying job would be impossible to implement because the group was running out of money. More likely the board of directors could not stomach my views on other matters such as the threat of international communism and support for the right to life of the unborn.

In 1984, I was approached by two well-known national conservative leaders who are closet gays with the request I serve as a public figure in a group that would appeal to the many conservative and Republican gays and lesbians. Out of this came Concerned Americans for Individual Rights (CAIR) patterned after similar local groups in California, New York, and Texas. After a year of talk, meetings, and more talk, I dropped out of the group along with two of its original founders when it became evident it was quickly getting nowhere. The principal obstacle was gay conservatives who did not wish to come out of the closet in spite of their obviously gay private lives. They did not want their names on even a "secret" mailing list or even to write contribution checks that contained their names. CAIR could fill a suburban Washington home for a cocktail party with nearly a hundred gay men representing positions from the White House staff, to offices of the most conservative Republican senators and congressmen, the Republican National Committee, and all parts of the Reagan administration. But only two of them, myself and one other, were willing to publicly acknowledge their role in the group.

Indeed, the closets of Washington are full of gay Republicans, and gay conservatives. Many of them serve in high Reagan administration posts, some in the White House. They serve in the Congress and populate the circles of power that exist in law firms, public relations firms, lobbying groups, political action committees, even conservative organizations and the Republican party structure as well. Their names appear on the White House guest list and feature articles on them can be seen in the *Washington Post* "Style" or "Business" sections.

It would startle no one except the totally uninitiated to know that the following dialogue took place one evening at the "Lost and Found," one of the Capitol's more "preppie" gay nightclubs:

Early-middle-aged gentleman: "Where do you work?"
Earnest preppie in early twenties: "On Capitol Hill."
Middle-aged gentleman: "Oh? Where on the Hill?"
Preppie: "I just got a job on the staff of the subcommittee on such-and-so. I start next Monday."

Middle-aged gentleman: "That's fabulous. I'm a member of that subcommittee."

When last seen they were leaning on the bar chatting merrily.

Many of these gay conservatives are well known to other gays, even though some are married and have children. Their all-male social events are discreetly conducted in Georgetown gardens and Foggy Bottom townhouses, in Capitol Hill condominiums and in the hot summer months, at Cape Cod or Rehoboth Beach in Delaware. Like their politically liberal gay counterparts, they value their anonymity but not so much that the possibility of exposure prevents them from quietly living their sexuality. And, of course, it can be argued their lives are the essence of hypocrisy.

For a time I harbored the thought of returning to public office but my abortive 1982 congressional candidacy convinced me it was not worth it. I was encouraged by gay leaders and some Republican party officials to move to an area where my sexuality would not be a major issue, to run for Congress in California or Houston. Some in my own Maryland district urged me to run again but I viewed this as charitable personal encouragement rather than practical politics.

That I would like to serve in government, usefully employing my extensive experience, is true. But repeated attempts for federal service have been met with quiet but firm rebuffs from officials of the Reagan Administration. In late 1982 my name was on a list of former Republican congressmen and senators submitted to top White House officials for consideration as federal appointees. A friendly official then acting as head of White House personnel pushed a decision on my acceptability; the answer was a blue pencil through my name. The veto came, I was told, from one of the triumvirate of Reagan aides then in charge: Ed Meese, James Baker, and Michael Deaver. All are now gone to other glory and unofficially I was told in 1985 I might be considered for some position "not requiring Senate confirmation."

Ironically I was turned down for a government position by a

close friend, the head of a federal agency who told me he could use my talents "but I do not have the courage to name you to a post." Citing the inevitable publicity, he said, "I'm in enough hot water now without adding to it." He might as well have named me to his department. Two years later the Senate rejected his reappointment by President Reagan because of my friend's political and policy decisions. I also applied through regular Civil Service channels for a position as a U.S. Justice Department attorney at a time when the department was seeking new legal aides. In spite of phone calls from ranking members of Congress on the Judiciary Committees of both Houses I never even got letters of acknowledgment for my applications. Insiders in the department told me bluntly, "They're all scared to touch you." One of those who told a member of Congress he would consider hiring me "after the 1984 elections" was William Bradford Reynolds, then head of the Civil Rights Division. Subsequently, Reynolds' own promotion was rejected by the Senate Judiciary Committee for various reasons, including his lack of candor in responding to senators' questions as well as his policy decisions. Even attempts to gain employment through answering ads for government jobs have met with silence or rejection. Similar responses have come from Washington law firms and lobbying groups. A not uncommon suggestion, probably meant in good faith but hardly encouraging, has been, "Why not just pull up stakes and go abroad or to some distant place where you are unknown?" Although my four children live in the Washington area and I do not wish to leave them, attempts to follow this well-meant advice for a "geographic cure" has so far failed to produce employment.

I certainly do not think the nervous rejection of my attempts to gain a government job reflects personal bias against gay people on the part of the President. I recall Lyn Nofziger's 1982 guarantee that President Reagan would support me if I became the congressional nominee in my Maryland district. My withdrawal from the race prevented having to honor that commitment, but it was made. (Nofziger himself refused to see me in 1985 when I called for an appointment. He relayed word through his secretary that he was "too busy with other projects" to meet with me and would continue to be so in the foreseeable future.)

Others close to the President, some of them gay, have told me Ronald Reagan has no personal bias against gay people, as evidenced by his public actions on many occasions. Perhaps the most memorable was in 1978 when California voters faced an election referendum question whether gays and lesbians should be prevented from teaching in public or private schools in the state. Reagan publicly rejected the "Briggs Initiative" and it was defeated by a huge margin. He said it made no sense to exclude people from the teaching profession because of their private sexual preference. What the public did not know was that Reagan arrived at his conclusion privately and against the violent objection of State Senator Briggs, the referendum sponsor. He also rejected the suggestion from Lyn Nofziger that he stay out of the battle by saying nothing. Characteristically, Ronald Reagan simply believed strongly that the Briggs position was wrong and felt compelled to say so. Both the President and Mrs. Reagan have not hesitated to invite gay persons to the White House, to associate with them, or even to send a message of friendship to actor Rock Hudson during his illness from AIDS (acquired immune deficiency syndrome), an illness associated with homosexual men.

In 1983, my declining economic state dictated I had to let go of the past and sell Glebe House. Our two youngest children, Vicky and Jimmy, were living with me, going to school in Easton and none of us wanted to disrupt our lives. The home place still served as a focal point for Genie and Teddy, our oldest children, and the Eastern Shore was the only place that truly had been "home" to all of us. Meanwhile Carol prospered in her government service and was named by the President to the Consumer Products Safety Commission, a top-level federal post in responsibility and salary.

In September 1983, we sold the house and Jimmy and Vicky

moved with their mother to a new home in suburban Washington. I moved to the Washington area which was better to pursue employment possibilities. About this time my public support of federal legislation to ban discrimination against gay people brought down the wrath of some of my fellow directors of the American Conservative Union. A move to impeach me from the board failed as did an attempt to revoke my membership in the organization. A founder and the senior member of the board, I quietly allowed my term to expire and did not seek re-election in 1985, although I refused to resign.

My treatment at the hands of some in the conservative movement has hurt, deeply so. But then I dismayed and deeply disappointed many who gave unquestioning loyalty to me. Some of my former colleagues in the Senate and House have been unstinting in their support, even personally extending help to my children in one case. One fellow conservative in particular has repeatedly gone out of his way to assist me. Another, however, lamented to me that he should have hired me when his term began so that the noise would have abated when he again faced re-election. "The gay thing would really hurt in my state," he said. Perhaps he does not know that two of his top aides regularly are seen weekends at Washington gay clubs.

What I have felt is a sense of deep frustration, knowing I have talents to offer the public and private sectors, but unable to do so. But I quickly learned my personal difficulties are shared by millions of other gays if statistical projections mean anything.

When I left public office in 1981, I experienced a disconcerting phenomenon, as though I did not have enough to deal with in my own life. Suddenly I began to receive letters, phone calls, and even visits from men, young and old, who had or were suffering the same difficult situation I experienced. They identified with my plight, and although they did not wish to make public their own sexual orientation, they desperately wanted to talk to someone who understood. The variety of people who "came out of the closet" surprised me.

A young Republican state legislator struggling with the same conflict of career and being gay called me in response to a television appearance I made. We have become good friends. (Another irony: the television reporter who interviewed me on that show was particularly brutal in his questioning. I later learned he is not only a closet homosexual, his preference is for young male hustlers.) I met a young businessman caught in a difficult financial situation because he refused to accept being gay; a leading Maryland community figure, wealthy and respected but lonely and closeted, looking for someone he could trust after years of secrecy; a reporter for a major national newspaper, married and with children; Catholic priests, Episcopal priests, Jewish rabbis, Protestant ministers, congressional aides, doctors, political party officials, local, state, and federal government officials; just about any occupation or background you might imagine, all gay, all trying to reach out to someone who would understand.

Though most non-gay people are unaware, gay people are everywhere, not just in your local beauty shop or florist. Being gay in America is not a condition which respects racial, ethnic, economic, geographic, political or any other arbitrary division. In 1982, *Harper's* magazine published a long article entitled "Closets of Power, the Double Life of Homosexuals in Politics," detailing the Washington gay scene without, of course, naming names. Largely the account of the private and public life of Dan Bradley, former head of the Federal Legal Services Corporation, the story touched upon many other examples of similar double lives. Naturally, Bob Bauman was cited as one of the exhibits.

In responding to the article, one liberal columnist wrote the account ". . . reminds me that Bauman, however offensive his politics, is a victim of the deepest prejudice still extant in this country, that against homosexuals." How deep that prejudice goes was brought home to me with a jolt when I appeared on a California radio call-in show. When I noted the struggle for civil rights of black Americans as an example of what gay Americans might expect, the lines lit up with blacks calling to denounce me for comparing "perverts" with blacks. Lost on my black callers was the double difficulty of being black and gay, a not unknown occurrence. But one group that has suffered most from irrational prejudice could not fathom the plight of another group in a similar situation.

Anti-gay sentiment in this nation is virulent. A leading Methodist theologian and television commentator in the Washington area, Edward W. Bauman (no relation), relates the reaction after he carefully researched and preached a sermon calling for understanding of, and compassion toward, gay people. "I was prepared for trouble," he wrote, "but the intensity of the storm took me by surprise." Reverend Bauman, defending his stand, realized from his research how little he knew about the subject of homosexuality and said:

> The thing that impressed me most, however, and moved me deeply was the discovery of the incredible amount of suffering experienced by homosexuals. For centuries the church refused to serve them Holy Communion. They were often stripped, castrated, marched through the streets and executed. In Hitler's Germany they were exterminated by the thousands in the furnaces and gas chambers. And in our own country, gay persons are disowned by their families, ridiculed and rejected by society, made the object of cruel jokes, and forced to laugh at the jokes lest their "secret" be revealed. They are barred from jobs and housing, often living in loneliness, seeking companionship in sordid places and in devious (and dangerous!) ways. They have become the "lepers" of our society. How many young people are there who lie awake at night, terrified by these "feelings," with no one to talk to? Is this one of the reasons for the increase in adolescent suicide?

I drew on my own experience when I spoke before the American Bar Association meeting in Atlanta in August 1983:

> Some aspects of prejudice and discrimination can never be reached by laws. I wish that my poor power of expression

permitted me to convey to those who are not gay the depth of despair and suffering society inflicts in a thousand subtle and not so subtle ways on the homosexual. I am not talking about the rejection for employment or housing, or even the rejection by an angry parent displeased with the conduct of a son or daughter.

What gays experience is a rejection not of their actions but of who they are constitutionally, a rejection of their very nature and being. As one writer has said: "We don't have a choice about being gay. There is nothing inherently destructive about our sexual orientation, and yet, once found out, gays are treated like lepers often by those who supposedly love them the most."

The really lucky ones are able to deal with this eventually and go on with life though few are ever reconciled fully to this cruel treatment. The less fortunate, and there are many, die by their own hand or seek escape in alcohol or other drugs.

It appears to me that from a very early age most children in this country, regardless of their eventual sexual identity, are taught "homophobia." A term popularized by George Weinberg in 1972, it is defined as an irrational fear, intolerance or dread of gay people. This homophobic education comes from countless sources, subtle and blatant. Peers ridicule a fellow adolescent who may appear effeminate. Persons fearful of their own sexual orientation often react negatively to gays because of their own discomfort. Small remarks and jokes about "fags," "queers," and "dykes" abound in locker rooms and offices. The closeted gay is forced to stand by and laugh along with the rest lest he be discovered. In a broader sense homophobia supports negative myths and stereotypes of gays which American mass media easily conveys to the general populace already conditioned to accept perjorative descriptions. And, of course, some of the more flamboyant sectors of the gay community eagerly and readily reenforce these unattractive impressions. Indeed, prejudice against homosexuals takes place on the part of gays and lesbians

themselves, appearing as self-hatred and internalizing the irrational fears of others. Of that I can speak with authority.

The locker room is not the only source for homophobia. It can
be traced to many individuals' own sexual insecurity, to ignorance and misinformation, to deeply held religious beliefs and,
yes, even to politicians and groups willing and eager to exploit a
highly inflammatory issue for their own personal gain. It all goes
to produce a near-hysteria that distorts the thinking of otherwise
decent people.

It is not a pleasant experience for any person to read some of
the letters I received in 1980, much less for the person to whom
they were directed. A Mr. R. M. Burnham from Virginia (more
courageous than most since he used his name) sent me a skillful
drawing of my face with my features those of a pig, calling me a
"schweinhund." A letter from New York addressed to "Dear Alcoholic Faggot" said in part: "Why don't you just have another
drink and try to forget all this? Maybe if we're lucky, you'll try to
drive while drunk and hit a telephone pole. You are the foulest
human being on the earth. I hope you die." And even in a small,
conservative community such as Easton it was some time before
the obscene phone calls stopped, usually from adolescents, but
not always. Even when I drove my children to school in the
morning young boys in the back of a school bus ahead of us
would make the universal sign of the limp wrist at me, laughing
heartily.

Why so strong a reaction against homosexuality?

In part I believe it is because most non-gay people have a great
personal investment in our society's majority orientation of heterosexuality. That investment is social, economic, political, and
sometimes very emotional. Often directed at gays, similar feelings
arise in reaction to claims made by women for equality of treatment, so called "equal rights." (Perhaps this is why most surveys
find men to be far more anti-gay than are women.) The "macho
image" of the American male, traditional paternal control of the

family unit, the unexpected (even exalted) aggressiveness of the male and the lesser role assigned to women all are threatened by homosexuality. Masculinity cannot be diluted if male control is to be retained.

Then, too, in spite of the fact that America is steeped in sex on television, radio, in plays, advertising, books, magazines and newspapers, we are essentially a people "up tight" about sex. In spite of soaring rates of illegitimate child birth, even among young girls, in spite of venereal disease and millions of abortions employed as a form of retroactive birth control, education in the schools about the nature and use of sexuality is opposed by many who say it should occur in the home. And in the home, often with only one parent, most children know more about sex at an earlier age than their parents ever did. They do not learn the facts of life from those parents, many of whom are disinclined to talk about the subject with each other, much less their offspring.

Introduce into such a nervous atmosphere the issue of homosexuality and many people, as it is said, "go right through the roof." Most people have an acquaintance with the physical acts of heterosexuality and thus can make a vicarious judgment about what they view to be the abnormality of homosexual acts. (The exception was the proverbial "little old lady" who called in to a KMOX talk-show I was on in St. Louis. Her comment/question: "I've been listening to all this talk about homosexuality and I just want to know what it is you people do in bed?" It being National Library Week, I referred her to her local library.)

And to some degree I believe there is resentment that gays claim a degree of sexual freedom heterosexuals are not supposed to have, but of course surely do. If gays are going to have such freedom, some seem to say, then at least they must be considered as sinners and punished as such. Thus it is a "good Catholic" such as Patrick J. Buchanan can state that the health crisis caused by the acquired immune deficiency syndrome (AIDS) is God's just punishment for the wanton and reckless life style of homosexuals.

270

Whatever their reasons, a large number of Americans see homosexuality as threatening the very foundations of society, or at the very least, the sexual strictures and mores society has created over the course of many centuries.

To talk to such people about the noble form of love as once viewed by the Greeks and Romans, the many societies in which homosexuality has been historically accepted, the thousands of famous and admired people who were gay, the popes, bishops, writers, kings, actors, even congressmen, all makes no difference. They have their minds made up on the issue of homosexuality; no amount of education or closet-opening is going to change their view. But, as one of my constituents told a reporter in October 1980, "I'm going to vote for him again, but if he's one of them, it makes you wonder who else could be one of them too!"

That *Baltimore Sun* editorial might have gone further to quote the entire speech by Polonius, Act 1, Scene 3, of Hamlet:

"This above all—to thine own self be true,
And it must follow, as the night the day,
Thou canst not then be false to any man."

For me the time for pretending is long passed. Even without the cataclysmic changes I have endured in the last five years, I would have been required to undergo that painful mid-life period so many experience; a time when it becomes necessary to explore the meaning and direction of life. Like Saul Bellow's character, Herzog, I too was beginning to feel "overcome by the need to explain, have it out, to justify, to put in perspective, to clarify, to make amends . . ."

The program I have so far successfully employed to hold my alcoholism in abeyance suggests the steps to recovery must include a searching and fearless moral inventory of myself, an admission to God, to myself, and another human being the exact nature of my wrongs, a recognition of those I may have harmed and a willingness to make amends to them if possible. Indeed that same program calls for a continuing taking of my own personal inventory and a prompt admission whenever I am wrong. For one who thought he was always right, that is not an easy task.

Tennessee Williams also wrote: "A man must live out his life's duration with his own set of fears and angers, suspicions and vanities, and his appetites, spiritual and carnal. Life is built of them and he is built of life." But what of my life, now that I have been forced to reexamine it in excruciating detail?

Who am I, really?

What am I?

After all these years, what have I become?

Henri Nouwen writes in *Reaching Out* (New York: Doubleday, 1975): ". . . there will be no hope for the future when the past remains unconfessed, unreceived or misunderstood." Similarly, wisdom suggests that in order to heal ourselves, to mature, we must learn that the past, in one important sense, can be changed. "When we forgive and become reconciled with our personal histories, they lose power over us. Emptied of much of its anger and guilt, our past can become a friend and a resource." Indeed if this possibility did not exist I think I would go insane.

Whatever has happened I must look back and give thanks to God for Carol, for the support and love of four wonderful children. At least we are able to talk without shame, seeking the truth and debating our differences. "We would have never known who you are," my daughter, Vicky, said in her youthful wisdom. And I would have never known my children fully, or myself.

Life and its unsuspected pathway offered me many more opportunities and honors than most people ever experience: high station, awards and public esteem, personal satisfaction from a profession I loved and will always cherish. At an early age I received the gift of my Catholic faith which, in spite of all its burdens, I have interpreted to sustain me. The shared association of the many good friends who sacrificed their time and energy for my political success and our common causes will always be in my memory.

Violent public exposure of my secret life forced me to eventual acceptance of my sexual nature and slowly I am coming to terms with myself. At last I realize the roots of my sexuality are far more diverse and complex than any conscious choice I might have made. But while the choice may not have been mine I am free to accept or reject its consequences. And I am freeing myself of the error and guilt engendered by the belief I was responsible for my nature. I am coming to understand the goal of human sexuality is not just self-satisfaction but human completeness. Without that goal of completeness satisfaction alone deteriorates into lust. Truthfully, I am not comfortable with the promiscuity of some portions of the gay community, precisely because I know firsthand of the emptiness, the squalid and sordid life it is. As one writer said: "Alcohol, drugs, and compulsive sexual activity may have been the strategies I used to maintain some sense of control over my life." What I seek now is stability, peace, the possibility of mutual love, all goals which for the gay person are difficult in the extreme to obtain. But that is so for almost everyone, isn't it?

In those middle days of 1980, after Carol spurred me to seek help and before the public scandal, my psychologist, Dr. Kay, surprised me and unnerved me with a profound question: "Haven't you ever wanted to surrender completely to another human being; to share with another your aspirations and hopes, your fears, your innermost thoughts? Haven't you ever wished to experience complete and total intimacy? To love someone so much that you trust them to listen to your heart?" My immediate response: "No, never!"

Belatedly I have come to understand the human need for intimacy. Now I long for a shared experience with another person I love and who loves me. That it comes so late and in the wake of turmoil makes this goal no less worthy of attainment. And I suppose I will always seek that goal, regretting the knowledge it was no farther than my wife of twenty-one years, yet still light-years away because of the insurmountable wall between us.

If only I had listened, been able to comprehend, I would have realized Carol understood this need for intimacy long years before I approached it in the wreckage of my old life. One night in 1970, before I took my seat in the State Senate, I was away. Carol was at home suffering from a cold, young children who would not stay in bed, telephone calls from soon-to-be constituents, and the many obligations of parenthood, politics and marriage.

She became so frustrated she sat down at her typewriter and wrote me a six-page letter on the topic "our personal relationship." "I'm not complaining. But I keep thinking what will happen if you go on to higher things? Will it get worse? And, finally, when you've got it made and my hair is gray and the children are in college, will you find another love? If so, the loss I suffer now may be irreparable. There may never be a time when I can feel complete as I was meant to be as a helpmate. (Sounds strange from a liberated woman, doesn't it?) I mean, if our marriage isn't close and intimate and satisfying now, when will it be?"

Peter Ilich Tchaikovsky's powerful Fourth Symphony, my favorite, has as its theme inexorable fate and destiny. In reviewing its meaning he reached the melancholy judgment: "So the whole of life is an endless alternation of dreadful reality and fleeting visions of happiness," and for the Russian composer it was certainly so.

Just as does any human being, whether they realize it or not, each of us needs loving relationships, affirmation, and the acceptance of others. And, most importantly, the acceptance of ourselves. That last is something I could never give myself and even now struggle to grant. Somehow I managed to survive what I did to myself. My fervent prayer is that those I harmed will forgive my transgressions as I now know a loving and merciful God will.

The sensational headlines of the Bauman scandal have long since faded from memory for most, but like Conrad's Lord Jim, I will go to my grave with the consequences of my actions.

In June 1917, Joseph Conrad, in the "Author's Note" to his masterpiece, *Lord Jim,* spoke worriedly about the rejection of this famous novel by an Italian lady who said "it is all so morbid." Said Conrad: ". . . no Latin temperament would have perceived anything morbid in the acute consciousness of loss of honor. Such a consciousness may be wrong, or it may be right, or it may be condemned as artificial; and perhaps my Jim is not a type of wide commonness. But I can safely assure my readers that it is not a product of coldly perverted thinking. He's not a figure of the Northern Mists either. One sunny morning in the commonplace surroundings of an Eastern [English] roadstead, I saw his form pass by—appealing—significant—under a cloud—perfectly silent. Which is as it should be. It was for me, with all the sympathy I was capable, to seek fit words for his meaning. He was 'one of us.' "

At the close of the Confiteor of the Latin Tridentine Mass the priest entoned: *"Misereatur vestri omnipotens Deus, et dismissis peccatis vestris, perducat vos ad vitam aeternam."* The message in English in the parallel column of my St. Joseph's Missal seems meant for me: "May almighty God have mercy on you, forgive you your sins, and bring you to life everlasting."

Traveling on the Milan Express from Mannheim, Germany, to Lugano, Switzerland, in September 1984, an American priest from Ohio, the Reverend Robert Thorsen, shared my train compartment. In a letter he wrote me the next day he summed it all up: "Christians, Bob, are a resurrection people. Whatever the human condition is for us now, however it came about, it will be different when we are created anew. It just won't be like 'this,' however 'this' is, forever. That is why we say and mean 'Come Lord Jesus.' For me Faith alone blunts the pain of the absurd."

I pray God, give me that faith.

EPILOGUE

From "Brigham Anderson's Book," *Advise and Consent* by Allen Drury:

Somewhere in a crowded hall a loud voice was saying, "And so I present to you the man who—" On Bethany Beach a tiny figure was wetting the water, a lost boy was crying on the telephone, and on the floor of the Senate the senior senator from Utah, that nice guy that everybody liked so much, was rising to seek recognition from the Chair.

Then it all ended, but not before, in one last moment of rigid and unflinching honesty, he realized that it was not only of his family that he was thinking as he died. It was of a beach in Honolulu on a long, hot, lazy afternoon.

The waves crashed and he heard for the last time the exultant cries of the surf riders, far out.